The American Pageant

Guidebook

The American Pageant

Guidebook

A Manual for Students
Volume II: Since 1865
THIRTEENTH EDITION

Mel Piehl

Valparaiso University

HOUGHTON MIFFLIN COMPANY   BOSTON   NEW YORK

Sponsoring Editor: Sally Constable
Development Editor: Lisa Kalner Williams
Editorial Assistant: Arianne Vanni
Manufacturing Coordinator: Karmen Chong
Senior Marketing Manager: Sandra McGuire

Printed in the U.S.A.

ISBN: 0-618-57428-X

789 – EB – 09 08

Contents

Foreword

This revised *Guidebook* is intended to assist you in comprehending American history as presented in *The American Pageant*, Thirteenth Edition, by David M. Kennedy, Lizabeth Cohen, and Thomas A. Bailey. The *Guidebook* focuses attention on the central themes and major historical developments of each chapter while presenting a variety of exercises and other material designed to reinforce your comprehension of the text and reinforce the broad historical perspective that the *The American Pageant* aims to foster. Factual knowledge of history is important, and some of the exercises will help you to review facts and recall their significance. But the *Guidebook* attempts to demonstrate that facts are best learned when they are understood in relation to key historical events and issues.

The *Guidebook* is available in a complete edition as well as in splits by volume. All chapters of the *Guidebook* correspond with those of *The American Pageant* and are best used in close association with the text. Each chapter of the *Guidebook* contains the same sequence of material and exercises, except for the Map Discrimination section, which is omitted from some chapters.

The **Checklist of Learning Objectives** in Part I ("Reviewing the Chapter") of each *Guidebook* chapter provides a summary of the essential chapter themes and underscores the major historical developments to be learned. The **Glossary** defines basic social science terms and illustrates their usage in the text. Learning this vocabulary will not only reinforce your understanding of *The American Pageant* but also familiarize you with terms often encountered in the study of politics, economics, geography, military science, and law, as well as history.

The various exercises in Part II ("Checking Your Progress") will assist in your careful reading of the text as well as foster your comprehension and spotlight the essential facts and concepts. **True-False**, **Multiple Choice**, and **Identification** exercises stress reading for understanding of important ideas and terms. **Matching People, Places, and Events** checks your knowledge of key historical figures, locations, and events. **Putting Things in Order** (which is specifically tied to the Chronology section at the end of each chapter of *The American Pageant*) and **Matching Cause and Effect** develop two essential principles of historical understanding: chronological sequence, and the causal relation between events. **Developing Historical Skills** is designed to hone your ability to use the diverse techniques employed in the study of history, including the interpretation of charts, maps, and visual evidence. **Map Mastery** includes Map Discrimination—specific questions focused on map reading—and Map Challenge, which asks you to use maps to discuss a historical issue or problem in a brief essay.

Completion of the exercises in Part II should enable you to address successfully the crucial interpretive questions in Part III ("Applying What You Have Learned"). Your instructor may ask you to use these questions as guides to study and review, or may assign them as essay questions to be answered following your reading of the chapter. The last question is an especially challenging one that often draws on earlier chapters of *The American Pageant* and asks you to make historical comparisons, draw conclusions, or consider broad historical issues.

You and your instructor hence may utilize the *Guidebook* in a variety of ways, and to suit a variety of academic goals. It can be used for class preparation and assignments, for guidance in your reading of the text, or for independent review of course contents in preparation for comprehensive subject examinations. The answers to all the exercises may be found by your careful rereading of the pertinent sections of *The American Pageant*. May your exploration of American history be stimulating and enriching.

M. P.

CHAPTER 22

The Ordeal of Reconstruction, 1865–1877

PART I: REVIEWING THE CHAPTER

A. CHECKLIST OF LEARNING OBJECTIVES

After mastering this chapter, you should be able to

1. define the major problems facing the South and the nation after the Civil War.

2. describe the responses of both whites and African Americans to the end of slavery.

3. analyze the differences between the presidential and congressional approaches to Reconstruction.

4. explain how the blunders of President Johnson and the white South opened the door to the radical Reconstruction policies of congressional Republicans.

5. describe the actual effects of congressional Reconstruction in the South.

6. indicate how militant white opposition gradually undermined the Republican attempt to empower Southern blacks.

7. explain why the radical Republicans impeached Johnson but failed to convict him.

8. explain the legacy of Reconstruction, and assess its successes and failures.

B. GLOSSARY

To build your social science vocabulary, familiarize yourself with the following terms:

1. **treason** The crime of betrayal of one's country, involving some overt act violating an oath of allegiance or providing illegal aid to a foreign state. In the United States, treason is the only crime specified in the Constitution. "What should be done with the captured Confederate ringleaders, all of whom were liable to charges of treason?" (p. 477)

2. **civil disabilities** Legally imposed restrictions of a person's civil rights or liberties. "But Congress did not remove all remaining civil disabilities until thirty years later. . . ." (p. 478)

3. **legalistically** In accord with the exact letter of the law, sometimes with the intention of thwarting its broad intent. "Some planters resisted emancipation more legalistically. . . ." (p. 479)

4. **mutual aid societies** Nonprofit organizations designed to provide their members with financial and social benefits, often including medical aid, life insurance, funeral costs, and disaster relief. "These churches . . . gave rise to other benevolent, fraternal, and mutual aid societies." (p. 480)

5. **confiscation (confiscated)** Legal government seizure of private property without compensation. ". . . the bureau was authorized to settle former slaves on forty-acre tracts confiscated from the Confederates. . . ." (p. 481)

6. **pocket veto** The presidential act of blocking a Congressionally passed law not by direct veto but by simply refusing to sign it at the end of a session. (A president can pocket-veto a bill within ten days of a session's end or after.) "Lincoln 'pocket-vetoed' this bill by refusing to sign it after Congress had adjourned." (p. 483)

7. **lease** To enter into a contract by which one party gives another use of land, buildings, or other property for a fixed time and fee. ". . . some [codes] even barred blacks from renting or leasing land." (p. 484)

8. **chain gang** A group of prisoners chained together while engaged in forced labor. "A black could be punished for 'idleness' by being sentenced to work on a chain gang." (p. 484)

9. **sharecrop** An agricultural system in which a tenant receives land, tools, and seed on credit and pledges in return a share of the crop to the creditor. ". . . former slaves slipped into the status of sharecropper farmers. . . ." (p. 484)

10. **peonage** A system in which debtors are held in servitude, to labor for their creditors. "Luckless sharecroppers gradually sank into a morass of virtual peonage. . . ." (p. 484)

11. **scalawag** A white Southerner who supported Republican Reconstruction after the Civil War. "The so-called scalawags were Southerners, often former Unionists and Whigs." (p. 492)

12. **carpetbagger** A Northern politician who came south to exploit the unsettled conditions after the Civil War; hence, any politician who relocates for political advantage. "The carpet-baggers, on the other hand, were supposedly sleazy Northerners. . . ." (p. 492)

13. **felony** A major crime for which severe penalties are exacted under the law. "The crimes of the Reconstruction governments were no more outrageous than the scams and felonies being perpetrated in the North at the same time. . . ." (p. 493)

14. **terror (terrorist)** Using violence or the threat of violence in order to create intense fear in the attempt to promote some political policy or objectives. "Such tomfoolery and terror proved partially effective." (p. 493)

15. **president pro tempore** In the United States Senate, the officer who presides in the absence of the vice president. "Under existing law, the president pro tempore of the Senate . . . would then become president." (p. 495)

PART II: CHECKING YOUR PROGRESS

A. True-False

Where the statement is true, circle **T**; where it is false, circle **F**.

1. T F   The South was economically devastated by the Civil War.

2. T F   Military defeat in the Civil War brought white Southerners to accept the reality of Northern political domination.

3. T F   The newly freed slaves often used their liberty to travel or seek lost loved ones.

4. T F   The focus of black community life after emancipation became the black church.

5. T F   Lincoln's "10 percent" Reconstruction plan was designed to return the Southern states to the Union quickly and with few restrictions.

6. T F   Southerners at first feared Andrew Johnson because he had been one of the few elite planters who backed Lincoln.

7. T F   The cause of black education was greatly advanced by Northern white female teachers who came South after the Civil War.

8. T F   The enactment of the Black Codes in the south strengthened those who supported a moderate approach to Reconstruction.

9.   T   F   Congressional Republicans demanded that the Southern states ratify the Fourteenth Amendment in order to be readmitted to the Union.

10. T   F   Radical Republicans succeeded in their goal of redistributing land to the former slaves.

11. T   F   During Reconstruction, blacks controlled most of the Southern state legislatures.

12. T   F   The Republican Reconstruction legislature enacted educational and other reforms in Southern state government.

13. T   F   The Ku Klux Klan was organized primarily because of white southerners' resentment of growing interracial marriage and corruption among radical black state legislators.

14. T   F   Johnson's impeachment was essentially an act of political vindictiveness by radical Republicans.

15. T   F   The moderate Republican plan for Reconstruction might have succeeded if the Ku Klux Klan had been suppressed.

B. Multiple Choice

Select the best answer and circle the corresponding letter.

1.   After emancipation, many blacks traveled in order to
   a.   return to Africa or the West Indies.
   b.   seek a better life in Northern cities.
   c.   find lost family members or seek new economic opportunities.
   d.   track down and punish cruel overseers.

2.   The Freedmen's Bureau was originally established to provide
   a.   land and supplies for black farmers.
   b.   labor registration.
   c.   food, clothes, and education for emancipated slaves.
   d.   political training in citizenship for black voters.

3.   Lincoln's original plan for Reconstruction in 1863 was that a state could be re-integrated into the Union when
   a.   it repealed its original secession act and took its soldiers out of the Confederate Army.
   b.   10 percent of its voters took an oath of allegiance to the Union and pledged to abide by emancipation.
   c.   it formally adopted a plan guaranteeing black political and economic rights.
   d.   it ratified the Fourteenth and Fifteenth Amendments to the Constitution.

4.   The Black Codes passed by many of the Southern state governments in 1865 aimed to
   a.   provide economic assistance to get former slaves started as sharecroppers.
   b.   ensure a stable and subservient labor force under white control.
   c.   permit blacks to vote if they met certain educational or economic standards.
   d.   gradually force blacks to leave the South.

5.   The congressional elections of 1866 resulted in
   a.   a victory for Johnson and his pro-Southern Reconstruction plan.
   b.   a further political stalemate between the Republicans in Congress and Johnson.
   c.   a decisive defeat for Johnson and a veto-proof Republican Congress.
   d.   a gain for Northern Democrats and their moderate compromise plan for Reconstruction.

6.   In contrast to radical Republicans, moderate Republicans generally
   a.   favored states' rights and opposed direct federal involvement in individuals' lives.
   b.   favored the use of federal power to alter the Southern economic system.
   c.   favored emancipation but opposed the Fourteenth Amendment.

    d.   favored returning the Southern states to the Union without significant Reconstruction.

7. Besides putting the South under the rule of federal soldiers, the Military Reconstruction Act of 1867 required that

    a.   Southern states give blacks the vote as a condition of readmittance to the Union.
    b.   blacks and carpetbaggers be given control of Southern legislatures.
    c.   former slaves be given land and education at federal expense.
    d.   former Confederate officials and military officers be tried for treason.

8. The Fourteenth amendment provided for

    a.   an end to slavery.
    b.   permanent disfranchisement of all Confederate officials.
    c.   full citizenship and civil rights for former slaves.
    d.   voting rights for women.

9. The Fifteenth Amendment provided for

    a.   readmitting Southern states to the Union.
    b.   full citizenship and civil rights for former slaves.
    c.   voting rights for former slaves.
    d.   voting rights for women.

10. Women's-rights leaders opposed the Fourteenth and Fifteenth Amendments because

    a.   they objected to racial integration in the women's movement.
    b.   the amendments granted citizenship and voting rights to black and white men but not to women.
    c.   they favored passage of the Equal Rights Amendment first.
    d.   most of them were Democrats who would be hurt by the amendments.

11. The right to vote encouraged southern black men to

    a.   form a third political party as an alternative to the Democrats and Republicans.
    b.   seek an apology and reparations for slavery.
    c.   organize the Union League as a vehicle for political empowerment and self-defense.
    d.   organize large-scale migrations out of the South to the West.

12. The radical Reconstruction regimes in the Southern states

    a.   took away white Southerners' civil rights and voting rights.
    b.   consisted almost entirely of blacks.
    c.   included white Northerners, white Southerners, and blacks.
    d.   eliminated the public education systems in most Southern states.

13. Most of the Northern "carpetbaggers" were actually

    a.   former Union soldiers, businessmen, or professionals.
    b.   undercover agents of the federal government.
    c.   former Southern Whigs and Unionists who had opposed the Confederacy.
    d.   Northern teachers and missionaries who wanted to aid the freedmen.

14. The radical Republicans' impeachment of President Andrew Johnson resulted in

    a.   Johnson's acceptance of the radicals' Reconstruction plan.
    b.   a failure to convict and remove Johnson by a margin of only one vote.
    c.   Johnson's conviction on the charge of violating the Tenure of Office Act.
    d.   Johnson's resignation and appointment of Ulysses Grant as his successor.

15. The skeptical public finally accepted Seward's purchase of Alaska because

    a.   there were rumors of extensive oil deposits in the territory.
    b.   it was considered strategically vital to American defense.
    c.   it would provide a new frontier safety valve after the settling of the West.
    d.   Russia had been the only great power friendly to the Union during the Civil War.

C. Identification

Supply the correct identification for each numbered description.

1. _____   Common term for the blacks newly liberated from slavery

2. _____   Federal agency that greatly assisted blacks educationally but failed in other aid efforts

3. _____   The largest African American denomination (church) after slavery

4. _____   Lincoln's 1863 program for a rapid Reconstruction of the South

5. _____   The constitutional amendment freeing all slaves

6. _____   The harsh Southern state laws of 1865 that limited black rights and imposed restrictions to ensure a stable black labor supply

7. _____   The constitutional amendment granting civil rights to freed slaves and barring former Confederates from office

8. _____   Republican Reconstructionists who favored a more rapid restoration of Southern state governments and opposed radical plans for drastic economic transformation of the South

9. _____   Republican Reconstructionists who favored keeping the South out of the federal government until a complete social and economic revolution was accomplished in the region

10. _____   The black political organization that promoted self-help and defense of political rights

11. _____   Supreme Court ruling that military tribunals could not try civilians when the civil courts were open

12. _____   Derogatory term for white Southerners who cooperated with the Republican Reconstruction governments

13. _____   Derogatory term for Northerners who came to the South during Reconstruction and sometimes took part in Republican state governments

14. _____   Constitutional amendment guaranteeing blacks the right to vote

15. _____   "Seward's Folly," acquired in 1867 from Russia

D. Matching People, Places, and Events

Match the person, place, or event in the left column with the proper description in the right column by inserting the correct letter on the blank line.

1. ___   Exodusters

2. ___   Oliver O. Howard

3. ___   Andrew Johnson

4. ___   Abraham Lincoln

5. ___   Civil Rights Bill of 1866

6. ___   Charles Sumner

7. ___   Thaddeus Stevens

a.   A constitutionally questionable law whose violation by President Johnson formed the basis for his impeachment

b.   The first congressional attempt to guarantee black rights in the South, passed over Johnson's veto

c.   Born a poor white southerner, he became the white South's champion against radical Reconstruction

8. ___   Military Reconstruction Act of 1867

9. ___   Hiram Revels

10. ___   Ku Klux Klan

11. ___   Force Acts of 1870 and 1871

12. ___   Tenure of Office Act

13. ___   Union League

14. ___   Benjamin Wade

15. ___   William Seward

d. Secretary of state who arranged an initially unpopular but valuable land deal in 1867

e. Laws designed to stamp out Ku Klux Klan terrorism in the South

f. Black Republican senator from Mississippi during Reconstruction

g. Secret organization that intimidated blacks and worked to restore white supremacy

h. Blacks who left the South for Kansas and elsewhere during Reconstruction

i. Congressional law that imposed military rule on the South and demanded harsh conditions for readmission of the seceded states

j. Beaten in the Senate chamber before the Civil War, he became the leader of Senate Republican radicals during Reconstruction

k. Pro-black general who led an agency that tried to assist the freedmen

l. Leading Black political organization during Reconstruction

m. Author of the moderate "10 percent" Reconstruction plan that ran into congressional opposition

n. The president pro tempore of the Senate who hoped to become president of the United States after Johnson's impeachment conviction

o. Leader of radical Republicans in the House of Representatives

E. Putting Things in Order

Put the following events in correct order by numbering them from 1 to 5.

1. _____   Constitution is amended to guarantee former slaves the right to vote.

2. _____   Lincoln announces a plan to rapidly restore southern states to the Union.

3. _____   Northern troops are finally withdrawn from the South, and Southern state governments are re-constituted without federal constraint.

4. _____   An unpopular antiradical president escapes conviction and removal from office by one vote.

5. _____   Johnson's attempt to restore the South to the Union is overturned because of congressional hostility to ex-Confederates and southern passage of the Black Codes.

F. Matching Cause and Effect

Match the historical cause in the left column with the proper effect in the right column by writing the correct letter on the blank line.

Cause	Effect
1. ___ The South's military defeat in the Civil War	a. Provoked a politically motivated trial to remove the president from office
2. ___ The Freedmen's Bureau	b. Intimidated black voters and tried to keep blacks "in their place"
3. ___ The Black Codes of 1865	c. Prompted Republicans to refuse to seat Southern delegations in Congress
4. ___ The election of ex-Confederates to Congress in 1865	d. Destroyed the southern economy but strengthened Southern hatred of "yankees"
5. ___ Johnson's "swing around the circle" in the election of 1866	e. Successfully educated former slaves but failed to provide much other assistance to them
6. ___ Military Reconstruction and the Fourteenth and Fifteenth Amendments	f. Forced all the Southern states to establish governments that upheld black voting and other civil rights
7. ___ The "radical" Southern state Reconstruction governments	g. Embittered white Southerners while doing little to really help blacks
8. ___ The Ku Klux Klan	h. Engaged in some corruption but also enacted many valuable social reforms
9. ___ The radical Republicans' hatred of Johnson	i. Weakened support for mild Reconstruction policies and helped elect overwhelming Republican majorities to Congress
10. ___ The whole Reconstruction era	j. Imposed slaverylike restrictions on blacks and angered the North

G. Developing Historical Skills

Interpreting Photographs and Drawings

Answer the following questions about the photographs and drawings in this chapter.

1. *The Faculty of a Freedmen's Bureau School near Norfolk, Virginia* (p. 481)

   What is the ratio of black to white teachers on the freedmen's school staff? Who appears to be the principal of the school? Where are the black teachers positioned in the photograph? Might this suggest anything about the relations between white and black teachers in the school?

2.   *A Family of Sharecroppers at the End of the Civil War* (photograph, p. 485)

      What physical details suggest the poverty of these former slaves? How would you characterize the attitudes of the people in the photograph?

3.   *Freedmen Voting, Richmond, Virginia, 1871* (drawing, p. 482)

      What appears to be the economic status of the new black voters portrayed here? How does their condition differ from that of the voting officials, black and white? What does the drawing suggest about the power of the newly enfranchised freedmen?

PART III: APPLYING WHAT YOU HAVE LEARNED

1.   What were the major problems facing the South and the nation after the Civil War? How did Reconstruction address them, or fail to do so?

2.   How did freed blacks react to the end of slavery? How did both Southern and Northern whites react?

3.   How did the white South's intransigence and President Johnson's political bungling open the way for the congressional Republican program of military Reconstruction?

4.   What was the purpose of congressional Reconstruction, and what were its actual effects in the South?

5.   What did the attempt at black political empowerment achieve? Why did it finally fail? Could it have succeeded with a stronger Northern political will behind it?

6.   How did African Americans take advantage of the political, economic, and social opportunities of Reconstruction, despite their limitations?

7.   How effective was the Ku Klux Klan and other white resistance movements in undermining the interracial governments even before the collapse of Reconstruction in 1877?

8.   Was the North in general, and the Republican Party in particular, ever really committed to transforming the political, economic, and racial conditions of the South?

9.   Why did Reconstruction apparently fail so badly? Was the failure primarily one of immediate political circumstances, or was it more deeply rooted in the history of American sectional and race relations?

10.   What was the greatest success of Reconstruction? Would you agree with historians who argue that even if Reconstruction failed at the time, it laid the foundations for the later successes of the civil rights movement?

CHAPTER 23

Political Paralysis in the Gilded Age, 1869–1896

PART I: REVIEWING THE CHAPTER

A. CHECKLIST OF LEARNING OBJECTIVES

After mastering this chapter, you should be able to

1. describe the political corruption of the Grant administration and the mostly unsuccessful efforts to reform politics in the Gilded Age.

2. describe the economic crisis of the 1870s and explain the growing conflict between "hard-money" and "soft-money" advocates.

3. explain the intense political partisanship of the Gilded age, despite the parties' lack of ideological difference and poor quality of political leadership.

4. indicate how the disputed Hayes-Tilden election of 1876 led to the Compromise of 1877 and the end of Reconstruction.

5. describe how the end of Reconstruction led to the loss of black rights and the imposition of the Jim Crow system of segregation in the South.

6. explain the rise of class conflict between business and labor in the 1870s and the growing hostility to immigrants, especially the Chinese.

7. explain the rise of political conflict in the early 1890s, and the failure of Cleveland to address growing farm and labor discontent.

8. show how the farm crisis of the depression of the 1890s stirred growing social protests and class conflict, and fueled the rise of the radical Populist Party.

B. GLOSSARY

To build your social science vocabulary, familiarize yourself with the following terms:

1. **coalition** A temporary alliance of political factions or parties for some specific purpose. "The Republicans, now freed from the Union party coalition of war days, enthusiastically nominated Grant. . . ." (p. 503)

2. **corner** To gain exclusive control of a commodity in order to fix its price. "The crafty pair concocted a plot in 1869 to corner the gold market." (p. 503)

3. **censure** An official statement of condemnation passed by a legislative body against one of its members or some other official of government. While severe, a censure itself stops short of penalties or **expulsion**, which is removal from office. "A newspaper exposé and congressional investigation led to formal censure of two congressmen. . . ." (p. 504)

4. **amnesty** A general pardon for offenses or crimes against a government. "The Republican Congress in 1872 passed a general amnesty act. . . ." (p. 506)

5. **civil service** Referring to regular employment by government according to a standardized system of job descriptions, merit qualifications, pay, and promotion, as distinct from **political appointees** who receive positions based on affiliation and party loyalty. "Congress also moved to reduce high Civil War tariffs and to fumigate the Grant administration with mild civil service reform." (p. 506)

6. **unsecured loans** Money loaned without identification of collateral (existing assets) to be forfeited in case the borrower defaults on the loan. "The Freedman's Savings and Trust Company had made unsecured loans to several companies that went under." (p. 506)

7. **contraction** In finance, reducing the available supply of money, thus tending to raise interest rates and lower prices. "Coupled with the reduction of greenbacks, this policy was called 'contraction.' " (p. 507)

8. **deflation (ary)** An increase in the value of money in relation to available goods, causing prices to fall. **Inflation**, a decrease in the value of money in relation to goods, causes prices to rise. "It had a noticeable deflationary effect—the amount of money per capita in circulation actually *decreased* . . . ." (p. 507)

9. **fraternal organization** A society of men drawn together for social purposes and sometimes to pursue other common goals. ". . . the Grand Army of the Republic [was] a politically potent fraternal organization of several hundred thousand Union veterans of the Civil War." (p. 507)

10. **consensus** Common or unanimous opinion. "How can this apparent paradox of political consensus and partisan fervor be explained?" (p. 507)

11. **kickback** The return of a portion of the money received in a sale or contract, often secretly or illegally, in exchange for favors. "The lifeblood of both parties was patronage—disbursing jobs by the bucketful in return for votes, kickbacks, and party service." (p. 507)

12. **lien** A legal claim by a lender or another party on a borrower's property as a guarantee against repayment, and prohibiting any sale of the property. " . . . storekeepers extended credit to small farmers for food and supplies and in return took a lien on their harvest." (p. 510)

13. **assassination** Politically motivated murder of a public figure. " . . . he asked all those who had benefited politically by the assassination to contribute to his defense fund." (p. 514)

14. **laissez-faire** The doctrine of noninterference, especially by the government, in matters of economics or business (literally, "leave alone"). "[The new president was] a staunch apostle of the hands-off creed of laissez-faire. . . ." (p. 518)

15. **pork barrel** In American politics, government appropriations for political purposes, especially projects designed to please a legislator's local constituency. "One [way to reduce the surplus] was to squander it on pensions and 'pork-barrel' bills. . . ." (p. 519)

PART II: CHECKING YOUR PROGRESS

A. True-False

Where the statement is true, circle **T**; where it is false, circle **F**.

1. T (F)   Ulysses Grant's status as a military hero enabled him to become a successful president who stood above partisan politics.

2. (T) F   The scandals of the Grant administration included bribes and corrupt dealings reaching to the cabinet and the vice president of the United States.

3. T (F)   The Liberal Republican movement's political skill enabled it to clean up the corruption of the Grant administration.

4. (T) F   The severe economic downturn of the 1870s caused business failures, labor conflict, and battles over currency.

5. T (F)   The close, fiercely contested elections of the Gilded Age reflected the deep divisions between Republicans and Democrats over national issues.

6. (T) F   The battles between the "Stalwart" and "Half-Breed" Republican factions were mainly over who would get patronage and spoils.

7. T (F)   The disputed Hayes-Tilden election was settled by a political deal in which Democrats got the presidency and Republicans got economic and political concessions.

8. (T) F   The Compromise of 1877 purchased political peace between North and South by sacrificing southern blacks and removing federal troops in the South.

9. (T) F   The sharecropping and tenant farming systems forced many Southern blacks into permanent economic debt and dependency.

10. (T) F   Western hostility to Chinese immigrants arose in part because the Chinese provided a source of cheap labor that competed with white workers.

11. (T) F   By reducing politicians' use of patronage, the new civil-service system inadvertently made them more dependent on big campaign contributors.

12. T (F)   The Cleveland-Blaine campaign of 1884 was conducted primarily as a debate about the issues of taxes and the tariff.

13. (T) F   The Republican party in the post–Civil War era relied heavily on the political support of veterans' groups, to which it gave substantial pension benefits in return.

14. (T) F   The Populist party's attempt to form a coalition of farmers and workers failed partly because of the racial division between poor whites and blacks in the South.

15. T (F)   President Cleveland's deal to save the gold standard by borrowing $65 million from J.P. Morgan enhanced his popularity among both Democrats and Populists.

B. Multiple Choice

Select the best answer and circle the corresponding letter.

1. Financiers Jim Fisk and Jay Gould tried to involve the Grant administration in a corrupt scheme to
    a.   skim funds from the Bureau of Indian Affairs.
    b.   sell "watered" railroad stock at high prices.
    c.   corner the gold market.
    d.   bribe congressmen in exchange for federal land grants.

2. Boss Tweed's widespread corruption was finally brought to a halt by
    a.   federal prosecutors who uncovered the theft.
    b.   outraged citizens who rebelled against the waste of public money.
    c.   the journalistic exposés of *The New York Times* and cartoonist Thomas Nast.
    d.   Tweed's political opponents in New York City.

3. The Credit Mobilier scandal involved
    a.   the abuse of federal credit intended for urban development.
    b.   railroad corporation fraud and the subsequent bribery of congressmen.
    c.   Secretary of War Belknap's fraudulent sale of contracts to supply Indian reservations.
    d.   the attempt of insiders to gain control of New York's gold and stock markets.

4. Grant's greatest failing in the scandals that plagued his administration was
    a.   his refusal to turn over evidence to congressional investigators.

    b.   his toleration of corruption and his loyalty to crooked friends.

    c.   his acceptance of behind-the-scenes payments for performing his duties as president.

    d.   his use of large amounts of "dirty" money in his political campaigns.

5.   The depression of the 1870s led to increasing demands for

    a.   inflation of the money supply by issuing more paper or silver currency.

    b.   federal programs to create jobs for the unemployed.

    c.   restoration of sound money by backing all paper currency with gold.

    d.   stronger regulation of the banking system.

6.   The political system of the "Gilded Age" was generally characterized by

    a.   "split-ticket" voting, low voter turnout, and single-issue special-interest groups.

    b.   strong party loyalties, low voter turnout, and deep ideological differences.

    c.   "third-party" movements, high voter turnout and strong disagreement on foreign-policy issues.

    d.   strong party loyalties, high voter turnout, and few disagreements on national issues.

7.   The primary goal for which all factions in both political parties contended during the Gilded Age was

    a.   racial justice.

    b.   a sound financial and banking system.

    c.   patronage.

    d.   a more assertive American foreign policy.

8.   The key tradeoff featured in the Compromise of 1877 was that,

    a.   Republicans got the presidency in exchange for the final removal of federal troops from the South.

    b.   Democrats got the presidency in exchange for federal guarantees of black civil rights.

    c.   Republicans got the presidency in exchange for Democratic control of the cabinet.

    d.   Democrats got the presidency in exchange for increased immigration quotas from Ireland.

9.   Which of the following was *not* among the changes that affected African Americans in the South after federal troops were withdrawn in the Compromise of 1877?

    a.   The forced relocation of black farmers to the Kansas and Oklahoma "dust bowl"

    b.   The imposition of literacy requirements and poll taxes to prevent black voting

    c.   The development of the tenant farming and share-cropping systems

    d.   The introduction of legal systems of racial segregation

10.   The Supreme Court's ruling in *Plessy* v. *Ferguson* upholding "separate but equal" public facilities in effect legalized

    a.   southern blacks' loss of voting rights.

    b.   the system of unequal segregation between the races.

    c.   the program of separate black and white economic development endorsed by Booker T. Washington.

    d.   the rights to "equal protection of the law" guaranteed by the Fourteenth Amendment.

11.   The great railroad strike of 1877 revealed

    a.   the growing strength of American labor unions.

    b.   the refusal of the U.S. federal government to intervene in private labor disputes.

    c.   the ability of American workers to cooperate across ethnic and racial lines.

    d.   the growing threat of class warfare in response to the economic depression of the mid-1870s.

12.   The final result of the widespread anti-Chinese agitation in the West was

    a.   a program to encourage Chinese students to enroll in American colleges and universities.

    b.   a Congressional law to prohibit any further Chinese immigration.

    c.   the stripping of citizenship even from native-born Chinese Americans.

    d.   legal segregation of all Chinese into "Chinatown" districts in San Francisco and elsewhere.

13. President James Garfield was assassinated by
   a. a fanatically anti-Republican Confederate veteran.
   b. a mentally unstable disappointed office seeker.
   c. an anticapitalist immigrant anarchist.
   d. a corrupt gangster under federal criminal indictment.
14. In its first years, the Populist Party advocated, among other things
   a. free silver, a graduated income tax, and government ownership of the railroads, telegraph, and telephone.
   b. higher tariffs and federally sponsored unemployment insurance and pensions.
   c. tighter restriction on black economic, social, and political rights.
   d. a Homestead Act to permit farmers and unemployed workers to obtain free federal land in the West.
15. Grover Cleveland stirred a furious storm of protest when, in response to the extreme financial crisis of the 1890s, he
   a. lowered tariffs to permit an influx of cheaper foreign goods into the country.
   b. signed a bill introducing a federal income tax that cut into workers' wages.
   c. pushed the Federal Reserve Board into sharply raising interest rates.
   d. borrowed $65 million dollars from J.P. Morgan and other bankers in order to save the monetary gold standard.

C. Identification

Supply the correct identification for each numbered description.

1. _____ The symbol of the Republican political tactic of attacking Democrats with reminders of the Civil War
2. _____ Corrupt construction company whose bribes and payoffs to congressmen and others created a major Grant administration scandal
3. _____ Short-lived third party of 1872 that attempted to curb Grant administration corruption
4. _____ Precious metal that "soft-money" advocates demanded be coined again to compensate for the "Crime of '73"
5. _____ "Soft-money" third party that polled over a million votes and elected fourteen congressmen in 1878 by advocating inflation
6. _____ Mark Twain's sarcastic name for the post–Civil War era, which emphasized its atmosphere of greed and corruption
7. _____ Civil War Union veterans' organization that became a potent political bulwark of the Republican party in the late nineteenth century
8. _____ Republican party faction led by Senator Roscoe Conkling that opposed all attempts at civil-service reform
9. _____ Republican party faction led by Senator James G. Blaine that paid lip service to government reform while still battling for patronage and spoils
10. _____ The complex political agreement between Republicans and Democrats that resolved the bitterly disputed election of 1876
11. _____ Asian immigrant group that experienced discrimination on the West Coast

12. _____ System of choosing federal employees on the basis of merit rather than patronage introduced by the Pendleton Act of 1883

13. _____ Sky-high Republican tariff of 1890 that caused widespread anger among farmers in the Midwest and the South

14. _____ Insurgent political party that gained widespread support among farmers in the 1890s

15. _____ Notorious clause in southern voting laws that exempted from literacy tests and poll taxes anyone whose ancestors had voted in 1860, thereby excluding blacks

D. Matching People, Places, and Events

Match the person, place, or event in the left column with the proper description in the right column by inserting the correct letter on the blank line.

1. ___ Ulysses S. Grant

2. ___ Jim Fisk

3. ___ Boss Tweed

4. ___ Horace Greeley

5. ___ Jay Cooke

6. ___ Denis Kearney

7. ___ Tom Watson

8. ___ Roscoe Conkling

9. ___ James G. Blaine

10. ___ Rutherford B. Hayes

11. ___ James Garfield

12. ___ Jim Crow

13. ___ Grover Cleveland

14. ___ William Jennings Bryan

15. ___ J. P. Morgan

a. Heavyweight New York political boss whose widespread fraud landed him in jail in 1871

b. Bold and unprincipled financier whose plot to corner the U.S. gold market nearly succeeded in 1869

c. Winner of the contested 1876 election who presided over the end of Reconstruction and a sharp economic downturn

d. Great military leader whose presidency foundered in corruption and political ineptitude

e. Term for the racial segregation laws imposed in the 1890s

f. Eloquent young Congressman from Nebraska who became the most prominent advocate of "free silver" in the early 1890s

g. President whose assassination after only a few months in office spurred the passage of a civil-service law

h. Irish-born leader of the anti-Chinese movement in California

i. Radical Populist leader whose early success turned sour, and who then became a vicious racist

j. Wealthy New York financier whose bank collapse in 1873 set off an economic depression

k. Imperious New York senator and leader of the "Stalwart" faction of Republicans

l. First Democratic president since the Civil War; defender of *laissez-faire* economics and low tariffs

m. Enormously wealthy banker whose secret bailout of the federal government in 1895 aroused fierce public anger

n. Colorful, eccentric newspaper editor who carried the Liberal Republican and Democratic banners against Grant in 1872

o. Charming but corrupt "Half-Breed" Republican senator and presidential nominee in 1884

E. Putting Things in Order

Put the following events in correct order by numbering them from 1 to 5.

1. _____ A bitterly disputed presidential election is resolved by a complex political deal that ends Reconstruction in the South.

2. _____ Two unscrupulous financiers use corrupt means to manipulate New York gold markets and the U.S. Treasury.

3. _____ A major economic depression causes widespread social unrest and the rise of the Populist Party as a vehicle of protest.

4. _____ Grant administration scandals split the Republican party, but Grant overcomes the inept opposition to win reelection.

5. _____ Monetary deflation and the high McKinley Tariff lead to growing agitation for "free silver" by Congressman William Jennings Bryan and others.

F. Matching Cause and Effect

Match the historical cause in the left column with the proper effect in the right column by writing the correct letter on the blank line.

Cause	Effect
1. ___ Favor-seeking business-people and corrupt politicians	a. Created fierce partisan competition and high voter turnouts, even though the parties agreed on most national issues
2. ___ *The New York Times* and cartoonist Thomas Nast	b. Caused anti-Chinese violence and restrictions against Chinese immigration
3. ___ Upright Republicans' disgust with Grant administration scandals	c. Led to the formation of the Liberal Republican party in 1872
4. ___ The economic crash of the mid-1870s	d. Induced Grover Cleveland to negotiate a secret loan from J. P. Morgan's banking syndicate
5. ___ Local cultural, moral, and religious differences	e. Forced Boss Tweed out of power and into jail
6. ___ The Compromise of 1877 that settled the disputed Hayes-Tilden election	f. Helped ensure passage of the Pendleton Act
7. ___ White workers' resentment of Chinese labor competition	g. Caused numerous scandals during President Grant's administration
8. ___ Public shock at Garfield's assassination by Guiteau	h. Led to failure of the third party revolt in the South and a growing racial backlash
9. ___ The 1890s depression and the drain of gold from the federal treasury	i. Caused unemployment, railroad strikes, and a demand for "cheap money"
10. ___ The inability of Populist leaders to overcome divisions between white and black farmers	j. Led to the withdrawal of troops from the South and the virtual end of federal

efforts to protect black rights there

G. Developing Historical Skills

Historical Fact and Historical Explanation

Historians uncover a great deal of information about the past, but often that information takes on significance only when it is analyzed and interpreted. In this chapter, many facts about the presidents and elections of the Gilded Age are presented: for example, the very close elections in 1876, 1884, 1888, and 1892; the large voter turnouts; and the lack of significant issues in most elections.

These facts take on larger meaning, however, when we examine the *reasons* for them. Reread the section "Pallid Politics in the Gilded Age" (pp. 507–508) and answer each of the following questions in a sentence or two.

1. What *fundamental* difference between the two parties made partisan politics so fiercely contested in the Gilded Age?

2. Why did this underlying difference *not* lead to differences over issues at the national level?

3. Why were so many of the elections extremely close, no matter who the candidates were?

4. Why was winning each election so very important to both parties, even though there was little disagreement on issues?

H. Map Mastery

Map Discrimination

Using the maps and charts in Chapter 23, answer the following questions:

1. *Hayes-Tilden Disputed Election of 1876*: In the controversial Hayes-Tilden election of 1876, how many *undisputed* electoral votes did Republican Hayes win in the former Confederate states?

2. *Hayes-Tilden Disputed Election of 1876*: Democrat Tilden carried four states in the North—states that did not have slavery before 1865. Which were they?

3. *Growth of Classified Civil Service*: The *percentage* of offices classified under civil service was approximately how many times greater under President McKinley than under President Arthur: two, three, four, five, or ten?

4. *Presidential Election of 1884*: Which of the following states gained the most electoral votes between 1876 and 1884: New York, Indiana, Missouri, or Texas?

5. *Presidential Election of 1884*: How many states that were carried by Republican Hayes in 1876 were carried by Democrat Cleveland in 1884?

Map Challenge

Using the election map on p. 508 and the account of the Compromise of 1877 in the text (pp. 508–509), discuss the election of 1876 in relation to both Reconstruction and the political balance of the Gilded Age. Include some analysis of the reasons why this was the last time for nearly a century that the states in the Deep South voted Republican.

PART III: APPLYING WHAT YOU HAVE LEARNED

1. What made politics in the Gilded Age extremely popular—with over 80 percent voter participation—yet so often corrupt and unconcerned with issues?

2. What caused the end of the Reconstruction? What did the North and South each gain from the Compromise of 1877?

3. What were the results of the Compromise of 1877 for race relations? How were the political, economic, and social conditions of southern African Americans interrelated?

4. What caused the rise of the "money issue" in American politics? What were the backers of "greenback" and silver money trying to achieve?

5. What were the causes and political results of the rise of agrarian protest in the 1880s and 1890s? Why were the Populists' attempts to form a coalition of white and black farmers and industrial workers ultimately unsuccessful?

6. White laborers in the West fiercely resisted Chinese immigration, and white farmers in the South turned toward race-baiting rather than forming a populist alliance with black farmers. How and why did racial "trump" the apparent economic self-interests of these lower class white?

7. In what ways did the political conflicts of the Gilded Age still reflect the aftermath of the Civil War and Reconstruction? (See Chapter 22.) To what extent did the political leaders of the time address issues of race and sectional conflict, and to what extent did they merely shove them under the rug?

8. Was the apparent failure of the American political system to address the industrial conflicts of the Gilded Age a result of the two parties' poor leadership and narrow self-interest, or was it simply the natural inability of a previously agrarian, local, democratic nation to face up to a modern, national industrial economy?

CHAPTER 24

Industry Comes of Age, 1865–1900

PART I: REVIEWING THE CHAPTER

A. CHECKLIST OF LEARNING OBJECTIVES

After mastering this chapter, you should be able to

1. explain how the transcontinental railroad network provided the basis for the great post–Civil War industrial transformation.

2. identify the abuses in the railroad industry and discuss how these led to the first efforts at industrial regulation by the federal government.

3. describe how the economy came to be dominated by giant "trusts," such as those headed by Carnegie and Rockefeller in the steel and oil industries.

4. discuss the growing class conflict caused by industrial growth and combination, and the early efforts to alleviate it.

5. indicate how industrialists and their supporters attempted to explain and justify great wealth and increasing class division through "natural law" and the "Gospel of Wealth."

6. explain why the South was generally excluded from industrial development and fell into a "third world" economic dependency.

7. analyze the social changes brought by industrialization, particularly the altered position of working men and women.

8. explain the failures of the Knights of Labor and the modest success of the American Federation of Labor.

B. GLOSSARY

To build your social science vocabulary, familiarize yourself with the following terms:

1. **pool** In business, an agreement to divide a given market in order to avoid competition. "The earliest form of combination was the 'pool'. . . . " (p. 535)

2. **rebate** A return of a portion of the amount paid for goods or services. "Other rail barons granted secret rebates. . . ." (p. 535)

3. **free enterprise** An economic system that permits unrestricted entrepreneurial business activity; capitalism. "Dedicated to free enterprise . . . , they cherished a traditionally keen pride in progress." (p. 535)

4. **regulatory commission** In American government, any of the agencies established to control a special sphere of business or other activity; members are usually appointed by the president and confirmed by Congress. "It heralded the arrival of a series of independent regulatory commissions in the next century. . . ." (p. 536)

5. **trust**   A combination of corporations, usually in the same industry, in which stockholders trade their stock to a central board in exchange for trust certificates. (By extension, the term came to be applied to any large, semi-monopolistic business.) "He perfected a device for controlling bothersome rivals—the 'trust.'" (p. 538)

6. **syndicate**   An association of financiers organized to carry out projects requiring very large amounts of capital. "His prescribed remedy was to . . . ensure future harmony by placing officers of his own banking syndicate on their various boards of directors." (p. 538)

7. **patrician**   Characterized by noble or high social standing. "An arrogant class of 'new rich' was now elbowing aside the patrician families. . . ." (p. 542)

8. **plutocracy**   Government by the wealthy. "Plutocracy . . . took its stand firmly on the Constitution." (p. 542)

9. **Third World**   Term developed during the Cold War for the non-Western (first world) and noncommunist (second world) nations of the world, most of them formerly under colonial rule and still economically poor and dependent. "The net effect was to keep the South in a kind of 'Third World' servitude to the Northeast. . . ." (p. 544)

10. **socialist (socialism)**   Political belief in promoting social and economic equality through the ownership and control of the major means of production by the whole community rather than by individuals or corporations. "Some of it was envious, but much of it rose from the small and increasingly vocal group of socialists. . . ." (p. 548)

11. **radical**   One who believes in fundamental change in the political, economic, or social system. ". .don't split . much of [this criticism] rose from . . . socialists and other radicals, many of whom were recent European immigrants." (p. 548)

12. **lockout**   The refusal by an employer to allow employees to work unless they agree to his or her terms. "Employers could lock their doors against rebellious workers—a process called the 'lockout'. . . ." (p. 549)

13. **yellow dog contract**   A labor contract in which an employee must agree not to join a union as a condition of holding the job. "[Employers] could compel them to sign 'ironclad oaths' or 'yellow dog contracts'. . . ." (p. 549)

14. **cooperative**   An organization for producing, marketing, or consuming goods in which the members share the benefits. ". . . they campaigned for . . . producers' cooperatives. . . ."

15. **anarchist (anarchism)**   Political belief that all organized, coercive government is wrong in principle, and that society should be organized solely on the basis of free cooperation. (Some anarchists practiced violence against the state, while others were nonviolent pacifists.) "Eight anarchists were rounded up, although nobody proved that they had anything to do directly with the bomb." (p. 551)

PART II: CHECKING YOUR PROGRESS

A. True-False

Where the statement is true, circle **T**; where it is false, circle **F**.

1.   T   F   Private railroad companies built the transcontinental rail lines by raising their own capital funds without the assistance of the federal government.

2.   T   F   The rapid expansion of the railroad industry was often accompanied by rapid mergers, bankruptcies, and reorganizations.

3. T F The railroads created an integrated national market, stimulated the growth in cities, and encouraged European immigration.

4. T F Railroad owners were generally fair and honest in their dealings with shippers, the government, and the public.

5. T F The early, weak federal efforts at railroad regulation did bring some order and stability to industrial competition.

6. T F The Rockefeller oil company technique of "horizontal integration" involved combining into one organization all the phases of manufacturing from the raw material to the customer.

7. T F Rockefeller, Morgan, and others organized monopolistic trusts and "interlocking directorates" in order to consolidate business and eliminate cutthroat competition.

8. T F Defenders of unrestrained capitalism like Herbert Spencer and William Graham Sumner primarily used "natural law" and laissez-faire economics rather than Charles Darwin's theories to justify the "survival of the fittest."

9. T F The pro-industry ideology of the "New South" enabled that region to make rapid economic gains by 1900.

10. T F Two new inventions that brought large numbers of women into the workplace were the typewriter and the telephone.

11. T F Industrialization generally gave the industrial wage earner greater status and control over his or her own life.

12. T F The impact of new machines and mass immigration held down wages and gave employers advantages in their dealings with labor.

13. T F The Knights of Labor organized skilled and unskilled workers, blacks and whites, women and men.

14. T F The Knights of Labor were severely hurt by the Haymarket Square episode, even though they had no connection with the bombing.

15. T F The American Federation of Labor tried hard but failed to organize unskilled workers, women, and blacks.

B. Multiple Choice

Select the best answer and circle the corresponding letter.

1. The federal government contributed to the building of the national rail network by
    a. importing substantial numbers of Chinese immigrants to build the railroads.
    b. providing free grants of federal land to the railroad companies.
    c. building and operating the first transcontinental rail lines.
    d. transporting the mail and other federal shipments over the rail lines.

2. The most efficient and public-minded of the early railroad-building industrialists was
    a. Collis P. Huntington.
    b. Leland Stanford.
    c. Cornelius Vanderbilt.
    d. James J. Hill.

3. The railroad most significantly stimulated American industrialization by
    a. opening up the West to settlement.

b.   creating a single national market for raw materials and consumer goods.

c.   eliminating the inefficient canal system.

d.   inspiring greater federal investment in technical research and development.

4.   The railroad barons aroused considerable public opposition by practices such as

a.   forcing Indians off their traditional hunting grounds.

b.   refusing to pay their employees decent wages.

c.   refusing to build railroad lines in less settled areas.

d.   stock watering and bribery of public officials.

5.   The railroads affected even the organization of time in the United States by

a.   introducing regularly scheduled departures and arrivals on railroad timetables.

b.   introducing the concept of daylight savings time.

c.   introducing four standard time zones across the country.

d.   turning travel that had once taken days into a matter of hours.

6.   The first important federal law aimed at regulating American industry was

a.   the Federal Communications Act.

b.   the Pure Food and Drug Act.

c.   the Interstate Commerce Act.

d.   the Federal Trade Commission.

7.   Financier J. P. Morgan exercised his economic power most effectively by

a.   developing "horizontal integration" in the oil industry.

b.   lending money to the federal government.

c.   consolidating rival industries through "interlocking directorates."

d.   serving as the middleman between American industrialists and foreign governments.

8.   Two late-nineteenth-century technological inventions that especially drew women out of the home and into the workforce were

a.   the railroad and the telegraph.

b.   the electric light and the phonograph.

c.   the cash register and the stock ticker.

d.   the typewriter and the telephone.

9.   Andrew Carnegie's industrial system of "vertical integration" involved

a.   the construction of large, vertical steel factories in Pittsburgh and elsewhere.

b.   the cooperation between manufacturers like Andrew Carnegie and financiers like J. P. Morgan.

c.   the integration of diverse immigrant ethnic groups into the steel industry labor force.

d.   the combination of all phases of the steel industry from mining to manufacturing into a single organization.

10.   The large trusts like Standard Oil and Swift and Armour justified their economic domination of their industries by claiming that

a.   they were fundamentally concerned with serving the public interest over private profit.

b.   only large-scale methods of production and distribution could provide superior products at low prices.

c.   competition among many small firms was contrary to the law of economics.

d.   only large American corporations could compete with huge British and German international companies.

11.   The oil industry first thrived in the late 1880s by producing

a.   natural gas and heating oil for home heating purposes.

b.   kerosene for oil lamps.

c.   gasoline for automobiles.

d.   heavy-duty diesel fuel for the railroads and industry.

12. Andrew Carnegie's "Gospel of Wealth" proclaimed his belief that
    a. wealth was God's reward for hard work, while poverty resulted from laziness and immorality.
    b. churches needed to take a stronger stand on the economic issues of the day.
    c. faith in capitalism and progress should take the place once reserved for religion.
    d. those who acquired great wealth were morally responsible to use it for the public good.
13. The attempt to create an industrialized "New South" in the late nineteenth century generally failed because
    a. the South was discriminated against and held down as a supplier of raw materials to northern industry.
    b. Southerners were too bitter at the Union to pursue national goals.
    c. continued political violence made the South an unattractive place for investment.
    d. there was little demand for southern products like textiles and cigarettes.
14. For American workers, industrialization generally meant
    a. a steady, long-term decline in wages and the standard of living.
    b. an opportunity to create small businesses that might eventually produce large profits.
    c. a long-term rise in the standard of living but a loss of independence and control of work.
    d. a stronger sense of identification with their jobs and employers.
15. In contrast to the Knights of Labor, the American Federation of Labor advocated
    a. uniting both skilled and unskilled workers into a single large union.
    b. concentrating on improving wages and hours and avoiding general social reform.
    c. working for black and female labor interests as well as those of white men.
    d. using secrecy and violence against employers.

C. Identification

Supply the correct identification for each numbered description.

1. _____ Federally owned acreage granted to the railroad companies in order to encourage the building of rail lines

2. _____ The original transcontinental railroad, commissioned by Congress, which built its rail line west from Omaha

3. _____ The California-based railroad company, headed by Leland Stanford, that employed Chinese laborers in building lines across the mountains

4. _____ The northernmost of the transcontinental railroad lines, organized by economically wise and public-spirited industrialist James J. Hill

5. _____ Dishonest device by which railroad promoters artificially inflated the price of their stocks and bonds

6. _____ Supreme Court case of 1886 that prevented states from regulating railroads or other forms of interstate commerce

7. _____ Federal regulatory agency often used by rail companies to stabilize the industry and prevent ruinous competition

8. _____ Late-nineteenth-century invention that revolutionized communication and created a large new industry that relied heavily on female workers

9. _____ First of the great industrial trusts, organized through a principle of "horizontal integration" that ruthlessly incorporated or destroyed competitors

10. _____   The first billion-dollar American corporation, organized when J. P. Morgan bought out Andrew Carnegie

11. _____   Term that identified southern promoters' belief in a technologically advanced industrial South

12. _____   Black labor organization that briefly flourished in the late 1860s

13. _____   Secret, ritualistic labor organization that enrolled many skilled and unskilled workers but collapsed suddenly after the Haymarket Square bombing

14. _____   Skilled labor organizations, such as those of carpenters and printers, that were most successful in conducting strikes and raising wages

15. _____   The conservative labor group that successfully organized a minority of American workers but left others out

D. Matching People, Places, and Events

Match the person, place, or event in the left column with the proper description in the right column by inserting the correct letter on the blank line.

1. ___   Leland Stanford

2. ___   Russell Conwell

3. ___   James J. Hill

4. ___   Cornelius Vanderbilt

5. ___   Charles Dana Gibson

6. ___   Alexander Graham Bell

7. ___   Thomas Edison

8. ___   Andrew Carnegie

9. ___   John D. Rockefeller

10. ___   J. Pierpont Morgan

11. ___   Henry Grady

12. ___   Terence V. Powderly

13. ___   William Graham Sumner

14. ___   John P. Altgeld

15. ___   Samuel Gompers

a. Inventive genius of industrialization who worked on devices such as the electric light, the phonograph, and the motion picture

b. The only businessperson in America wealthy enough to buy out Andrew Carnegie and organize the United States Steel Corporation

c. Illinois governor who pardoned the Haymarket anarchists

d. Southern newspaper editor who tirelessly promoted industrialization as the salvation of the economically backward South

e. Aggressive energy-industry monopolist who used tough means to build a trust based on "horizontal integration"

f. Magazine illustrator who created a romantic image of the new, independent woman

g. Aggressive eastern railroad builder and consolidator who scorned the law as an obstacle to his enterprise

h. Pro-business clergyman whose "Acres of Diamonds" speeches criticized the poor

i. Scottish immigrant who organized a vast new industry on the principle of "vertical integration"

j.   Former California governor and organizer of the Central Pacific Railroad

k.   Organizer of a conservative craft-union group and advocate of "more" wages for skilled workers

l.   Eloquent leader of a secretive labor organization that made substantial gains in the 1880s before it suddenly collapsed

m.   Public-spirited railroad builder who assisted farmers in the northern areas served by his rail lines

n.   Intellectual defender of laissez-faire capitalism who argued that the wealthy owed "nothing" to the poor

o.   Former teacher of the deaf whose invention created an entire new industry

E. Putting Things in Order

Put the following events in correct order by numbering them from 1 to 5.

1. _____   J. P. Morgan buys out Andrew Carnegie to form the first billion-dollar U.S. corporation.

2. _____   The first federal law regulating railroads is passed.

3. _____   The killing of policemen during a labor demonstration results in the execution of radical anarchists and the decline of the Knights of Labor.

4. _____   A teacher of the deaf invents a machine that greatly eases communication across distance.

5. _____   A golden spike is driven, fulfilling the dream of linking the nation by rail.

F. Matching Cause and Effect

Match the historical cause in the left column with the proper effect in the right column by writing the correct letter on the blank line.

	Cause		Effect
1. ___	Federal land grants and subsidies	a.	Eliminated competition and created monopolistic "trusts" in many industries
2. ___	The building of a transcontinental rail network		
3. ___	Corrupt financial dealings and political manipulations by the railroads	b.	Fostered growing class divisions and public demands for restraints on corporate trusts
4. ___	New developments in steel making, oil refining, and communication	c.	Created a strong but narrowly based union organization
5. ___	The ruthless competitive techniques of Rockefeller and other industrialists	d.	Stimulated the growth of a huge unified national market for American manufactured goods
6. ___	The growing concentration of wealth and power in the new corporate "plutocracy"	e.	Created a public demand for railroad regulation, such as the Interstate Commerce Act
7. ___	The North's use of discriminatory price practices against the South	f.	Often made laborers feel powerless and vulnerable to their well-off corporate employers
8. ___	The growing mechanization and depersonalization of factory work	g.	Helped destroy the Knights of Labor and increased public fear of labor agitation
9. ___	The Haymarket Square bombing	h.	Laid the technological basis for huge new industries and spectacular economic growth
10. ___	The American Federation of Labor's concentration on skilled craft workers	i.	Encouraged the railroads to build their lines across the North American continent
		j.	Kept the South in economic dependency as a poverty-stricken supplier of farm products and raw materials to the Northeast

G. Developing Historical Skills

Interpreting Historical Paintings and Photographs

Historical paintings, lithographs, and photographs not only convey substantive information; they can also tell us how an artist or photographer viewed and understood the society and events of his or her day. Examine the photographs and painting indicated below and answer the following questions about them.

1. Examine the working people in the images on pp. 542, 544, 546, and 547. What is the relationship of the workers in each image to their workplace? What is their relation to one another? What does each of the photos reveal about the nature of industrial labor?

2. Examine the painting of "The Strike" by Robert Koehler on p.550. Where is the scene taking place? What is the relationship between the place of work and the scene in the painting? What has likely happened to bring the workers to this scene?

3. Analyze the clothing of all the figures in the Koehler painting. What does it tell you about the economic and social condition of the various people?

4. Two main conversations seem to be taking place in the foreground of the painting. What might each be about? What is the artist suggesting by presenting *both* conversations?

PART III: APPLYING WHAT YOU HAVE LEARNED

1. What was the impact of the transcontinental rail system on the American economy and society in the late nineteenth century?

2. How did the huge industrial trusts develop in industries such as steel and oil, and what was their effect on the economy?

3. What early efforts were made to control the new corporate industrial giants, and how effective were these efforts?

4. What was the effect of the new industrial revolution on American laborers, and how did various labor organizations attempt to respond to the new conditions?

5. Compare the impact of the new industrialization on the North and the South. Why was the "New South" more a slogan than a reality?

6. William Graham Sumner argued that the wealth and luxury enjoyed by millionaires was justifiable as a "good bargain for society" and that "natural law" should prevent the wealthy

classes from aiding the working classes and poor. Why were such views so popular during the Gilded Age? What criticisms of such views might be offered?

7. The text states that "no single group was more profoundly affected by the new industrial age than women." Why was women's role in society so greatly affected by these economic changes?

8. In what ways did industrialization bring a revolution in cultural views of labor, opportunity, and even time?

9. How did the industrial transformation after the Civil War compare with the earlier phase of American economic development? (See Chapter 14.) Why were the economic developments of 1865–1900 often seen as a threat to American democracy, whereas those of 1815–1860 were not?

10. What strains did the new industrialization bring to the American ideals of democracy and equality? Was the growth of huge corporations and great fortunes a successful realization of American principles or a threat to them?

CHAPTER 25

America Moves to the City, 1865–1900

PART I: REVIEWING THE CHAPTER

A. CHECKLIST OF LEARNING OBJECTIVES

After mastering this chapter, you should be able to

1.   describe the new industrial city and its impact on American society.

2.   describe the "New Immigration" and explain why it aroused opposition from many native-born Americans.

3.   discuss the efforts of social reformers and churches to aid the New Immigrants and alleviate urban problems.

4.   analyze the changes in American religious life in the late nineteenth century, including the reaction to Charles Darwin's evolutionary theories and the expansion of Catholicism and Judaism.

5.   explain the changes in American education from elementary to the college level.

6.   describe the literary and cultural life of the period, including the widespread trend towards "realism."

7.   explain the growing national debates about morality in the late nineteenth century, particularly in relation to the changing roles of women and the family.

B. GLOSSARY

To build your social science vocabulary, familiarize yourself with the following terms:

1.   **megalopolis** An extensive, heavily populated area, containing several dense urban centers. " . . . gave way to the immense and impersonal megalopolis. . . ." (p. 558)

2.   **tenement** A multidwelling building, often poor or overcrowded. "The cities . . . harbored . . . towering skyscrapers and stinking tenements." (p. 560)

3.   **affluence** An abundance of wealth. "These leafy 'bedroom communities' eventually ringed the brick-and-concrete cities with a greenbelt of affluence." (p. 560)

4.   **despotism** Government by an absolute or tyrannical ruler. ". . . people had grown accustomed to cringing before despotism." (p. 561)

5.   **parochial** Concerning a religious parish or small district. (By extension, the term is used, often negatively, to refer to narrow or local perspectives as distinct from broad or cosmopolitan outlooks.) "Catholics expanded their parochial-school system. . . ." (p. 565)

6.   **sweatshop** A factory where employees are forced to work long hours under difficult conditions for meager wages. "The women of Hull House successfully lobbied in 1893 for an Illinois antisweatshop law that protected women workers. . . ." (p. 568)

7.   **pauper** A poor person, often one who lives on tax-supported charity. "The first restrictive law . . . banged the gate in the faces of paupers. . . ." (p. 570)

8.   **convert** A person who turns from one religion or set of beliefs to another. "A fertile field for converts was found in America's harried, nerve-racked, and urbanized civilization. . . ." (p. 572)

9.   **Fundamentalist** A conservative Protestant who rejects religious modernism and adheres to a strict and literal interpretation of Christian doctrine and Scriptures. "Conservatives, or 'Fundamentalists,' stood firmly on the Scripture. . . ." (p. 572)

10.   **agnostic** One who believes that there can be no human knowledge of any God or gods. "The . . . skeptic . . . lectured widely on 'Some Mistakes of Moses' and 'Why I Am an Agnostic." (p. 573)

11.   **behavioral psychology** The branch of psychology that examines human action, often considering it more important than mental or inward states. "His [work] helped to establish the modern discipline of behavioral psychology." (p. 576)

12.   **syndicated** In journalism, material that is sold by an organization for publication in several newspapers. "Bare-knuckle editorials were, to an increasing degree, being supplanted by feature articles and non-controversial syndicated material." (p. 577)

13.   **tycoon** A wealthy businessperson, especially one who openly displays power and position. "Two new journalistic tycoons emerged." (p. 577)

14.   **feminist (feminism)** One who promotes complete political, social, and economic equality of opportunity for women. " . . . in 1898 they heard the voice of a major feminist prophet." (p. 583)

15.   **prohibition** Forbidding by law the manufacture, sale, or consumption of liquor. (**Temperance** is the voluntary abstention from liquor consumption.) "Statewide prohibition . . . was sweeping new states into the 'dry' column." (p. 586)

PART II: CHECKING YOUR PROGRESS

A. True-False

Where the statement is true, circle **T**; where it is false, circle **F**.

1.   T   F   Rapid and uncontrolled growth made American cities places of both exciting opportunity and severe social problems.

2.   T   F   After 1880, most immigrants to America came from northern and western Europe.

3.   T   F   Most of the New Immigrants who arrived in America were escaping from the slums and poverty of European cities.

4.   T   F   Female social workers established settlement houses to aid struggling immigrants and promote social reform.

5.   T   F   American Protestantism was dominated by "liberal" denominations that adapted religious ideas to modern culture and promoted a "social gospel" rather than biblical literalism.

6.   T   F   Two religions that gained strength in the United States from the New Immigrants were Roman Catholicism and Judaism.

7.   T   F   Charles Darwin's theories of evolution were overwhelmingly rejected by the majority of both Protestant and Catholic religious thinkers in the late nineteenth century.

8.   T   F   In the late nineteenth century, secondary (high school) education was increasingly carried on by private schools.

9. T F   Booker T. Washington believed that blacks should try to achieve social equality with whites but not economic equality.

10. T F   American higher education depended on both public "land-grant" funding and private donations for its financial support.

11. T F   Urban newspapers often promoted a sensational "yellow journalism" that emphasized sex and scandal rather that politics or social reform.

12. T F   Post–Civil War writers like Mark Twain and William Dean Howells turned from social realism toward fantasy and science fiction in their novels.

13. T F   There was growing tension in the late nineteenth century between women's traditionally defined "sphere" of family and home and the social and cultural changes of the era.

14. T F   The new urban environment generally weakened the family but offered new opportunities for women to achieve social and economic independence.

15. T F   Voices like Victoria Woodhull, Kate Chopin, and Charlotte Perkins Gilman signaled women's growing dissatisfaction with Victorian ideas about sex and gender roles.

B. Multiple Choice

Select the best answer and circle the corresponding letter.

1. The new cities' glittering consumer economy was symbolized especially by the rise of
    a.   separate districts for retail merchants.
    b.   fine restaurants and food shops.
    c.   large, elegant department stores.
    d.   large, carefully constructed urban parks.

2. One of the most difficult new problems generated by the rise of cities and the urban American life-style was
    a.   dealing with horses and other animals in crowded urban settings.
    b.   developing means of communication in densely populated city centers.
    c.   disposing of large quantities of consumer-generated waste material.
    d.   finding effective methods of high-rise construction for limited urban space.

3. Two new technical developments of the late nineteenth century that contributed to the spectacular growth of American cities were
    a.   the telegraph and the railroads.
    b.   the compressor and the internal combustion engine.
    c.   the electric trolley and the skyscraper.
    d.   the oil furnace and the air conditioner.

4. Countries from which many of the "New Immigrants" came included
    a.   Sweden and Great Britain.
    b.   Germany and Ireland.
    c.   Poland and Italy.
    d.   China and Japan.

5. Among the factors driving millions of European peasants from their homeland to America were
    a.   American food imports and religious persecution.
    b.   The rise of European nation-states and the decline of the Catholic Church.
    c.   the rise of communist and fascist regimes.
    d.   major international wars among the European great powers.

6.   Besides providing direct services to immigrants, the reformers of Hull House worked for general goals like

     a.   the secret ballot and direct election of senators.
     b.   antisweatshop laws to protect women and child laborers.
     c.   social security and unemployment compensation.
     d.   conservation and federal aid to municipal governments.

7.   The one immigrant group that was totally banned from America after 1882 as a result of nativist agitation was the

     a.   Irish.
     b.   Greeks.
     c.   Africans.
     d.   Chinese.

8.   Two religious groups that grew most dramatically because of the "New Immigration" were

     a.   Methodists and Baptists.
     b.   Christian Scientists and the Salvation Army.
     c.   Episcopalians and Unitarians.
     d.   Jews and Roman Catholics.

9.   The phrase "social Gospel" refers to

     a.   the fact that many people were turning to God seeking solutions to social conflicts.
     b.   the theory developed by religious liberals to reconcile Darwinian theories with the biblical views of human origins.
     c.   the efforts of some Christian reformers to apply their religious beliefs to new social problems.
     d.   the conflict between socialists and traditional religious believers.

10.   Besides aiding immigrants and promoting social reforms, settlement houses like Jane Addams's Hull House demonstrated that

     a.   it was almost impossible to bring about real economic reform in the cities.
     b.   the cities offered new challenges and opportunities for women.
     c.   women could not bring about successful social change without the vote.
     d.   labor was unsympathetic to middle-class reform efforts.

11.   Traditional American Protestant religion received a substantial blow from

     a.   the psychological ideas of William James.
     b.   the theological ideas of the Fundamentalists.
     c.   the chemical theories of Charles Eliot.
     d.   the biological ideas of Charles Darwin.

12.   Unlike Booker T. Washington, W. E. B. Du Bois advocated

     a.   economic opportunity for blacks.
     b.   integration and social equality for blacks.
     c.   practical as well as theoretical education for blacks.
     d.   that blacks remain in the South rather than move north.

13.   In the late nineteenth century, American colleges and universities benefited especially from

     a.   federal and state "land-grant" assistance and the private philanthropy of wealthy donors.
     b.   the growing involvement of the churches in higher education.
     c.   the fact that a college degree was becoming a prerequisite for employment in industry.
     d.   the growth of federal grants and loans to college students.

14.   American social reformers like Henry George and Edward Bellamy advocated

     a.   utopian reforms to end poverty and eliminate class conflict.
     b.   an end to racial prejudice and segregation.
     c.   the resettlement of the urban poor on free western homesteads.

    d.   a transformation of the traditional family through communal living arrangements.

15.   Authors like Mark Twain, Stephen Crane, and Jack London turned American literature toward a greater concern with

    a.   close observation and contemplation of nature.

    b.   postmodernism and deconstruction of traditional narratives.

    c.   fantasy and romance.

    d.   social realism and contemporary problems.

C. Identification

Supply the correct identification for each numbered description.

1. _____ High-rise urban buildings that provided barrackslike housing for urban slum dwellers

2. _____ Term for the post-1880 newcomers who came to America primarily from southern and eastern Europe

3. _____ Immigrants who came to America to earn money for a time and then returned to their native land

4. _____ The religious doctrines preached by those who believed the churches should directly address economic and social problems

5. _____ Settlement house in the Chicago slums that became a model for women's involvement in urban social reform

6. _____ Profession established by Jane Addams and others that opened new opportunities for women while engaging urban problems

7. _____ Nativist organization that attacked "New Immigrants" and Roman Catholicism in the 1880s and 1890s

8. _____ The church that became the largest American religious group, mainly as a result of the "New Immigration"

9. _____ Black educational institution founded by Booker T. Washington to provide training in agriculture and crafts

10. _____ Organization founded by W. E. B. Du Bois and others to advance black social and economic equality

11. _____ Henry George's best-selling book that advocated social reform through the imposition of a "single tax" on land

12. _____ Federal law promoted by a self-appointed morality crusader and used to prosecute moral and sexual dissidents

13. _____ Charlotte Perkins Gilman's book urging women to enter the work force and advocating cooperative kitchens and child-care centers

14. _____ Organization formed by Elizabeth Cady Stanton and others to promote the vote for women

15. _____ Women's organization founded by reformer Frances Willard and others to oppose alcohol consumption

D. Matching People, Places, and Events

Match the person, place, or event in the left column with the proper description in the right column by inserting the correct letter on the blank line.

1. ___   Louis Sullivan

2. ___   Walter Rauschenbusch

3. ___   Jane Addams

4. ___   Dwight L. Moody

5. ___   Mary Baker Eddy

6. ___   Booker T. Washington

7. ___   W. E. B. Du Bois

8. ___   William James

9. ___   Henry George

10. ___   Emily Dickinson

11. ___   Mark Twain

12. ___   Victoria Woodhull

13. ___   Anthony Comstock

14. ___   Charlotte Perkins Gilman

15. ___   Henry Adams

a. Controversial reformer whose book *Progress and Poverty* advocated solving problems of economic inequality by a tax on land

b. Midwestern-born writer and lecturer who created a new style of American literature based on social realism and humor

c. Well-connected and socially prominent historian who feared modern trends and sought relief in the beauty and culture of the past

d. Author and founder of a popular new religion based on principles of spiritual healing

e. Leading Protestant advocate of the "social gospel" who tried to make Christianity relevant to urban and industrial problems

f. Former slave who promoted industrial education and economic opportunity but not social equality for blacks

g. Harvard scholar who made original contributions to modern psychology and philosophy

h. Radical feminist propagandist whose eloquent attacks on conventional social morality shocked many Americans in the 1870s

i. Brilliant feminist writer who advocated cooperative cooking and child-care arrangements to promote women's economic independence and equality

j. Leading social reformer who lived with the poor in the slums and pioneered new forms of activism for women

k. Vigorous nineteenth-century crusader for sexual "purity" who used federal law to enforce his moral views

l. Harvard-educated scholar and advocate of full black social and economic equality through the leadership of a "talented tenth"

m. Chicago-based architect whose high-rise innovation allowed more people to crowd into limited urban space

n. Popular evangelical preacher who brought the tradition of old-time revivalism to the industrial city

o.   Gifted but isolated New England poet, the bulk of whose works were not published until after her death

E. Putting Things in Order

Put the following events in correct order by numbering them from 1 to 5.

1. _____   Well-educated young midwesterner moves to Chicago slums and creates a vital center of social reform and activism.

2. _____   Introduction of a new form of high-rise slum housing drastically increases the overcrowding of the urban poor.

3. _____   Nativist organization is formed to limit the "New Immigration" and attack Roman Catholicism.

4. _____   The formation of a new national organization signals growing strength for the women's suffrage movement.

5. _____   A western territory becomes the first U.S. government to grant full voting rights to women.

F. Matching Cause and Effect

Match the historical cause in the left column with the proper effect in the right column by writing the correct letter on the blank line.

Cause

1. ___ New industrial jobs and urban excitement

2. ___ Uncontrolled rapid growth and the "New Immigration" from Europe

3. ___ Cheap American grain exports to Europe

4. ___ The cultural strangeness and poverty of southern and eastern European immigrants

5. ___ Social gospel ministers and settlement-house workers

6. ___ Darwinian science and growing urban materialism

7. ___ Government land grants and private philanthropy

8. ___ Popular newspapers and "yellow journalism"

9. ___ Changes in moral and sexual attitudes

10. ___ The difficulties of family life in the industrial city

Effect

a. Encouraged the mass urban public's taste for scandal and sensation

b. Created intense poverty and other problems in the crowded urban slums

c. Weakened the religious influence in American society and created divisions within the churches

d. Led women and men to delay marriage and have fewer children

e. Helped uproot European peasants from their ancestral lands and sent them seeking new opportunities in America and elsewhere

f. Supported the substantial improvements in American undergraduate and graduate education in the late nineteenth century

g. Lured millions of rural Americans off the farms and into the cities

h. Assisted immigrants and other slum dwellers and pricked middle-class consciences about urban problems

i. Provoked sharp hostility from some native-born Americans and organized labor groups

j. Created sharp divisions about the "new morality" and issues such as divorce

G. Developing Historical Skills

Interpreting a Line Graph

A line graph is another visual way to convey information. It is often used to present notable historical changes occurring over substantial periods of time. Study the line graph on p.561 and answer the following questions.

1. There are five major "peaks" of immigration, and four major "valleys." What factors helped cause each of the periods of heavy immigration? What helped cause each of the sharp declines?

2.   About how long did each of the first four periods of major immigration last? About how long did each of the four "valleys" last? How long has the current (to 1997) phase of rising or steady immigration lasted?

3.   During what five-year period was there the sharpest rise in immigration? What five-year period saw the sharpest fall?

4.   In about what *three* years did approximately 800,000 immigrants enter the United States? In about what *seven* years did approximately 200,000 immigrants enter the United States?

5.   Approximately how many fewer immigrants came in 1920 than in 1914? About how many more immigrants came in 1990 than in 1950?

PART III: APPLYING WHAT YOU HAVE LEARNED

1.   What new opportunities did the cities create for Americans?

2.   What new social problems did urbanization create? How did Americans respond to these problems?

3.   How did the "New Immigration" differ from the "Old Immigration," and how did Americans respond to it?

4.   How was American religion affected by the urban transformation, the New Immigration, and cultural and intellectual changes?

5.   Why was Darwinian evolution such a controversial challenge for American religious thinkers? Why were religious "liberals" able to dominate Americans' cultural response to evolution? How did a minority resistance to evolution lay the basis for the later rise of fundamentalism?

6.   How did American social criticism, imaginative writing, and art all relate to the urban industrial changes of the late nineteenth century?

7.   How and why did women assume a larger place in American society at this time? (Compare their status in this period with that of the pre–Civil War period described in Chapter 16.) How were changes in their condition related to changes in both the family and the larger social order?

8.   What was the greatest single cultural transformation of the Gilded Age?

9.   Why did American culture and writing actually flourish amidst the troubling and conflict-ridden politics and economics of the period (See Chapters 23 and 24)? Can it be argued that American intellectuals and writers of the period actually "benefited" from economic upheaval and social disruption?

CHAPTER 26

The Great West and the Agricultural Revolution, 1865–1896

PART I: REVIEWING THE CHAPTER

A. CHECKLIST OF LEARNING OBJECTIVES

After mastering this chapter, you should be able to

1. describe the nature of the cultural conflicts and battles that accompanied the white American migration into the Great Plains and the Far West.

2. explain the development of federal policy towards Native Americans in the late nineteenth century.

3. analyze the brief flowering and decline of the cattle and mining frontiers.

4. explain the impact of the closing of the frontier, and the long-term significance of the frontier for American history.

5. describe the revolutionary changes in farming on the Great Plains.

6. describe the economic forces that drove farmers into debt, and describe how the Grange, the Farmers' Alliances, and the Populist Party organized to protest their oppression.

B. GLOSSARY

To build your social science vocabulary, familiarize yourself with the following terms:

1. **nomadic (nomad)** A way of life characterized by frequent movement from place to place for economic sustenance. ". . . the Sioux transformed themselves from foot-traveling, crop-growing villagers to wide-ranging nomadic traders. . . ." (p. 591)

2. **immunity** Freedom or exemption from some imposition. ". . . [the] militia massacred . . . four hundred Indians who apparently thought they had been promised immunity." (p. 593)

3. **reservation** Public lands designated for use by Indians. "The vanquished Indians were finally ghettoized on reservations. . . ." (p. 595)

4. **ward** Someone considered incompetent to manage his or her own affairs and therefore placed under the legal guardianship of another person or group. ". . . there [they had] to eke out a sullen existence as wards of the government." (p. 595)

5. **probationary** Concerning a period of testing or trial, after which a decision is made based on performance. "The probationary period was later extended. . . ." (p. 597)

6. **folklore** The common traditions and stories of a people. "These bowlegged Knights of the Saddle . . . became part of American folklore." (p. 602)

7. **irrigation** Watering land artificially, through canals, pipes, or other means. ". . . irrigation projects . . . caused the 'Great American Desert' to bloom. . . ." (p. 604)

    d.   developing programs of bilingual education in reservation schools.

7.   Both the mining and cattle frontiers saw

    a.   an increase of ethnic and class conflict.

    b.   a loss of economic viability after an initial boom.

    c.   a turn from large-scale investment to the individual entrepreneur.

    d.   a movement from individual operations to large-scale corporate businesses.

8.   The problem of developing agriculture in the arid West was solved most successfully through

    a.   concentrating agriculture in the more fertile mountain valleys.

    b.   the use of small-scale family farms rather than large "bonanza" farms.

    c.   the use of irrigation from dammed western rivers.

    d.   the turn to desert crops like olives and dates.

9.   The "safety valve" theory of the frontier holds that

    a.   Americans were able to divert the most violent elements of the population to the West.

    b.   the conflict between farmers and ranchers was relieved by the Homestead Act.

    c.   unemployed city dwellers could move west and thus relieve labor conflict in the East.

    d.   political movements such as the Populists provided relief for the most serious grievances of western farmers.

10.   Which one of these factors did *not* make the trans-Mississippi West a unique part of the American frontier experience?

    a.   The large numbers of Indians, Hispanics, and Asian Americans in the region

    b.   The problem of applying new technologies in a hostile wilderness

    c.   The scale and severity of environmental challenges in an arid environment

    d.   The large role of the federal government in economic and social development

11.   By the 1880s, most western farmers faced hard times because

    a.   free land was no longer available under the Homestead Act.

    b.   they were unable to increase grain production to keep up with demand.

    c.   they were being strangled by excessive federal regulation of agriculture.

    d.   they were forced to sell their grain at low prices in a depressed world market.

12.   Which of the following was *not* among the political goals advocated by the Populist Party in the 1890s?

    a.   Nationalizing the railroad, telegraph, and telephone

    b.   Creation of a national system of unemployment insurance and old-age pensions

    c.   A graduated income tax

    d.   Free and unlimited coinage of silver money

13.   The U.S. government's response to the Pullman strike aroused great anger from organized labor because

    a.   it seemed to represent "government by injunction" designed to destroy labor unions.

    b.   it broke apart the growing alliance between urban workers and farmers.

    c.   it undermined efforts to organize federal workers like those in the postal service.

    d.   it turned their most effective leader, Eugene V. Debs, into a cautious conservative.

14.   William Jennings Bryan gained the Democratic nomination in 1896 because he strongly advocated

    a.   unlimited coinage of silver in order to inflate currency.

    b.   higher tariffs in order to protect the American farmer.

    c.   government ownership of the railroads and the telegraph system.

    d.   a coalition between white and black farmers in the South and Midwest.

15.   McKinley defeated Bryan primarily because he was able to win the support of

    a.   white southern farmers.

    b.   eastern wage earners and city dwellers.

c.   urban and rural blacks.

d.   former Populists and Greenback Laborites.

C. Identification

Supply the correct identification for each numbered description.

1. _____   Major northern Plains Indian nation that fought and eventually lost a bitter war against the U.S. Army, 1876–1877

2. _____   Southwestern Indian tribe led by Geronimo that carried out some of the last fighting against white conquest

3. _____   Generally poor areas where vanquished Indians were eventually confined under federal control

4. _____   Indian religious movement, originating out of the sacred Sun Dance that the federal government attempted to stamp out in 1890

5. _____   Federal law that attempted to dissolve tribal landholding and establish Indians as individual farmers

6. _____   Huge silver and gold deposit that brought wealth and statehood to Nevada

7. _____   General term for the herding of cattle from the grassy plains to the railroad terminals of Kansas, Nebraska, and Wyoming

8. _____   Federal law that offered generous land opportunities to poorer farmers but also provided the unscrupulous with opportunities for hoaxes and fraud

9. _____   Improved type of fencing that enabled farmers to enclose land on the treeless plains

10. _____   Former "Indian Territory" where "sooners" tried to get the jump on "boomers" when it was opened for settlement in 1889

11. _____   Third political party that emerged in the 1890s to express rural grievances and mount major attacks on the Democrats and Republicans

12. _____   Popular pamphlet written by William Hope Harvey that portrayed pro-silver arguments triumphing over the traditional views of bankers and economics professors

13. _____   Bitter labor conflict in Chicago that brought federal intervention and the jailing of union leader Eugene V. Debs

14. _____   Spectacular convention speech by a young pro-silver advocate that brought him the Democratic presidential nomination in 1896

15. _____   Popular term for those who favored the "status quo" in metal money and opposed the pro-silver Bryanites in 1896

D. Matching People, Places, and Events

Match the person, place, or event in the left column with the proper description in the right column by inserting the correct letter on the blank line.

1. ___   Sand Creek, Colorado

2. ___   Little Big Horn

a.   Ohio industrialist and organizer of McKinley's victory over Bryan in the election of 1896

3.	___	Sitting Bull	
4.	___	Chief Joseph	
5.	___	Geronimo	
6.	___	Helen Hunt Jackson	
7.	___	John Wesley Powell	
8.	___	William Hope Harvey	
9.	___	Eugene V. Debs	
10.	___	James B. Weaver	
11.	___	Mary E. Lease	
12.	___	Mark Hanna	

b. Leader of the Nez Percé tribe who conducted a brilliant but unsuccessful military campaign in 1877

c. Author of the popular pro-silver pamphlet "Coin's Financial School"

d. Former Civil War general and Granger who ran as the Greenback Labor party candidate for president in 1880

e. Leader of the Sioux during wars of 1876–1877

f. Explorer and geologist who warned that traditional agriculture could not succeed west of the 100th meridian

g. Leader of the Apaches of Arizona in their warfare with the whites

h. Site of Indian massacre by militia forces in 1864

i. Massachusetts writer whose books aroused sympathy for the plight of the Native Americans

j. Site of major U.S. Army defeat in the Sioux War of 1876–1877

k. Railway union leader who converted to socialism while serving jail time during the Pullman strike

l. Eloquent Kansas Populist who urged farmers to "raise less corn and more hell"

E. Putting Things in Order

Put the following events in correct order by numbering them from 1 to 5.

1. _____ A sharp economic depression leads to a major railroad strike and the intervention of federal troops in Chicago.

2. _____ The violation of agreements with the Dakota Sioux leads to a major Indian war and a military disaster for the U.S. cavalry.

3. _____ A federal law grants 160 acres of land to farmers at token prices, thus encouraging the rapid settlement of the Great West.

4. _____ The U.S. Census Bureau declares that there is no longer a clear line of frontier settlement, ending a formative chapter of American history.

5. _____ Despite a fervent campaign by their charismatic young champion, pro-silver Democrats lose a pivotal election to "Gold Bug" Republicans.

F. Matching Cause and Effect

Match the historical cause in the left column with the proper effect in the right column by writing the correct letter on the blank line.

Cause

1. ___ The encroachment of white settlement and the violation of treaties with Indians

2. ___ Railroad building, disease, and the destruction of the buffalo

3. ___ Reformers' attempts to make Native Americans conform to white ways

4. ___ The coming of big-business mining and stock-raising to the West

5. ___ "Dry farming," barbed wire, and irrigation

6. ___ The passing of the frontier of 1890

7. ___ The growing economic specialization of western farmers

8. ___ The rise of the Populist Party in the early 1890s

9. ___ The economic depression that began in 1893

10. ___ The return of prosperity after 1897 and new gold discoveries in Alaska, South Africa, and elsewhere

Effect

a. Caused widespread protests and strikes like the one against the Pullman Company in Chicago

b. Threatened the two-party domination of American politics by the Republicans and Democrats

c. Created new psychological and economic problems for a nation accustomed to a boundlessly open West

d. Ended the romantic, colorful era of the miners' and the cattlemen's frontier

e. Decimated Indian populations and hastened their defeat at the hands of advancing whites

f. Effectively ended the free-silver agitation and the domination of the money question in American politics

g. Made settlers vulnerable to vast industrial and market forces beyond their control

h. Made it possible to farm the dry, treeless areas of the Great Plains and the West

i. Further undermined Native Americans' traditional tribal culture and morale

j. Led to nearly constant warfare with Plains Indians from 1868 to about 1890

G. Developing Historical Skills

Comparing Election Maps

Comparing maps of two consecutive elections enables you to see what political changes have occurred in a relatively brief historical period. The election map on p. 628 shows the vote by county; the one on p. 637 shows the vote by state. Keep that difference in mind as you answer the following questions:

1. Six western states had significant votes for the Populist Weaver in 1892. Who carried them in 1896?

2. List six states where Democrat Cleveland had strong support in 1892 that turned around and voted Republican in 1896. In which region were most such states located?

3. List five states that stayed solidly Republican in both 1892 and 1896, and five states that stayed solidly Democratic. In which regions were each of these groups of "solid" states located?

4. In 1892, nine midwestern and western states had substantial concentrations of Populist voters. In the election of 1896, how many of those nine states went Democratic, and how many went Republican?

H. Map Mastery

Map Discrimination

Using the maps and charts in Chapter 26, answer the following questions:

1. In the election of 1892, which three western states had no counties that backed the Populist party?

2. Which four southern states had the most Populist support in the election of 1892 (that is, at least three counties that went Populist)?

3. In the election of 1896, how many electoral votes did McKinley win from states west of the Mississippi River?

4. How many electoral votes did McKinley win in the southern states of the old Confederacy?

Map Challenge

Using the maps of *American Agriculture in 1900* (p. 609) and *Presidential Election of 1896* (p. 620, discuss the relationship between the Populist and pro-silver movements and the patterns of American agriculture. Include in your analysis some analysis of those Midwestern agricultural states that may have been influenced by Populism but did not vote for Bryan in 1896.

PART III: APPLYING WHAT YOU HAVE LEARNED

1. How did whites finally overcome resistance of the Plains Indians, and what happened to the Indians after their resistance ceased?

2. What social, ethnic, environmental, and economic factors made the trans-Mississippi West a unique region among the successive American frontiers?

3. What were the actual effects of the frontier on American society at different stages of its development? What was valuable in Frederick Jackson Turner's "frontier thesis," despite its being discredited by subsequent historians?

4. How did the forces of economic class conflict and race figure into the farmer and labor revolt of the 1880s and 1890s? Was there ever any chance that a bi-racial coalition of farmers could have succeeded not only in economic change but in overcoming the South's racial divisions? Were race relations actually worse after the Populist revolt failed?

5. Were the Populist and pro-silver movements of the 1880s and 1890s essentially backward-looking protests by a passing rural America, or were they, despite their immediate political failure, genuine prophetic voices raising central critical questions about democracy and economic justice in the new corporate industrial America?

6. What were the major issues in the crucial campaign of 1896? Why did McKinley win, and what were the long-term effects of his victory?

7. Some historians have seen Bryan as the political heir of Jefferson and Jackson, and McKinley as the political heir of Hamilton and the Whigs. Are such connections valid? Why or why not? (See Chapters 10, 12, and 13.)

8. The settlement of the "Great West" and the farmers' revolt occurred at the same time as the rise of industrialism and the growth of American cities. To what extent were the defeat of the Indians, the destruction and exploitation of western resources, and the populist revolt of the farmers caused by the Gilded Age forces of industrialization and urbanization?

CHAPTER 27

Empire and Expansion, 1890–1909

PART I: REVIEWING THE CHAPTER

A. CHECKLIST OF LEARNING OBJECTIVES

After mastering this chapter, you should be able to

1. Explain why the United States suddenly abandoned its isolationism and turned outward at the end of the nineteenth century.

2. Describe the forces pushing for American overseas expansion, and the causes of the Spanish-American War.

3. Describe and explain the unintended results of the Spanish-American War, especially the conquest of Puerto Rico and the Philippines.

4. Explain McKinley's decision to keep the Philippines, and list the opposing arguments in the debate about imperialism.

5. Analyze the consequences of the Spanish-American War, including the Filipino rebellion against U.S. rule and the war to suppress it.

6. Explain the growing U.S. involvement in East Asia, and summarize America's "Open Door" policy toward China.

7. Discuss the significance of the "pro-imperialist" Republican victory in 1900 and the rise of Theodore Roosevelt as a strong advocate of American power in international affairs.

8. Describe Roosevelt's assertive policies in Panama and elsewhere in Latin America, and explain why his "corollary" to the Monroe Doctrine aroused such controversy.

9. Discuss Roosevelt's foreign policies and diplomatic achievements, especially regarding Japan.

B. GLOSSARY

To build your social science vocabulary, familiarize yourself with the following terms:

1. **arbitration** An arrangement in which a neutral third party conclusively determines the outcome of a dispute between two parties. (In **mediation** the third party only proposes solutions that the disputing parties may or may not accept.) "A simmering argument between the United States and Canada . . . was resolved by arbitration in 1893."

2. **scorched-earth policy** The policy of burning and destroying all the property in a given area so as to deny it to an enemy. "The desperate insurgents now sought to drive out their Spanish overlords by adopting a scorched-earth policy." (p. 628)

3. **reconcentration** The policy of forcibly removing a population to confined areas in order to deny support to enemy forces. " He undertook to crush the rebellion by herding many civilians into barbed-wire reconcentration camps." (p. 629)

4.   **atrocity** A specific act of extreme cruelty. "Where atrocity stories did not exist, they were invented." (p. 629)

5.   **proviso** An article or clause in a statute, treaty, or contract establishing a particular stipulation or condition affecting the whole document. "This proviso proclaimed . . . that when the United States had overthrown Spanish misrule, it would give the Cubans their freedom. . . ." (p. 631)

6.   **hostage** A person or thing forcibly held in order to obtain certain goals or agreements. "Hereafter these distant islands were to be . . . a kind of indefensible hostage given to Japan." (p. 642)

7.   **Americanization** The process of assimilating American character, manner, ideals, culture, and so on. "The Filipinos, who hated compulsory Americanization, preferred liberty." (p. 648)

8.   **sphere of influence** In international affairs, the territory where a powerful state exercises the dominant control over weaker states or territories. ". . . they began to tear away valuable leaseholds and economic spheres of influence from the Manchu government." (p. 648)

9.   **partition** In politics, the act of dividing a weaker territory or government among several more powerful states. "Those principles helped to spare China from possible partition in those troubled years. . . . (p. XXX)

10.   **blue blood** A person of supposedly "pure blood," presumed to be descended from nobility or aristocracy. "Born into a wealthy and distinguished New York family, Roosevelt, a red-blooded blue blood. . . ." (p. XXX)

11.   **bellicose** Disposed to fight or go to war. "Incurably boyish and bellicose, Roosevelt ceaselessly preached the virile virtues. . . ." (p. 654)

12.   **preparedness** The accumulation of sufficient armed forces and matériel to go to war. "An ardent champion of military and naval preparedness. . . ." (p. 654)

13.   **corollary** A secondary inference or deduction from a main proposition that is assumed to be established or proven. "[Roosevelt] therefore devised a devious policy of 'preventive intervention,' better known as the Roosevelt Corollary of the Monroe Doctrine." (p. 657)

14.   **indemnity** A payment assessed to compensate for an injury or illegal action. "Japan was forced to drop its demands for a cash indemnity. . . ." (p. 659)

PART II: CHECKING YOUR PROGRESS

A. True-False

Where the statement is true, circle **T**; where it is false, circle **F**.

1.   T   F   The American people and their government were deeply involved in the key international developments of the 1860s and 1870s.

2.   T   F   The South American boundary dispute over Guyana in 1895–1896 nearly resulted in a U.S. war with Venezuela.

3.   T   F   President Cleveland refused to annex Hawaii because he believed that the white American planters there had unjustly deposed Hawaii's Queen Liliuokalani.

4.   T   F   Americans first became involved in Cuba because they sympathized with the Cubans' revolt against imperialist Spain.

5.   T   F   Admiral Dewey's squadron attacked Spanish forces in the Philippines because of secret orders given by Assistant Navy Secretary Theodore Roosevelt.

6.   T   F   American forces received assistance in capturing Manila by native Filipino insurgents who were rebelling against Spain.

7.   T   F   The American military conquest of Cuba was efficient but very costly in battlefield casualties.

8.   T   F   President McKinley declared that religion played a crucial role in his decision to keep the Philippines as an American colony.

9.   T   F   The peace treaty with Spain that made the Philippines an American colony was almost universally popular with the U. S. Senate and the American public.

10. T   F   The Supreme Court decided in the insular cases that American constitutional law and the Bill of Rights applied to the people under American rule in Puerto Rico and the Philippines.

11. T   F   The Filipino insurrection against U.S. rule was larger and more costly in lives than the Spanish-American War.

12. T   F   John Hay's Open Door notes effectively rescued China from foreign intervention and partition.

13. T   F   Theodore Roosevelt believed that America and its president should exercise restraint in international involvements.

14. T   F   Roosevelt encouraged and assisted the Panamanian revolution against Colombia in 1903.

15. T   F   The Roosevelt Corollary to the Monroe Doctrine stated that only the United States had the right to intervene in Latin American nations' affairs.

16. T   F   The Japanese crisis of 1906 forced President Roosevelt to intervene in the policies of the San Francisco School Board.

B. Multiple Choice

Select the best answer and circle the corresponding letter.

1.   Alfred Thayer Mahan promoted American overseas expansion by
   a.   developing a lurid "yellow press" that stimulated popular excitement.
   b.   arguing that domination of the seas through naval power was the key to world domination.
   c.   provoking naval incidents with Germany and Britain in the Pacific.
   d.   arguing that the Monroe Doctrine implied American control of Latin America.

2.   Which of the following was *not* among the factors propelling America toward overseas expansion in the 1890s?
   a.   The desire to expand overseas agricultural and manufacturing exports
   b.   The "yellow press" of Joseph Pulitzer and William Randolph Hearst
   c.   The need to find new African and Asian sources of raw materials for American industry
   d.   The ideologies of Anglo-Saxon superiority and social Darwinism
   e.   The intervention of the German kaiser in Latin America

3.   President Grover Cleveland refused to annex Hawaii because
   a.   white planters had illegally overthrown Queen Liliuokalani against the wishes of most native Hawaiians.
   b.   there was no precedent for the United States to acquire territory except by purchase.
   c.   the Germans and the British threatened possible war.
   d.   he knew the public disapproved and the Senate would not ratify a treaty of annexation.

4. Americans first became concerned with the situation in Cuba because
    a. Spanish control of Cuba violated the Monroe Doctrine.
    b. imperialists and business leaders were looking to acquire colonial territory for the United States.
    c. Americans sympathized with Cuban rebels in their fight for freedom from Spanish rule.
    d. the Battleship *Maine* exploded in Havana harbor.
5. Even before the sinking of the *Maine*, the American public's indignation at Spain had been whipped into a frenzy by
    a. Spanish Catholics' persecution of the Protestant minority in Cuba.
    b. Spain's aggressive battleship-building program.
    c. William Randolph Hearst's sensational newspaper accounts of Spanish atrocities in Cuba.
    d. the Spanish government's brutal treatment of American sailors on leave in Havana.
6. Even after the *Maine* exploded, the United States did not immediately declare war on Cuba because
    a. the public was reluctant to get into a war.
    b. President McKinley was reluctant to get into a war.
    c. the Cubans did not want Americans to intervene in their affairs.
    d. there was no clear evidence that the Spanish had really blown up the *Maine*.
7. Emilio Aguinaldo was
    a. the leader of Cuban insurgents against Spanish rule.
    b. the leader of Filipino insurgents against Spanish rule.
    c. the commander of the Spanish navy in the Battle of Manila Bay.
    d. the first native Hawaiian to become governor of the islands after the American takeover.
8. Which of the following was *not* among the colonial territories that the United States acquired in the Spanish-American War?
    a. The Virgin Islands
    b. Puerto Rico
    c. The Philippines
    d. Guam.
9. President William McKinley based his decision to make the Philippines an American colony on
    a. the belief in white Anglo-Saxon superiority to the Asian Filipinos.
    b. a combination of religious piety and material economic interests.
    c. the belief that the Philippines would be the first step toward an American empire in China.
    d. the strong agitation for empire coming from the Hearst and Pulitzer yellow press.
10. Pro-imperialist Americans argued that the Philippines should be seized because of
    a. patriotism, religion, and economic opportunities.
    b. the Monroe Doctrine and national security.
    c. the Declaration of Independence and the wishes of the Philippine people.
    d. overpopulation and the need to acquire new land for American settlers.
11. The most immediate consequence of American acquisition of the Philippines was
    a. the establishment of Manila as a crucial American defense post in East Asia.
    b. an agreement between Americans and Filipinos to move toward Philippine independence.
    c. a guerrilla war between the United States and Filipino rebels.
    d. threats by Japan to seize the Philippines from American control.
12. In the Open Door notes, Secretary of State John Hay called on all the imperial powers to
    a. guarantee American control of the Philippines.
    b. reduce the arms race in China and the Pacific.
    c. respect Chinese rights and permit economic competition in their spheres of influence.
    d. grant the United States an equal share in the colonization of China.

13.   As president, Theodore Roosevelt gained political strength especially through

    a.   his careful use of traditional diplomacy.

    b.   his willingness to follow Congress's lead in domestic policy.

    c.   his personal popularity with the public and his belief in direct action.

    d.   his ability to subordinate his own personality to that of his cabinet.

    e.   Colombia.

14.   Roosevelt overcame Colombia's refusal to approve a canal treaty by

    a.   increasing the amount of money the United States was willing to pay for a canal zone.

    b.   encouraging Panamanian rebels to revolt and declare independence from Colombia.

    c.   looking for another canal site elsewhere in Central America.

    d.   seeking mediation of the dispute by other Latin American nations.

15.   Theodore Roosevelt's slogan that stated his essential foreign policy principle was

    a.   "Open covenants openly arrived at."

    b.   "Millions for defense but not one cent for tribute."

    c.   "Speak softly and carry a big stick."

    d.   "Democracy and Liberty in a New World Order."

C. Identification

Supply the correct identification for each numbered description.

1.   _____   Remote Pacific site of a naval clash between the United States and Germany in 1889

2.   _____   South American nation that nearly came to blows with the United States in 1892 over an incident involving the deaths of American sailors

3.   _____   The principle of American foreign policy invoked by Secretary of State Olney to justify American intervention in the Venezuelan boundary dispute

4.   _____   Term for the sensationalistic and jingoistic prowar journalism practiced by W. R. Hearst and Joseph Pulitzer

5.   _____   American battleship sent on a "friendly" visit to Cuba that ended in disaster and war

6.   _____   Site of the dramatic American naval victory that led to U.S. acquisition of rich, Spanish-owned Pacific islands

7.   _____   Colorful volunteer regiment of the Spanish-American War led by a militarily inexperienced but politically influential colonel

8.   _____   The Caribbean island conquered from Spain in 1898 that became an important American colony

9.   _____   Supreme Court cases of 1901 that determined that the U.S. Constitution and Bill of Rights did not apply in colonial territories under the American flag

10.   _____   John Hay's clever diplomatic efforts to preserve Chinese territorial integrity and maintain American access to China

11.   _____   Antiforeign Chinese revolt of 1900 that brought military intervention by Western troops, including Americans

12.   _____   Diplomatic agreement of 1901 that permitted the United States to build and fortify a Central American canal alone, without British involvement

13. _____ Nation whose senate in 1902 refused to ratify a treaty permitting the United States to build a canal across its territory

14. _____ Questionable extension of a traditional American policy; declared an American right to intervene in Latin American nations under certain circumstances

15. _____ Diplomatic understanding of 1907–1908 that ended a Japanese American crisis over treatment of Japanese immigrants to the U.S.

D. Matching People, Places, and Events

Match the person, place, or event in the left column with the proper description in the right column by inserting the correct letter on the blank line.

1. ___ Josiah Strong

2. ___ Alfred Thayer Mahan

3. ___ Emilio Aguinaldo

4. ___ Queen Liliuokalani

5. ___ Grover Cleveland

6. ___ "Butcher" Weyler

7. ___ William R. Hearst

8. ___ William McKinley

9. ___ George E. Dewey

10. ___ Theodore Roosevelt

11. ___ John Hay

12. ___ Philippe Bunau-Varilla

13. ___ William James

14. ___ William Jennings Bryan

15. ___ Thomas Platt

a. Imperialist advocate, aggressive assistant navy secretary, Rough Rider

b. Harvard philosopher and one of the leading anti-imperialists opposing U.S. acquisition of the Philippines

c. Spanish general whose brutal tactics against Cuban rebels outraged American public opinion

d. Native Hawaiian ruler overthrown in a revolution led by white planters and aided by U.S. troops

e. Scheming French engineer who helped stage a revolution in Panama and then became the new country's "instant" foreign minister

f. American naval officer who wrote influential books emphasizing sea power and advocating a big navy

g. Naval commander whose spectacular May Day victory in 1898 opened the doors to American imperialism in Asia

h. Vigorous promoter of sensationalistic anti-Spanish propaganda and eager advocate of imperialistic war

i. New York politician who successfully schemed to get TR out of New York and into the vice presidency in Washington

j. American clergyman who preached Anglo-Saxon superiority and called for stronger U.S. missionary effort overseas

k. Filipino leader of a guerilla war against American rule from 1899 to

1901

l.   President who initially opposed war with Spain but eventually supported U.S. acquisition of the Philippines

m.   Leading Democratic politician whose intervention narrowly tipped the Senate vote in favor of acquiring the Philippines in 1899

n.   American president who refused to annex Hawaii on the grounds that the native ruler had been unjustly deposed

o.   American secretary of state who attempted to preserve Chinese independence and protect American interests in China

E. Putting Things in Order

Put the following events in correct order by numbering them from 1 to 5.

1. _____   American rebels in Hawaii seek annexation by the United States, but the American president turns them down.

2. _____   A battleship explosion arouses fury in America and leads the nation into a "splendid little war" with Spain.

3. _____   A South American boundary dispute leads to aggressive American assertion of the Monroe Doctrine against Britain.

4. _____   Questionable Roosevelt actions in Central America help create a new republic and pave the way for a U.S.-built canal.

5. _____   A San Francisco School Board dispute leads to intervention by President Roosevelt and a "Gentleman's Agreement" to prohibit further Japanese immigration to the United States.

F. Matching Cause and Effect

Match the historical cause in the left column with the proper effect in the right column by writing the correct letter on the blank line.

Cause		Effect
1. ___ Economic expansion, the yellow press, and competition with other powers	a.	Brought American armed forces onto the Asian mainland for the first time
2. ___ The Venezuelan boundary dispute	b.	Created an emotional and irresistible public demand for war with Spain
3. ___ The white planter revolt against Queen Liliuokalani	c.	Strengthened the Monroe Doctrine and made Britain more willing to accommodate U.S. interests
4. ___ The Cuban revolt against Spain		

5. ___ The *Maine* explosion

6. ___ Theodore Roosevelt's secret orders to Commodore Dewey

7. ___ The Boxer Rebellion that attempted to drive all foreigners out of China

8. ___ McKinley's decision to keep the Philippines

9. ___ Colombia's refusal to permit the United States to build a canal across its province of Panama

10. ___ The Spanish-American War

d. Led to the surprising U.S. victory over Spain at Manila Bay

e. Set off the first debate about the wisdom and rightness of American overseas imperialism

f. Turned America away from isolationism and toward international involvements in the 1890s

g. Aroused strong sympathy from most Americans

h. Enhanced American national pride and made the United States an international power in East Asia

i. Set off a bitter debate about imperialism in the Senate and the country

j. Led President Theodore Roosevelt to encourage a revolt for Panamanian independence

G. Map Mastery

Map Discrimination

Using the maps and charts in Chapter 27, answer the following questions:

1. *The Venezuela-British Guiana Boundary Dispute*: In the Venezuelan boundary conflict, which nation—Britain or Venezuela—gained more of the disputed territory in the final settlement?

2. *The Pacific*: What two prime naval harbors did the United States acquire in (a) Samoa and (b) Hawaii?

3. *Dewey's Route in the Philippines, 1898*: Manila Bay lies off the coast of which island of the Philippine archipelago?

4. *The Cuban Campaign, 1898*: Which of the two battles fought by Rough Riders—San Juan Hill and El Caney—occurred nearer Santiago Harbor?

5.   *The Cuban Campaign, 1898*: Which of the two Spanish-owned Caribbean islands conquered by the United States in 1898 was farthest from Florida?

Map Challenge

Using the map of *The Pacific* on p. 627, discuss the exact geographical relation of each of America's new Pacific colonies—Samoa, Hawaii, the Philippines—to (a) the United States mainland and (b) China and Japan. Which of the colonies was most strategically important to America's position in the Pacific, which least, and which was most vulnerable? Why?

PART III: APPLYING WHAT YOU HAVE LEARNED

1.   What were the causes and signs of America's sudden turn toward international involvement at the end of the nineteenth century?

2.   How did the United States get into the Spanish-American War over the initial objections of President McKinley?

3.   What role did the press and public opinion play in the origin, conduct, and results of the Spanish-American War?

4.   What were the key arguments for and against U. S. imperialism?

5.   What were some of the short-term and long-term results of American acquisition of the Philippines and Puerto Rico?

6.   How was U. S. overseas imperialism in 1898 similar to and different from earlier American expansion across North America, or "Manifest Destiny"? (See especially Chapter 13.) Was this "new imperialism" a fundamental departure from America's traditions, or simply a further extension of "westward migration"?

7.   What were the effects of America's new East Asian involvement in both the Philippines and China in 1899–1901?

8.   What were the essential principles of Theodore Roosevelt's foreign policy, and how did he apply them to specific situations?

9.   How did Roosevelt's policies in Latin America demonstrate American power in the region, and why did they arouse opposition from Latin Americans?

10.   What were the central issues in America's relations with China and Japan? How did Roosevelt handle tense relations with Japan?

11.   What were the strengths and weaknesses of Theodore Roosevelt's aggressive foreign policy? What were the benefits of TR's activism and what were its drawbacks?

12.   The text states that the Roosevelt corollary to the Monroe Doctrine distorted the original policy statement of 1823. How did it do so? (See Chapter 10.) Compare the circumstances and purposes of the two policies.

CHAPTER 28

Progressivism and the Republican Roosevelt, 1901–1912

PART I: REVIEWING THE CHAPTER

A. CHECKLIST OF LEARNING OBJECTIVES

After mastering this chapter, you should be able to

1.   discuss the origins and nature of the progressive movement.

2.   describe how the early progressive movement developed its roots at the city and state level.

3.   identify the critical role that women played in progressive social reform.

4.   tell how President Roosevelt began applying progressive principles to the national economy.

5.   explain why Taft's policies offended progressives, including Roosevelt.

6.   describe how Roosevelt led a progressive revolt against Taft that openly divided the Republican party.

B. GLOSSARY

To build your social science vocabulary, familiarize yourself with the following terms:

1.   **progressive** In politics, one who believes in continuing social advancement, improvement, or reform. "The new crusaders, who called themselves 'progressives,' waged war on many evils. . ." (p. 664)

2.   **conspicuous consumption** The theory, developed by economist Thorstein Veblen, that much spending by the affluent occurs primarily to display wealth and status to others rather than from enjoyment of the goods or services. " . . . a savage attack on 'predatory wealth' and 'conspicuous consumption.' " (p. 665)

3.   **direct primary** In politics, the nomination of a party's candidates for office through a special election of that party's voters. "These ardent reformers pushed for direct primary elections. . . ." (p. 667)

4.   **initiative** In politics, the procedure whereby voters can, through petition, present proposed legislation directly to the electorate. "They favored the 'initiative' so that voters could directly propose legislation. . . ." (p. 667)

5.   **referendum** The submission of a law, proposed or already in effect, to a direct vote of the electorate. "Progressives also agitated for the 'referendum.' " (p. 667)

6.   **recall** In politics, a procedure for removing an official from office through popular election or other means. "The 'recall' would enable the voters to remove faithless elected officials. . . ." (p. 667)

7. **city manager** An administrator appointed by the city council or other elected body to manage affairs, supposedly in a nonpartisan or professional way. "Other communities adopted the city-manager system. . . ." (p. 669)

8. **red-light district** A section of a city where prostitution is officially or unofficially tolerated. ". . . wide-open prostitution (vice-at-a-price) . . . flourished in red-light districts. . . ." (p. 669)

9. **franchise** In government, a special privilege or license granted to a company or group to perform a specific function. "Public-spirited city-dwellers also moved to halt the corrupt sale of franchises for streetcars. . . ." (p. 669)

10. **bureaucracy (bureaucrat)** The management of government or business through departments and subdivisions manned by a system of officials (bureaucrats) following defined rules and processes. (The term is often thought not necessarily disparaging.) "These wedges into the federal bureaucracy, however small, gave female reformers a national stage. . . ." (p. 670)

11. **workers' (workmen's) compensation** Insurance, provided either by government or employers or both, providing benefits to employees suffering work-related injury or disability. " . . . by 1917 thirty states had put workers' compensation laws on the books. . . ." (p. 672)

12. **reclamation** The process of bringing or restoring wasteland to productive use. "Settlers repaid the cost of reclamation. . . ." (p. 676)

13. **collectivism** A political or social system in which individuals are subordinated to mass organization and direction. "He strenuously sought the middle road between unbridled individualism and paternalistic collectivism." (p. 683)

14. **insubordination** Deliberate disobedience to proper authority. ". . . Taft dismissed Pinchot on the narrow grounds of insubordination. . . ." (p. 685)

PART II: CHECKING YOUR PROGRESS

A. True-False

Where the statement is true, circle **T**; where it is false, circle **F**.

1.   T F   The progressive movement believed that social and economic problems should be solved at the community level without involvement by the federal government.

2.   T F   Muckraking journalists, social-gospel ministers, and women reformers all aroused Americans' concern about economic and social problems.

3.   T F   The leading progressive reformers were primarily immigrants and urban industrial workers.

4.   T F   Many female progressives saw the task of improving life in factories and slums as an extension of their traditional roles as wives and mothers.

5.   T F   President Theodore Roosevelt ended the anthracite coal strike by threatening to use federal troops to break the miners' union.

6.   T F   Roosevelt promoted stronger federal legislation to regulate the railroads and other major industries.

7.   T F   Roosevelt believed that all the monopolistic corporate trusts should be broken up and competition restored among smaller businesses.

8.   T F   Upton Sinclair's novel *The Jungle* was intended to arouse consumers' concern about unsanitary practices in the meat industry.

9.   T   F   Conservation policies like land reclamation and forest preservation were probably Theodore Roosevelt's most popular and enduring presidential achievements.

10.   T   F   Defenders of nature became divided between fervent "preservationists" who wanted to stop all human intrusions and more moderate "conservationists."

11.   T   F   Roosevelt effectively used the power of the presidency and the federal government to tame unrestricted capitalism while preserving the basic foundations of American business.

12.   T   F   William Howard Taft demonstrated his skill as a political campaigner and leader throughout his presidency.

13.   T   F   Progressive Republicans became angry with President Taft because he began to form alliances with Democrats and Socialists.

14.   T   F   The Ballinger-Pinchot conservation controversy pushed Taft into alliance with the Republican "Old Guard" against the pro-Roosevelt progressives.

15.   T   F   President Taft used his control of the Republican party machinery to deny Roosevelt the nomination in 1912.

B. Multiple Choice

Select the best answer and circle the corresponding letter.

1. The primary emphasis of the progressive movement was on
   a. freeing individuals and business from federal control.
   b. protecting farmers and small business from corporate power.
   c. strengthening government as an instrument of social betterment.
   d. organizing workers into a unified and class-conscious political party.
2. Prominent among those who aroused the progressive movement by stirring the public's sense of concern were
   a. socialists, social gospelers, women, and muckraking journalists.
   b. union leaders, machine politicians, immigrant spokespeople, and engineers.
   c. bankers, advertising people, congressmen, and scientists.
   d. athletes, entertainers, filmmakers, and musicians.
3. Which of the following was *not* among the targets of muckraking journalistic exposés?
   a. Urban politics and government
   b. The oil, insurance, and railroad industries
   c. The U.S. Army and Navy
   d. Child labor and the "white slave" traffic in women
4. Most progressives were
   a. poor farmers.
   b. urban workers.
   c. urban middle-class people.
   d. wealthy people.
5. Among the political reforms sought by the progressives were
   a. an end to political parties, political conventions, and the Supreme Court's right to judicial review of legislation.
   b. an Equal Rights Amendment, federal financing of elections, and restrictions on negative campaigning.
   c. civil-service reform, racial integration, and free silver.
   d. initiative and referendum, direct election of senators, and women's suffrage.

6.   The states where progressivism first gained great influence were

a.   Massachusetts, Maine, and New Hampshire.
b.   Wisconsin, Oregon, and California.
c.   Michigan, Kansas, and Nevada.
d.   New York, Florida, and Texas.

7.   The Supreme Court case of *Muller* v. *Oregon* was seen as a victory for both progressivism and women's rights because

a.   it upheld the constitutionality of laws granting special protection to women in the workplace.
b.   it held that women should receive "equal pay for equal work."
c.   it upheld workplace safety regulations to prevent disasters like the Triangle Shirtwaist fire.
d.   it opened almost all categories of the new industrial employment to women.

8.   Roosevelt ended the Pennsylvania coal strike by

a.   urging labor and management to negotiate a settlement.
b.   passing federal legislation legalizing unions.
c.   forcing mediation by threatening to seize the coal mines and operate them with federal troops.
d.   declaring a national state of emergency and ordering the miners back to work.

9.   The Roosevelt-backed Elkins Act and Hepburn Act were aimed at

a.   better protection for industrial workers.
b.   more effective regulation of the railroad industry.
c.   protection for consumers of beef and produce.
d.   breaking up the Standard Oil monopoly.

10.   The controversy over the Hetch Hetchy Valley in Yosemite National Park revealed

a.   a philosophical disagreement between wilderness "preservationists" and more moderate "conservationists."
b.   President Roosevelt's hostility toward creating any more national parks.
c.   a political conflict between the lumber industry and conservationists.
d.   a split between urban California's need for water and environmentalists' concerns to preserve free-flowing streams.

11.   Two areas where Roosevelt's progressivism made its substantial headway were

a.   agricultural and mining legislation.
b.   stock-market and securities legislation.
c.   immigration and racial legislation.
d.   consumer and conservation legislation.

12.   Roosevelt was blamed for the "Panic of 1907" because

a.   his "boat-rocking tactics" had allegedly unsettled industry.
b.   his policies of regulating and protecting industrial workers had caused a depression.
c.   his inability to establish a stable monetary policy led to a wall street crash.
d.   the public wanted him to run again for president in 1908.

13.   As a result of his successful campaign in 1908, William Howard Taft was expected to

a.   continue and extend Roosevelt's progressive policies.
b.   forge a coalition with William Jennings Bryan and the Democrats.
c.   emphasize foreign policy instead of Roosevelt's domestic reforms.
d.   turn away from Roosevelt and toward the conservative wing of the Republican party.

14.   Progressive Republicans grew disillusioned with Taft primarily over the issues of

a.   dollar diplomacy and military intervention in the Caribbean and Central America.
b.   labor union rights and women's concerns.
c.   trust-busting, tariffs, and conservation.
d.   regulation of the banking and railroad industries.

15. Roosevelt finally decided to break with the Republicans and form a third party because
   a. he had always regarded the Republican party as too conservative.
   b. he could no longer stand to be in the same party with Taft.
   c. Taft used his control of the Republican convention to deny Roosevelt the nomination.
   d. Roosevelt believed that he would have a better chance of winning the presidency as a third-party candidate.

C. Identification

Supply the correct identification for each numbered description.

1. _____ A largely middle-class movement that aimed to use the power of government to correct the economic and social problems of industrialism

2. _____ Popular journalists who used publicity to expose corruption and attack abuses of power in business and government

3. _____ Progressive proposal to allow voters to bypass state legislatures and propose legislation themselves

4. _____ Progressive device that would enable voters to remove corrupt or ineffective officials from office

5. _____ Roosevelt's policy of having the federal government promote the public interest by dealing evenhandedly with both labor and business

6. _____ Effective railroad-regulation law of 1906 that greatly strengthened the Interstate Commerce Commission

7. _____ Disastrous industrial fire of 1911 that spurred workmen's compensation laws and some state regulation of wages and hours in New York

8. _____ Upton Sinclair's novel that inspired proconsumer federal laws regulating meat, food, and drugs

9. _____ Powerful women's reform organization led by Frances Willard

10. _____ Brief but sharp economic downturn of 1907, blamed by conservatives on the supposedly dangerous president

11. _____ Generally unsuccessful Taft foreign policy in which government attempted to encourage overseas business ventures

12. _____ Powerful corporation broken up by a Taft-initiated antitrust suit in 1911

D. Matching People, Places, and Events

Match the person, place, or event in the left column with the proper description in the right column by inserting the correct letter on the blank line.

1. ___ Thorstein Veblen
2. ___ Lincoln Steffens
3. ___ Ida Tarbell
4. ___ Seventeenth Amendment
5. ___ Robert La Follette
6. ___ Triangle Shirtwaist Company fire

a. Politically inept inheritor of the Roosevelt legacy who ended up allied with the reactionary Republican "Old Guard"

b. Case that upheld protective legislation on the grounds of women's supposed physical weakness

7. ___ Anthracite coal strike

8. ___ Meat Inspection Act of 1906

9. ___ *Muller* v. *Oregon*

10. ___ William Howard Taft

11. ___ *Lochner* v. *New York*

12. ___ Gifford Pinchot

c. New York City disaster that underscored urban workers' need for government protection

d. The most influential of the state-level progressive governors and a presidential aspirant in 1912

e. Eccentric economist who criticized the wealthy for "conspicuous consumption" and failure to serve real human needs

f. Leading muckraking journalist whose articles documented the Standard Oil Company's abuse of power

g. Proconservation federal official whose dismissal by Taft angered Roosevelt progressives

h. Dangerous labor conflict resolved by Rooseveltian negotiation and threats against business people

i. Early muckraker who exposed the political corruption in many American cities

j. Progressive law aimed at curbing practices like those exposed in Upton Sinclair's *The Jungle*

k. Progressive measure that required U.S. senators to be elected directly by the people rather than by state legislatures

l. Supreme court ruling that overturned a progressive law mandating a ten-hour workday

E. Putting Things in Order

Put the following events in correct order by numbering them from 1 to 5.

1. _____ A former president opposes his handpicked successor for the Republican presidential nomination.

2. _____ Sensational journalistic accounts of corruption and abuse of power in politics and business spur the progressive movement.

3. _____ A progressive forestry official feuds with Taft's secretary of the interior, deepening the division within the Republican party.

4. _____ A novelistic account of Chicago's meat-packing industry sparks new federal laws to protect consumers.

5. _____ A brief but sharp financial crisis leads to conservative criticism of Roosevelt's progressive policies.

F. Matching Cause and Effect

Match the historical cause in the left column with the proper effect in the right column by writing the correct letter on the blank line.

Cause	Effect
1. ___ Old-time Populists, muckraking journalists, social-gospel ministers, and European socialist immigrants	a. Ended the era of uncontrolled exploitation of nature and involved the federal government in preserving natural resources
2. ___ Progressive concern about political corruption	b. Led to reforms like the initiative, referendum, and direct election of senators
3. ___ Governors like Robert La Follette	
4. ___ Roosevelt's threat to seize the anthracite coal mines	c. Forced a compromise settlement of a strike that threatened the national well-being
5. ___ Settlement Houses and women's clubs	d. Outraged consumers and led to the Meat Inspection Act and the Pure Food and Drug Act
6. ___ Upton Sinclair's *The Jungle*	
7. ___ Roosevelt's personal interest in conservation	e. Laid the basis for a third-party crusade in the election of 1912
8. ___ Taft's political mishandling of tariff and conservation policies	f. Incensed pro-Roosevelt progressives and increased their attacks on the Republican "Old Guard"
9. ___ Russia's and Japan's hostility to an American role in China	g. Led the way in using universities and regulatory agencies to pursue progressive goals
10. ___ Roosevelt's feeling that he was cheated out of the Republican nomination by the Taft machine	h. Made Taft's dollar-diplomacy policy a failure
	i. Provided the pioneering forces who laid the foundations for the Progressive movement.
	j. Served as the launching pads for widespread female involvement in progressive reforms

G. Developing Historical Skills

Classifying Historical Information

Often a broad historical movement, such as progressivism, can best be understood by breaking it down into various component parts. Among the varieties of progressive reform discussed in this chapter are (A) political progressivism, (B) economic or industrial progressivism, (C) consumer progressivism, and (D) environmental progressivism.

Put each of the following progressive acts, policies, or court cases into one of those categories by writing in the correct letter.

1. _____   The Newlands Act of 1902

2. _____   The ten-hour law for bakers

3. _____   The movement for women's suffrage

4. _____   The anthracite coal strike of 1902

5. _____   Direct election of senators

6. _____   The Meat Inspection Act of 1906

7. _____   The Pure Food and Drug Act

8. _____   Initiative, referendum, and recall

9. _____   *Muller* v. *Oregon*

10. _____   The Hepburn Act of 1906

11. _____   Yosemite and Grand Canyon National Parks

12. _____   Workmen's compensation laws

PART III: APPLYING WHAT YOU HAVE LEARNED

1. What caused the progressive movement, and how did it get under way?

2. What did the progressive movement accomplish at the local, state, and national levels?

3. What made women such central forces in the progressive crusade? What specific backgrounds and ideologies did they bring to the public arena? What were the strengths and limitations of the progressive emphasis on providing special protection to children and women?

4. Discuss Roosevelt's support for conservation and consumer protection. Why were these among the most successful progressive achievements?

5. What caused the Taft-Roosevelt split, and how did it reflect the growing division between "Old Guard" and "progressive" Republicans?

6. How was progressivism a response to the development of the new urban and industrial order in America? (See Chapters 24 and 25.)

7. It is sometimes argued that progressivism was a uniquely American phenomenon because it addressed the most profound social and economic problems without engaging in the rhetoric of class conflict or economic warfare. Is this true? How did progressives address the problems of the working classes and poor without adopting the ideologies of socialism or communism?

8. If it is true that progressivism was largely a movement of the middle classes, was that a source of strength or weakness for its ideology and social policies?

CHAPTER 29

Wilsonian Progressivism at Home and Abroad, 1912–1916

PART I: REVIEWING THE CHAPTER

A. CHECKLIST OF LEARNING OBJECTIVES

After mastering this chapter, you should be able to

1. discuss the key issues of the pivotal 1912 election and the basic principles of Wilsonian progressivism.

2. describe how Wilson successfully reformed the "triple wall of privilege."

3. state the basic features of Wilson's moralistic foreign policy and explain how they first drew him into intervention in Latin America.

4. describe America's initial response to World War I, and explain the increasingly sharp conflict over America's policies toward Germany.

5. explain how domestic and foreign controversies affected Wilson's narrow victory over Hughes in 1916.

B. GLOSSARY

To build your social science vocabulary, familiarize yourself with the following terms:

1. **entrepreneurship** The process whereby an individual initiates a business at some risk in order to expand it and thereby earn a profit. "Wilson's New Freedom, by contrast, favored small enterprise, entrepreneurship, and the free functioning of . . . markets." (p. 688)

2. **self-determination** In politics, the right of a people to shape its own national identity and form of government, without outside coercion or influence. ". . . [the Confederacy] . . . partly inspired his ideal of self-determination for people of other countries." (p. 690)

3. **piety** Devotion to religious duty and practices. ". . . Wilson was reared in an atmosphere of fervent piety." (p. 690)

4. **graduated income tax** A tax on income in which the taxation rates grow progressively higher for those with higher income. "Congress enacted a graduated income tax. . . ." (p. 691)

5. **levy** A forcible tax or other imposition. ". . . [the] income tax [began] with a modest levy on income over $3,000. . . ." (p. 691)

6. **inelasticity** The inability to expand or contract rapidly. "[The] most serious shortcoming [of the country's financial structure] was the inelasticity of the currency." (p. 691)

7. **commercial paper** Any business document having monetary or exchangeable value. "The . . . paper money [was] backed by commercial paper. . . ." (p. 692)

8. **promissory note** A written pledge to pay a certain person a specified sum of money at a certain time. "The . . . paper money [was] backed by commercial paper, such as promissory notes of business people." (p. 692)

9. **Magna Carta** The "Great Charter" of England, which feudal nobles of England forced King John I to sign in 1215. As the first written guarantee of certain traditional rights, such as trial by a jury of peers, against arbitrary royal power, it served as a model for later assertions of Anglo-Saxon liberties. "Union leader Samuel Gompers hailed the [Clayton] act as the Magna Carta of labor...." (p. 692)

10. **agricultural extension** The system of providing services and advice to farmers through dispersed local agents. "Other laws benefited rural America by providing for . . . the establishment of agricultural extension work in the state colleges." (p. 693)

11. **enclave** A small territory surrounded by foreign or hostile territory. "Though often segregated in Spanish-speaking enclaves, they helped to create a unique borderland culture. . . ." (p. 695)

12. **gringo** Contemptuous Latin American term for North Americans. "Challenging Carranza's authority while also punishing the gringos. . . ." (p. 696)

13. **censor** An official who examines publications, mail, literature, and so forth in order to remove or prohibit the distribution of material deemed dangerous or offensive. "Their censors sheared away war stories harmful to the Allies . . . ." (p. 697)

14. **torpedo** To launch from a submarine or airplane a self-propelled underwater explosive designed to detonate on impact. ". . . the British passenger liner *Lusitania* was torpedoed and sank. . . ." (p. 699)

15. **draft** In politics, to choose an individual to run for office without that person's prior solicitation of the nomination. (A *military* draft, or conscription, legally compels individuals into the armed services.) "Instead, they drafted Supreme Court Justice Charles Evans Hughes, a cold intellectual who had achieved a solid record as governor of New York." (p. 701)

PART II: CHECKING YOUR PROGRESS

A. True-False

Where the statement is true, circle **T**; where it is false, circle **F**.

1. T   F   Wilson won the election of 1912 largely because the Republican party split in two.

2. T   F   In the 1912 campaign, Wilson's "New Freedom" favored a socially activist government and preserving large regulated trusts, while Roosevelt's "New Nationalist" favored small enterprise and strict antitrust laws.

3. T   F   Wilson believed that the president should provide national leadership by appealing directly to the people.

4. T   F   Wilson successfully used his popular appeal to push through progressive reforms of the tariff, monetary systems, and trusts.

5. T   F   Wilson's progressive outlook showed itself clearly in his attempt to improve the conditions and treatment of blacks.

6. T   F   Wilson initially attempted to overturn the imperialistic big-stick and dollar-diplomacy foreign policies of Roosevelt and Taft, especially in Latin America.

7. T   F   Wilson consistently refused to send American troops to intervene in the Caribbean.

8. T F   Wilson's initial policy toward the revolutionary Mexican government of General Huerta was to show his disapproval without sending in American troops.

9. T F   The mediation of three Latin American nations saved Wilson from a full-scale war with Mexico.

10. T F   General Pershing's expedition into Mexico was an attempt to bring the pro-American faction of Mexican revolutionaries to power.

11. T F   In the early days of World War I, more Americans sympathized with Germany than with Britain.

12. T F   The American economy benefited greatly from supplying goods to the Allies.

13. T F   After the *Lusitania*'s sinking, the Midwest and West favored war with Germany, while the East generally favored attempts at negotiation.

14. T F   After the sinking of the *Sussex*, Wilson successfully pressured Germany into stopping submarine attacks against neutral shipping.

15. T F   In the 1916 campaign, Wilson ran on the slogan "He Kept Us Out of War," while his opponent Hughes tried to straddle the issue of a possible war with Germany.

B. Multiple Choice

Select the best answer and circle the corresponding letter in the space provided.

1. The basic contrast between the two progressive candidates, Roosevelt and Wilson, was that
    a. Roosevelt wanted genuine political and social reforms, while Wilson wanted only to end obvious corruption.
    b. Roosevelt wanted to promote free enterprise and competition, while Wilson wanted the federal government to regulate the economy and promote social welfare.
    c. Roosevelt wanted the federal government to regulate the economy and promote social welfare, while Wilson wanted to restore economic competition and social equality.
    d. Roosevelt wanted to focus on issues of jobs and economic growth, while Wilson wanted social legislation to protect women, children, and city-dwellers.

2. Wilson won the election of 1912 primarily because
    a. his policies were more popular with the public.
    b. Taft and Roosevelt split the former Republican vote.
    c. the Socialists took nearly a million votes from Roosevelt.
    d. he was able to win over many of the Roosevelt supporters to his cause.

3. Wilson's primary weakness as a politician was
    a. his lack of skill in public speaking.
    b. his inability to grasp the complexity of governmental issues.
    c. his tendency to be inflexible and refuse to compromise.
    d. his lack of overarching political ideals.

4. The "triple wall of privilege" that Wilson set out to reform consisted of
    a. farmers, shippers, and the military.
    b. the tariffs, the banks, and the trusts.
    c. the universities, private dining clubs, and political bosses.
    d. congressional leaders, lobbyists, and lawyers.

5. During the Wilson administration, Congress exercised the authority granted by the newly enacted Sixteenth Amendment to pass
    a. prohibition of liquor.

b.   women's suffrage.

c.   voting rights for blacks.

d.   a federal income tax.

6.   The new regulatory agency created by the Wilson administration in 1914 that attacked monopolies, false advertising, and consumer fraud was

a.   the Federal Trade Commission.

b.   the Interstate Commerce Commission.

c.   the Federal Reserve System.

d.   the Consumer Products Safety Commission.

7.   While it attacked business monopolies, the Clayton Anti-Trust Act exempted from antitrust prosecution

a.   industries essential to national defense.

b.   agricultural and labor organizations.

c.   the oil and steel industries.

d.   professional organizations of doctors and lawyers.

8.   Wilson effectively reformed the banking and financial system by

a.   establishing a third Bank of the United States to issue and regulate the currency.

b.   taking the United States off the gold standard.

c.   establishing a publicly controlled Federal Reserve Board with regional banks under bankers' control.

d.   transferring authority to regulate banking and currency to the states and the private sector.

9.   Wilson's progressive policies and laws substantially aided all of the following groups *except*

a.   workers.

b.   blacks.

c.   farmers.

d.   children.

10.   Wilson's initial attitude toward the Mexican revolutionary government was

a.   to refuse recognition of General Huerta's regime but avoid American intervention.

b.   to intervene with troops on behalf of threatened American business interests.

c.   to provide military and economic assistance to the Huerta regime.

d.   to mobilize other Latin American governments to oust Huerta.

11.   The threatened war between the United States and Mexico in 1914 was avoided by the mediation of the ABC powers, which consisted of

a.   Australia, Britain, and Canada.

b.   Antigua, Brazil, and Cuba.

c.   Argentina, Brazil, and Chile.

d.   the Association of British Commonwealth nations.

12.   General Pershing's expedition into Mexico was sent in direct response to

a.   the refusal of Huerta to abandon power.

b.   the threat of German intervention in Mexico.

c.   the arrest of American sailors in the Mexican port of Tampico.

d.   the killing of American citizens in New Mexico by "Pancho" Villa.

13.   The sympathy of a majority of Americans for the Allies and against Germany was especially conditioned by

a.   British bribes and payoffs to American journalists.

b.   the Germans' involvement in overseas imperialism.

c.   the German invasion of neutral Belgium.

d.   the British refusal to use poison gas in warfare.

14. After the *Lusitania*, *Arabic*, and *Sussex* sinkings, Wilson successfully pressured the German government to
    a. end the use of the submarine against British warships.
    b. end its attempt to blockade the British Isles.
    c. publish warnings to all Americans considering traveling on unarmed ships.
    d. cease from sinking neutral merchant and passenger ships without warning.
15. Wilson's most effective slogan in the campaign of 1916 was
    a. "The full dinner pail."
    b. "Free and unlimited coinage of silver in the ratio of sixteen to one."
    c. "A war to make the world safe for democracy."
    d. "He kept us out of war."

C. Identification

Supply the correct identification for each numbered description.

1. _____ Four-footed symbol of Roosevelt's Progressive third party in 1912

2. _____ A fourth political party, led by a former labor union leader, that garnered nearly a million votes in 1912

3. _____ Wilson's political philosophy of restoring democracy through trust-busting and economic competition

4. _____ A twelve-member agency appointed by the president to oversee the banking system under a new federal law of 1913

5. _____ New presidentially appointed regulatory commission designed to prevent monopoly and guard against unethical trade practices

6. _____ Wilsonian law that tried to curb business monopoly while permitting labor and agricultural organizations

7. _____ Wilsonian reform law that established an eight-hour day for railroad workers

8. _____ Troubled Caribbean island nation where a president's murder led Wilson to send in the marines and assume American control of the police and finances

9. _____ Term for the three Latin American nations whose mediation prevented war between the United States and Mexico in 1914

10. _____ World War I alliance headed by Germany and Austria-Hungary

11. _____ The coalition of powers—led by Britain, France, and Russia—that opposed Germany and its partners in World War I

12. _____ New underwater weapon that threatened neutral shipping and seemed to violate all traditional norms of international law

13. _____ Large British passenger liner whose sinking in 1915 prompted some Americans to call for war against Germany

14. _____ Germany's carefully conditional agreement in 1916 not to sink passenger and merchant vessels without warning

15. _____ Key electoral state where a tiny majority for Wilson tipped the balance against Hughes in 1916

D. Matching People, Places, and Events

Match the person, place, or event in the left column with the proper description in the right column by inserting the correct letter on the blank line.

1. ___ Thomas Woodrow Wilson

2. ___ Theodore Roosevelt

3. ___ Samuel Gompers

4. ___ Louis D. Brandeis

5. ___ Virgin Islands

6. ___ General Huerta

7. ___ Venustiano Carranza

8. ___ Vera Cruz

9. ___ "Pancho" Villa

10. ___ John J. Pershing

11. ___ Belgium

12. ___ Serbia

13. ___ Kaiser Wilhelm II

14. ___ Haiti

15. ___ Charles Evans Hughes

a. Small European nation in which an Austro-Hungarian heir was killed, leading to the outbreak of World War I

b. Mexican revolutionary whose assaults on American citizens and territory provoked a U.S. expedition into Mexico

c. Ports where clashes between Mexicans and American military forces nearly led to war in 1914

d. Caribbean territory purchased by the United States from Denmark in 1917

e. Narrowly unsuccessful presidential candidate who tried to straddle both sides of the fence regarding American policy toward Germany

f. Small European nation whose neutrality was violated by Germany in the early days of World War I

g. Commander of the American military expedition into Mexico in 1916–1917

h. Southern-born intellectual who pursued strong moral goals in politics and the presidency

i. Leading progressive reformer and the first Jew named to the U.S. Supreme Court

j. Caribbean nation where Wilson sent American marines in 1915

k. Energetic progressive and vigorous nationalist who refused to wage another third-party campaign in 1916

l. Labor leader who hailed the Clayton Anti-Trust Act as the "Magna Carta of labor"

m. Second revolutionary Mexican president, who took aid from the United States but strongly resisted American military intervention in his country

n. Autocratic ruler who symbolized

ruthlessness and arrogance to many pro-Allied Americans

o.   Mexican revolutionary whose bloody regime Wilson refused to recognize and nearly ended up fighting

E. Putting Things in Order

Put the following events in correct order by numbering them from 1 to 5.

1. _____   Wilson extracts a dangerously conditional German agreement to halt submarine warfare.

2. _____   Wilson's superb leadership pushes major reforms of the tariff and monetary system through Congress.

3. _____   The bull moose and the elephant are both electorally defeated by a donkey bearing the banner of "New Freedom."

4. _____   The heavy loss of American lives to German submarines nearly leads the United States into war with Germany.

5. _____   Despite efforts to avoid involvement in the Mexican revolution, Wilson's occupation of a Mexican port raises the threat of war.

F. Matching Cause and Effect

Match the historical cause in the left column with the proper effect in the right column by writing the correct letter on the blank line.

1. ___   The split between Taft and Roosevelt

2. ___   Wilson's presidential appeals to the public over the heads of Congress

3. ___   The Federal Reserve Act

4. ___   Conservative justices of the Supreme Court

5. ___   Political turmoil in Haiti and Santo Domingo (Dominican Republic)

6. ___   The Mexican revolution

7. ___   "Pancho" Villa's raid on Columbus, New Mexico

8. ___   America's close cultural and economic ties with Britain

9. ___   Germany's sinking of the *Lusitania, Arabic,* and *Sussex*

10. ___   Wilson's apparent success in keeping America at peace through

a.   Caused most Americans to sympathize with the Allies rather than the Central Powers

b.   Helped push through sweeping reforms of the tariff and the banking system in 1913

c.   Enabled the Democrats to win a narrow presidential victory in the election of 1916

d.   Allowed Wilson to win a minority victory in the election of 1912

e.   Declared unconstitutional progressive Wilsonian measures dealing with labor unions and child labor

f.   Caused President Wilson and other outraged Americans to demand an end to unrestricted submarine warfare

g.   Created constant political instability south of the border and undermined Wilson's hopes for better U.S. relations with Latin America

diplomacy

h.   Was the immediate provocation for General Pershing's punitive expedition into Mexico

i.   Finally established an effective national banking system and a flexible money supply

j.   Caused Wilson to send in U.S. marines to restore order and supervise finances

G. Developing Historical Skills

Understanding Documents in Context

Historical documents cannot usually be understood in isolation. Awareness of the circumstances and conditions under which they were written is essential to comprehending their importance. The text reproduces on p. 701 the advertisement with notice from the German government that appeared in the New York *Herald* on May 1, 1915, six days before the *Lusitania* was sunk. Read the ad carefully, and reread text pp. 698–703 to understand and evaluate the context in which the warning appeared. Then answer the following questions.

1.   What was the *policy* of the German government regarding submarine use at the time the ad was taken out?

2.   Why might the German government be particularly concerned about warning American passengers thinking of traveling on a British liner? How would the notice be useful even if some Americans did travel on the ship?

3.   What fact about the *Lusitania*'s cargo did the German government know that it did not put into the warning?

4.   Why were many Americans outraged about the *Lusitania* sinking despite the warning?

PART III: APPLYING WHAT YOU HAVE LEARNED

1.   What were the essential qualities of Wilson's presidential leadership, and how did he display them in 1913–1914?

2.   What were the results of Wilson's great reform assault on the "triple wall of privilege"—the tariff, the banks, and the trusts?

3.   How was Wilson's foreign policy an attempt to expand idealistic progressive principles from the domestic to the international arena? Why did Wilson's progressive democratic idealism lead to the kind of U.S. interventions he professed to dislike?

4.   What were the causes and consequences of U.S. entanglement with Mexico in the wake of the Mexican Revolution? Could the U.S. have avoided involvement in Mexican affairs?

5.   Why was it so difficult for Wilson to maintain America's neutrality from 1914–1916?

6.   How did Wilson's foreign policy differ from that of the other great progressive president, Theodore Roosevelt? (See Chapter 27.) Which president was more effective in foreign policy and why?

7.   "Wilsonianism" is defined as the inclination to use U.S. foreign policy as a means of spreading American political and economic values throughout the whole world. In what ways does Wilson's foreign policy from 1913-1916 fit this definition? In what ways was his administration's policy during this period *not* Wilsonian?

8.   Why was America so determined to stay out of World War I during the early years of the conflict? What were the factors that gradually turned the government and the majority of Americans against Germany?

CHAPTER 30

The War to End War, 1917–1918

PART I: REVIEWING THE CHAPTER

A. CHECKLIST OF LEARNING OBJECTIVES

After mastering this chapter, you should be able to

1. explain what caused America to enter World War I.

2. describe how Wilsonian idealism turned the war into an ideological crusade that inspired fervor and overwhelmed dissent.

3. discuss the mobilization of America for war.

4. explain the consequences of World War I for labor, women, and African Americans.

5. describe America's economic and military role in the war.

6. analyze Wilson's attempt to forge a peace based on his Fourteen Points and explain why developments at home and abroad forced him to compromise.

7. discuss the opposition of Lodge and others to Wilson's League and show how Wilson's refusal to compromise doomed the Treaty of Versailles.

B. GLOSSARY

To build your social science vocabulary, familiarize yourself with the following terms:

1. **isolationism** In American diplomacy, the traditional belief that the United States should refrain from involvement in overseas politics, alliances, or wars, and confine its national security interest to its own borders (sometimes along with the Caribbean and Central America). **Internationalism** or **Wilsonianism** is the contrasting belief that America's national security requires involvement and sometimes diplomatic or military alliances overseas. "But their obstruction was a powerful reminder of the continuing strength of American isolationism." (p. 706)

2. **collective security** In international affairs, reliance on a group of nations or an international organization as protection against aggressors, rather than on national self-defense alone. " . . . an international organization that Wilson dreamed would provide a system of collective security." (p. 707)

3. **mobilization** The organization of a nation and its armed forces for war. "Creel typified American war mobilization. . . ." (p. 708)

4. **pardon** The official release of a person from punishment for a crime. ". . . presidential pardons were rather freely granted. . . ." (p. 709)

5. **ration** A fixed allowance of food or other scarce commodity. "He deliberately rejected issuing ration cards. . . ." (p. 713)

6. **conscientious objector** A person who refuses to participate in war on grounds of conscience or belief. ". . . about 4,000 conscientious objectors were excused." (p. 715)

7. **Bolshevik** The radical majority faction of the Russian Socialist party that seized power in the October 1917 revolution; they later took the name *Communist*. (Bolshevik is the Russian word for "majority"; their rivals for power were **Mensheviks**, or minority.) "The Bolsheviks long resented these 'capitalistic' interventions. . . ." (p. 716)

8. **salient** A portion of a battle line that extends forward into enemy territory. ". . . nine American divisions . . . joined four French divisions to push the Germans from the St. Mihiel salient. . . ." (p. 717)

9. **parliamentary** Concerning political systems in which the government is constituted from the controlling party's members in the legislative assembly. "Unlike all the parliamentary statesmen at the table, [Wilson] did not command a legislative majority at home." (p. 719)

10. **protectorate** In international affairs, a weaker or smaller country held to be under the guidance or protection of a major power; the arrangement is a weaker form of imperialism or colonialism. (A **colony** is a territory owned outright by a more powerful nation.) ". . . preventing any vengeful parceling out of the former colonies and protectorates of the vanquished powers." (p. 720)

11. **trustee** A nation that holds the territory of a former colony as the conditional agent of an international body under defined terms. "The victors would . . . receive the conquered territory . . . only as trustees of the League of Nations." (p. 720)

12. **mandate** Under the League of Nations (1919–1939), a specific commission that authorized a trustee to administer a former colonial territory. "Japan was conceded the strategic Pacific islands under a League of Nations mandate. . . ." (p. 720)

13. **self-determination** The Wilsonian doctrine that each people should have the right to freely choose its own political affiliation and national future, e.g., independence or incorporation into another nation. "Faced with fierce Wilsonian opposition to this violation of self-determination...." (p. 721)

14. **reservation** A portion of a deed, contract, or treaty that places conditions or restrictions on the general obligations. ". . . he finally came up with fourteen formal reservations. . . ." (p. 723)

15. **demagogue** A politician who arouses fervor by appealing to the lowest emotions of a mass audience, such as fear, hatred, and greed. " . . . a debacle that played into the hands of the German demagogue Adolf Hitler." (p. 725)

PART II: CHECKING YOUR PROGRESS

A. True-False

Where the statement is true, circle **T**; where it is false, circle **F**.

1. T   F   Germany responded to Wilson's call for "peace without victory" by proposing a temporary armistice.

2. T   F   Wilson's proclamation of the war as a crusade to end all war and spread democracy around the world inspired intense ideological enthusiasm among Americans.

3. T   F   Among Wilson's Fourteen Points were freedom of the seas, national self-determination for minorities, and an international organization to secure peace.

4. T   F   The Committee on Public Information used an aroused American patriotism more than formal laws and censorship to promote the war cause.

5. T   F   The primary targets of prosecution under the Espionage and Sedition Acts were German and Austrian agents in the United States.

6. T F   Even during the war mobilization, Americans were extremely reluctant to grant the federal government extensive powers over the economy.

7. T F   Despite bitter and sometimes violent strikes, American labor made economic and organizational gains as a result of World War I.

8. T F   War-inspired black migration into northern cities led to major racial riots in 1917–1919.

9. T F   The passage of the Nineteenth Amendment granting women's suffrage guaranteed the permanence of women's wartime economic gains.

10. T F   American troops actually played only a small role in the Allies' final victory.

11. T F   When Woodrow Wilson arrived in Europe, the European public hailed him as a hero and a peacemaking savior.

12. T F   Wilson's skillful handling of Republican political opposition strengthened his hand at the Paris Peace Conference.

13. T F   Other Allied leaders forced Wilson to make serious compromises in his Fourteen Points in order to keep the League of Nations in the Treaty of Versailles.

14. T F   Wilson's unwillingness to compromise and accept Republican reservations to the Treaty of Versailles sent the whole treaty down to defeat.

15. T F   In the election of 1920, Republican Harding supported the League of Nations while Democrat Cox tried to evade the issue.

B. Multiple Choice

Select the best answer and circle the corresponding letter.

1. The immediate cause of American entry into World War I was

    a. German support for a possible Mexican invasion of the southwestern United States.
    b. Germany's resumption of unrestricted submarine warfare.
    c. the German defeat of France.
    d. desire of the American munitions makers for large profits.

2. Wilson aroused the somewhat divided American people to fervent support of the war by

    a. seizing control of the means of communication and demanding national unity.
    b. declaring the German people to be immoral Huns and barbarians.
    c. proclaiming an ideological war to end war and make the world safe for democracy.
    d. proclaiming the war a religious crusade.

3. The capstone "Fourteenth Point" of Wilson's declaration of war aims called for

    a. the establishment of parliamentary democracies throughout Europe.
    b. guarantees of basic human rights for all people in the world.
    c. an international organization to guarantee collective security.
    d. freedom of travel without restrictions.

4. The purpose of George Creel's Committee on Public Information was

    a. to develop information on American wartime industrial production.
    b. to whip up public support for the war and promote anti-German propaganda.
    c. to develop counterintelligence information on German spies and saboteurs in the United States.
    d. to recruit volunteers for the armed forces.

5. The two key laws aimed at enforcing loyalty and suppressing antiwar dissent were

    a.   the War Mobilization Act and the National Defense Act.
    b.   the Selective Service Act and the Public Information Act.
    c.   the Eighteenth Amendment and the Anti-German Language Act.
    d.   the Espionage Act and the Sedition Act.

6. Among the primary victims of the prowar propaganda campaign to enforce loyalty were

    a.   German Americans and socialists.
    b.   Russian Americans and communists.
    c.   Mexican Americans and immigrants.
    d.   African Americans and feminists.

7. The mobilization for war gave new momentum to the movement for

    a.   a constitutional amendment granting women the right to vote.
    b.   a law granting labor unions the right to strike.
    c.   a constitutional amendment guaranteeing African Americans the right to travel freely.
    d.   a constitutional amendment prohibiting child labor.

8. Particularly violent strikes erupted during and after World War I in the

    a.   shipping and railroad industries.
    b.   mining and steel industries.
    c.   textile and clothing manufacturing industries.
    d.   factories employing women war workers.

9. During World War I, African American military men served primarily in

    a.   segregated, non-combat support units.
    b.   the navy and the coast guard.
    c.   the most dangerous trenches in northern France.
    d.   in northern cities where their presence did not threaten the system of segregation.

10. A major difference between the World War I Selective Service Act and the Civil War draft was that

    a.   in World War I women as well as men were drafted.
    b.   in World War I it was not possible to purchase an exemption or to hire a substitute.
    c.   in World War I draftees were sent immediately into front line combat.
    d.   in World War I draftees received the same training as professional soldiers.

11. American soldiers were especially needed in France in the spring of 1918 because

    a.   the Allied invasion of Germany was faltering short of its goal.
    b.   Britain had moved many of its soldiers from the western front to Russia.
    c.   a renewed German offensive was threatening to break through to Paris.
    d.   the Russians were threatening to enter the war on the German side.

12. Most of the military supplies for General Pershing's expeditionary force came from

    a.   America's European allies.
    b.   factories in the United States.
    c.   captured German matériel.
    d.   Britain's colonies in Africa.

13. Wilson blundered when choosing the American peace delegation by failing to

    a.   have a set of clear diplomatic goals.
    b.   include any Republicans in the delegation.
    c.   consult with his key allies, Britain and France.
    d.   include experts who would understand the intricate politics of Europe.

14. The European powers and Japan weakened Wilson at the peace conference by

    a.   refusing to support his proposed League of Nations.

b.   supporting the Republicans who were criticizing Wilson at home.

c.   demanding continuing American aid and involvement in European affairs.

d.   forcing him to compromise his ideals on matters of self-determination and punishment of Germany.

15. Wilson bore considerable responsibility for the failure of the United States to join the League of Nations because

a.   he linked the League too closely to European politics.

b.   he ordered Democratic senators to defeat the pro-League treaty with the Lodge reservations.

c.   he failed to take the case for the League to the American public.

d.   he had agreed that America would pay most of the cost of the League.

C. Identification

Supply the correct identification for each numbered description.

1. _____   Wilson's appeal to all the belligerents in January 1917, just before the Germans resumed submarine warfare

2. _____   Message that contained a German proposal to Mexico for an anti-American alliance

3. _____   Wilson's idealistic statement of American war aims in January 1918 that inspired the Allies and demoralized their enemies

4. _____   American government propaganda agency that aroused zeal for Wilson's ideals and whipped up hatred for the kaiser

5. _____   Radical antiwar labor union whose members were prosecuted under the Espionage and Sedition Act

6. _____   Weak federal agency designed to organize and coordinate U.S. industrial production for the war effort

7. _____   Constitutional provision endorsed by Wilson as a war measure whose ratification achieved a long-sought goal for American women

8. _____   Treasury Department bond-selling drives that raised about $21 billion to finance the American war effort

9. _____   The nations that dominated the Paris Peace Conference—namely, Britain, France, Italy, and the United States

10. _____   Wilson's proposed international body that constituted the key provision of the Versailles treaty

11. _____   Controversial peace agreement that compromised many of Wilson's Fourteen Points but retained his League

12. _____   Senatorial committee whose chairman used delaying tactics and hostile testimony to develop opposition to Wilson's treaty and League of Nations

13. _____   A hard core of isolationist senators who bitterly opposed any sort of league; also called the "Battalion of Death"

14. _____   Amendments to the proposed Treaty of Versailles, sponsored by Wilson's hated senatorial opponent, that attempted to guarantee America's sovereign rights in relation to the League of Nations

15. _____   Wilson's belief that the presidential election of 1920 should constitute a direct
                     popular vote on the League of Nations

D. Matching People, Places, and Events

Match the person, place, or event in the left column with the proper description in the right column by inserting the correct letter on the blank line.

1. ___   George Creel

2. ___   Eugene V. Debs

3. ___   Bernard Baruch

4. ___   Herbert Hoover

5. ___   John J. Pershing

6. ___   Alice Paul

7. ___   Meuse-Argonne

8. ___   Kaiser Wilhelm II

9. ___   Woodrow Wilson

10. ___   Henry Cabot Lodge

11. ___   Georges Clemenceau

12. ___   William Borah

13. ___   James Cox

14. ___   Calvin Coolidge

15. ___   Warren G. Harding

a.   Inspirational leader of the Western world in wartime who later stumbled as a peacemaker

b.   Senatorial leader of the isolationist "irreconcilables" who absolutely opposed all American involvement in Europe

c.   Climactic final battle of World War I

d.   The "tiger" of France, whose drive for security forced Wilson to compromise at Versailles

e.   Head of the American propaganda agency that mobilized public opinion for World War I

f.   Folksy Ohio senator whose 1920 presidential victory ended the last hopes for U.S. participation in the League of Nations

g.   Hated leader of America's enemy in World War I

h.   Head of the Food Administration who pioneered successful voluntary mobilization methods

i.   Leader of the pacifist National Women's Party who opposed U.S. involvement in World War I

j.   Defeated Democratic presidential candidate in the election of 1920

k.   Commander of the overseas American Expeditionary Force in World War I

l.   Massachusetts governor and Warren G. Harding's vice presidential running mate in the election of 1920

m.   Wilson's great senatorial antagonist who fought to keep America out of the League of Nations

n.   Head of the War Industries Board, which attempted to impose some order on U.S. war production

o.   Socialist leader who won nearly a million votes as a presidential candidate while in federal prison for antiwar activities

E. Putting Things in Order

Put the following events in correct order by numbering them from 1 to 5.

1. _____ Germany's resumption of submarine warfare forces the United States onto a declaration of war.

2. _____ The Senate's final defeat of the Versailles treaty and a Republican election victory end Wilson's last hopes for American entry into the League of Nations.

3. _____ The United States takes the first hesitant steps toward preparedness in the event of war.

4. _____ The effectiveness of American combat troops in crucial battles helps bring about an Allied victory in World War I.

5. _____ Wilson struggles with other Allied leaders in Paris to hammer out a peace treaty and organize the postwar world.

F. Matching Cause and Effect

Match the historical cause in the left column with the proper effect in the right column by writing the correct letter on the blank line.

Cause

1. ___ Germany's resumption of unrestricted submarine warfare

2. ___ Wilson's Fourteen Points

3. ___ The wartime atmosphere of emotional patriotism and fear

4. ___ Women's labor in wartime factories

5. ___ The migration of African Americans to northern cities

6. ___ American troops' entry into combat in the spring and summer of 1918

7. ___ Wilson's political blunders in the fall of 1918

8. ___ The strong diplomatic demands of France, Italy, and Japan

9. ___ Senator Lodge's tactics of delaying and proposing reservations in the Versailles treaty

10. ___ Wilson's refusal to accept any reservations supported by Lodge.

Effect

a. Led to major racial violence in Chicago and East St. Louis, Illinois

b. Forced Democrats to vote against a modified treaty and killed American participation in the League of Nations

c. Stopped the final German offensive and turned the tide toward Allied victory

d. Allowed domestic disillusionment and opposition to the treaty and League to build strength

e. Finally pushed the United States into World War I

f. Weakened the president's position during the peacemaking process

g. Caused harsh attacks on German Americans and other Americans who opposed the war

h. Lifted Allied and American spirits and demoralized Germany and its allies

i. Forced Wilson to compromise his Fourteen Points in order to keep the League as part of the peace treaty

j. Helped pass the Nineteenth

Amendment but did not really change
society's emphasis on the maternal role

G. Developing Historical Skills

Analyzing Visual Propaganda

This exercise involves analyzing visual propaganda designed to make emotional appeals on behalf of a
cause. In this case, the propaganda was designed to enlist the American public's support for the war
effort against Germany. The kinds of propaganda used on behalf of a cause can tell the historian a great
deal about what issues were perceived to be at stake and what public values were being appealed to.

Answer the following questions about the cartoons and drawings in this chapter.

1. *Anti-German Propaganda* (p. 708): How do the words and image of this poster work together to
    persuade an American audience to buy liberty loans? Besides the specific message, what general
    portrait of Germany, the war, and America's reasons for fighting are conveyed?

2. *A Universal Draft, 1917*: How do the visual and verbal symbols in this cartoon convey the
    combination of invitation and threat implied in the War Department's 1918 wartime manpower
    rules? How would you characterize the depiction of "Uncle Sam's" mood here?

3. *Food for Thought* (p. 713): How does this poster visually make the connection between the
    patriotic war effort and gardens"? What specific words or phrases create the link between
    women's food-growing effort and military service on fields of combat? What specific appeal is
    this image making to women?

PART III: APPLYING WHAT YOU HAVE LEARNED

1. What caused American entry into World War I, and how did Wilson turn the war into an
    ideological crusade?

2. Did World War I substantially alter American society and culture (e.g., ethnic, class, gender, and
    race relations), or were its effects primarily an "affair of the mind," i.e., altering American ideas
    and world views?

3. What was America's military and ideological contribution to the Allied victory?

4. How were the goals of the war presented to the American public? What does the text mean when
    it says that the war and Wilson's ideals may have been "oversold?" (p. 708)

5. How was Wilson forced to compromise during the peace negotiations, and why did America in
    the end refuse to ratify the treaty and join the League of Nations?

6. Apart from such immediate factors as the Lodge-Wilson antagonism, what general features of
    earlier American history worked against American involvement in European affairs and
    participation in the League of Nations?

7.   Do you agree that the primary responsibility for the failure of America to join the League of Nations lies with Woodrow Wilson rather than with his opponents?

8.   Ever since World War I and its aftermath, many of the fundamental debates about American foreign policy have been defined by whether the United States should pursue "Wilsonianism" or not. Using the account of Wilson's policies in the text and "Varying Viewpoints," outline the essential principles of Wilsonianism and explain why they have been so powerful and controversial in American history.

CHAPTER 31

American Life in the "Roaring Twenties," 1919–1929

PART I: REVIEWING THE CHAPTER

A. CHECKLIST OF LEARNING OBJECTIVES

After mastering this chapter, you should be able to

1. analyze the movement toward social conservatism following World War I.

2. describe the cultural conflicts over such issues as immigration, cultural pluralism, prohibition, and evolution.

3. discuss the rise of the mass-consumption economy, led by the automobile industry.

4. describe the cultural revolution brought about by radio, films, and changing sexual standards.

5. explain how new ideas and values were reflected and promoted in the American literary renaissance of the 1920s.

6. explain how the era's cultural changes affected women and African Americans.

B. GLOSSARY

To build your social science vocabulary, familiarize yourself with the following terms:

1. **syndicalism** A theory or movement that advocates bringing all economic and political power into the hands of labor unions by means of strikes. ". . . a number of legislatures . . . passed criminal syndicalism laws." (p. 729)

2. **Bible Belt** The region of the American South, extending roughly from North Carolina west to Oklahoma and Texas, where Protestant Fundamentalism and belief in literal interpretation of the Bible have traditionally been strongest. ". . . the Klan spread with astonishing rapidity, especially in the Midwest and the 'Bible Belt' South." (p. 730)

3. **provincial** Narrow and limited; isolated from cosmopolitan influences. "Isolationist America of the 1920s, ingrown and provincial, had little use for the immigrants. . . ." (p. 730)

4. **racketeer** A person who obtains money illegally by fraud, bootlegging, gambling, or threats of violence. "Racketeers even invaded the ranks of local labor unions. . . ." (pp. 736–737)

5. **underworld** Those who live outside society's laws, by vice or crime. ". . . the annual 'take' of the underworld was estimated to be from $12 billion to $18 billion. . . ." (p. 737)

6. **credit** In business, the arrangement of purchasing goods or services immediately but making the payment at a later date. "Buying on credit was another innovative feature of the postwar economy." (p. 739)

   b.   the teachings of Darwin could be reconciled with those of religion.
   c.   Darwinian evolutionary science could be taught in the public schools.
   d.   Fundamentalist Protestantism could be taught in the public schools.

8.   The most highly acclaimed industrial innovator of the new mass-production economy was

   a.   Babe Ruth.
   b.   Bruce Barton.
   c.   Ransom E. Olds.
   d.   Henry Ford.

9.   Two major American industries that benefited economically from the widespread use of the automobile were

   a.   plastics and synthetic fibers.
   b.   rubber and petroleum.
   c.   textiles and leather.
   d.   electronics and aluminum.

10.   One of the primary *social* effects of the new automobile age was

   a.   a weakening of traditional family ties between parents and youth.
   b.   a strengthening of intergenerational ties among parents, children, and grandchildren.
   c.   a tightening of restrictions on women.
   d.   a closing of the gap between the working class and the wealthy.

11.   Radio and the movies both had the cultural effect of

   a.   increasing Americans' interest in history and literature.
   b.   increasing mass standardization and weakening traditional forms of culture.
   c.   undermining the tendency of industry toward big business and mass production.
   d.   encouraging creativity and cultural independence among the people.

12.   In the 1920s, the major changes pursued by American women were

   a.   voting rights and political equality.
   b.   economic equality and equal pay for equal work.
   c.   social reform and family welfare.
   d.   cultural freedom and expanded sexual experience.

13.   The primary achievement of Marcus Garvey's Universal Negro Improvement Association was

   a.   its promotion of black jazz and blues.
   b.   its positive impact on black racial pride.
   c.   its economic development program in Harlem.
   d.   its transportation of numerous blacks to Liberia.

14.   The literary figure who promoted many new writers of the 1920s in his magazine, *The American Mercury*, was

   a.   H. L. Mencken.
   b.   W. C. Handy.
   c.   F. Scott Fitzgerald.
   d.   Henry Adams.

15.   Many of the prominent new writers of the 1920s were

   a.   fascinated by their historical roots in old New England.
   b.   disgusted with European domination of American culture.
   c.   interested especially in nature and social reform.
   d.   highly critical of traditional American "Puritanism" and small-town life.

C. Identification

Supply the correct identification for each numbered description.

1. _____ The movement of 1919–1920, spawned by fear of Bolshevik revolution, that resulted in the arrest and deportation of many political radicals

2. _____ Hooded defenders of Anglo-Saxon and "Protestant" values against immigrants, Catholics, and Jews

3. _____ Restrictive legislation of 1924 that reduced the number of newcomers to the United States and discriminated against immigrants from southern and eastern Europe

4. _____ New constitutional provision, popular in the Midwest and South, that encouraged lawbreaking and gangsterism in big cities

5. _____ Term for area of the South where traditional evangelical and Fundamentalist religion remained strong

6. _____ Legal battle over teaching evolution that pitted modern science against Fundamentalist religion

7. _____ New industry spawned by the mass-consumption economy that encouraged still more consumption

8. _____ Henry Ford's cheap, mass-produced automobile

9. _____ Invented in 1903 and first used primarily for stunts and mail carrying

10. _____ One of the few new consumer products of the 1920s that encouraged people to stay at home rather than pulling them away from home and family

11. _____ Feminist Margaret Sanger's cause that contributed to changing sexual behaviors, especially for women

12. _____ Syncopated style of music created by blacks that attained national popularity in the 1920s

13. _____ Marcus Garvey's self-help organization that proposed leading blacks to Africa

14. _____ H. L. Mencken's monthly magazine that led the literary attack on traditional moral values, the middle class, and "Puritanism"

15. _____ The New York institution in which continuously rising prices and profits were fueled by speculation in the 1920s

D. Matching People, Places, and Events

Match the person, place, or event in the left column with the proper description in the right column by inserting the correct letter on the blank line.

1. ___ A. Mitchell Palmer

2. ___ Nicola Sacco and Bartolomeo Vanzetti

3. ___ Al Capone

4. ___ John Dewey

5. ___ William Jennings Bryan

6. ___ Henry Ford

7. ___ Bruce Barton

a. The "Poet Laureate" of Harlem and author of *The Weary Blues*

b. Innovative writer whose novels reflected the disillusionment of many Americans with propaganda and patriotic idealism

c. Italian American anarchists whose trial and execution aroused widespread protest

d. Mechanical genius and organizer of the

8. ___   Langston Hughes

9. ___   Charles A. Lindbergh

10. ___   Marcus Garvey

11. ___   Randolph Bourne

12. ___   H. L. Mencken

13. ___   F. Scott Fitzgerald

14. ___   Ernest Hemingway

15. ___   Andrew Mellon

mass-produced automobile industry

e. U.S. attorney general who rounded up thousands of alleged Bolsheviks in the red scare of 1919–1920

f. Baltimore writer who criticized the supposedly narrow and hypocritical values of American society

g. Top gangster of the 1920s, eventually convicted of income-tax evasion

h. Former presidential candidate who led the fight against evolution at the 1925 Scopes trial

i. U. S. treasury secretary who attempted to promote business investment by reducing taxes on the rich

j. A leader of the advertising industry and author of a new interpretation of Christ in *The Man Nobody Knows*

k. Cosmopolitan intellectual who advocated "cultural pluralism" and said America should be "not a nationality but a trans-nationality"

l. Leading American philosopher and proponent of "progressive education"

m. Humble aviation pioneer who became a cultural hero of the 1920s

n. Minnesota-born writer whose novels were especially popular with young people in the 1920s

o. Jamaican-born leader who enhanced African American pride despite his failed migration plans

E. Putting Things in Order

Put the following events in correct order by numbering them from 1 to 5.

1. _____   The trial of a Tennessee high-school biology teacher symbolizes a national conflict over values of religion and science.

2. _____   Fear of the Bolshevik revolution sparks a crusade against radicals and Communists in America.

3. _____   A modest young man becomes a national hero by accomplishing a bold feat of aviation.

4. _____   Two Italian immigrants are convicted of murder and robbery, provoking charges of prejudice against the judge and jury.

5. _____   A new immigration law tightens up earlier emergency restrictions and imposes discriminatory quotas against the "New Immigrants."

F. Matching Cause and Effect

Match the historical cause in the left column with the proper effect in the right column by writing the correct letter on the blank line.

Cause	Effect
1. ___ American fear of Bolshevism	a. Caused the rise of the Ku Klux Klan and the imposition of immigration restrictions
2. ___ Nativist American fear of immigrants and Catholics	b. Caused many influential writers of the 1920s to criticize traditional values and search for new moral standards
3. ___ Prohibition	c. Caused the red scare and the deportation of foreign radicals
4. ___ The automobile industry	
5. ___ The radio	d. Enabled many ordinary citizens to join in a speculative Wall Street boom
6. ___ Rising prosperity, new technologies, and the ideas of Sigmund Freud	e. Stimulated highway construction, petroleum production, and other related industries
7. ___ Resentment against conventional small-town morality	f. Helped stimulate mass attention to sports and entertainment while spreading the reach of advertising
8. ___ The economic boom of the 1920s	
9. ___ The ability to buy stocks with only a small down payment	g. Reduced the tax burden on the wealthy and contributed to the stock-market boom
10. ___ Andrew Mellon's tax policies	h. Greatly raised the incomes and living standards of many Americans
	i. Created a new atmosphere of sexual frankness and liberation, especially among the young
	j. Helped spawn "bootlegging" and large-scale organized crime

G. Developing Historical Skills

Understanding Cultural Developments in Historical Context

The first part of this chapter describes the major social and economic changes of the 1920s. The second part describes the cultural developments that also occurred in the 1920s. Since the artists, writers, and others who produced the culture and ideas of the period were living amidst these very same social changes, your knowledge of the historical context can help you understand why they created the kind of works they did.

Answer the following questions:

1. In what ways were the "movies," for all their glamour, similar to the automobile industry as developed by Henry Ford?

2. How did new technological and economic innovations like the automobile (pp. 739–742) and social changes like urbanization help bring about the cultural liberation of women?

3. In what ways did the novels of F. Scott Fitzgerald (pp. 749–750)) or musical developments like jazz (p. 746–747) especially appeal to people living amid the social and economic changes of the 1920s? Did these cultural developments simply mirror existing politics and society, or were they in some ways a challenge to them?

4. Why were writers like H. L. Mencken, Sinclair Lewis, and Sherwood Anderson so harshly critical of American rural and small-town life in their work? Why would writers with such attitudes have been unlikely to succeed in any period before the 1920s?

PART III: APPLYING WHAT YOU HAVE LEARNED

1. How and why did America turn toward domestic isolation and social conservatism in the 1920s?

2. How was the character of American culture affected by the social and political changes of the 1920s? (Include both white ethnic groups and blacks in your discussion.)

3. Why was immigration, which had existed for many generations, seen as such a great threat to American identity and culture in the prosperous 1920s?

4. Why did critics like Horace Kallen and Randolph Bourne dislike the pressure on immigrants to

5. "Americanize" and join the "melting pot"?   What did they envision that America should be like under their ideals of "cultural pluralism"?

6. How did some of the events of the 1920s reflect national conflicts over social, cultural, and religious values?

7. How did the automobile and other new products create a mass-consumption economy in the 1920s?

8. How did the new films, literature, and music of the 1920s affect American values in areas of religion, sexuality, and family life? Were African American cultural developments fundamentally different, or were they part of the *same* cultural movement?

9. In what ways were the twenties a social and cultural reaction against the progressive idealism that held sway before and during World War I? (See Chapters 29, 30, and 31.)

CHAPTER 32

The Politics of Boom and Bust, 1920–1932

PART I: REVIEWING THE CHAPTER

A. CHECKLIST OF LEARNING OBJECTIVES

After mastering this chapter, you should be able to

1.   analyze the domestic political conservatism and economic prosperity of the 1920s.

2.   explain the Republican administrations' policies of isolationism, disarmament, and high-tariff protectionism.

3.   compare the easygoing corruption of the Harding administration with the straight-laced uprightness of his successor Coolidge.

4.   describe the international economic tangle of loans, war debts, and reparations, and indicate how the United States dealt with it.

5.   discuss how Hoover went from being a symbol of twenties business success to a symbol of depression failure.

6.   explain how the stock-market crash set off the deep and prolonged Great Depression.

7.   indicate how Hoover's response to the depression was a combination of old-time individualism and the new view of federal responsibility for the economy.

B. GLOSSARY

To build your social science vocabulary, familiarize yourself with the following terms:

1.   **nationalization** Ownership of the major means of production by the national or federal government. ". . . wartime government operation of the lines might lead to nationalization." (p. 755)

2.   **dreadnought** A heavily armored battleship with large batteries of twelve-inch guns. ". . . Secretary Hughes startled the delegates . . . with a comprehensive, concrete plan for . . . scrapping some of the huge dreadnoughts. . . ." (p. 757)

3.   **accomplice** An associate or partner of a criminal who shares some degree of guilt. ". . . he and his accomplices looted the government to the tune of about $200 million. . . ." (p. 759)

4.   **reparations** Compensation by a defeated nation for damage done to civilians and their property during a war. "Overshadowing all other foreign-policy problems . . . was . . . a complicated tangle of private loans, Allied war debt, and German reparations payments." (p. 763)

5.   **pump priming** In economics, the spending or lending of a small amount of funds in order to stimulate a larger flow of economic activity. " 'Pump-priming' loans by the RFC were no doubt of widespread benefit. . . ." (p. 772)

PART II: CHECKING YOUR PROGRESS

A. True-False

Where the statement is true, circle **T**; where it is false, circle **F**.

1. T F   The most corrupt members of Harding's cabinet were the secretaries of state and the treasury.

2. T F   The Republican administrations of the 1920s believed in strict enforcement of antitrust laws to maintain strong business competition.

3. T F   The Republican administrations of the 1920s pursued their isolationist approach to national security by engaging in a large military buildup.

4. T F   The high tariff policies of the 1920s enhanced American prosperity but hindered Europe's economic recovery from World War I.

5. T F   Calvin Coolidge's image of honesty and thrift helped restore public confidence in the government after the Harding administration scandals.

6. T F   One sector of the American economy that did not share the prosperity of the 1920s was agriculture.

7. T F   The main sources of support for liberal third-party presidential candidate Robert La Follette in 1924 were urban workers and social reformers.

8. T F   The main exception to America's isolationist foreign policy in the 1920s was continuing U.S. armed intervention in the Caribbean and Central America.

9. T F   Britain and France did not begin to repay their war debts to the United States until the Dawes plan provided American loans to Germany.

10. T F   In the election of 1928, Democratic nominee Al Smith's urban, Catholic, and "wet" background cost him support from traditionally Democratic southern voters.

11. T F   The Hawley-Smoot Tariff strengthened the trend toward expanded international trade and economic cooperation.

12. T F   The American economic collapse of the Great Depression was the most severe suffered by any major industrial nation in the 1930s.

13. T F   The depression was caused partly by over-expansion of credit and excessive consumer debt.

14. T F   Throughout his term, Hoover consistently followed his belief that the federal government should play no role in providing economic relief and assisting the recovery from the depression.

15. T F   The United States strongly supported China against Japan in the Manchurian crisis even though it had greater economic interests in Japan.

B. Multiple Choice

Select the best answer and circle the corresponding letter.

1. As president, Warren G. Harding proved to be
    a.   thoughtful and ambitious but rather impractical.
    b.   an able administrator and diplomat but a poor politician.
    c.   politically competent and concerned for the welfare of ordinary people.

  d. weak-willed and tolerant of corruption among his friends.

2. The general policy of the federal government toward industry in the early 1920s was

  a. a weakening of federal regulation and encouragement of trade associations.
  b. an emphasis on federal regulation rather than state and local controls.
  c. an emphasis on vigorous antitrust enforcement rather than on regulation.
  d. a turn toward direct federal control of key industries like the railroads.

3. Two groups who suffered severe political setbacks in the immediate post–World War I environment were

  a. Protestants and Jews.
  b. organized labor and blacks.
  c. small businesses and farmers.
  d. women and city dwellers.

4. Two terms that describe the Harding and Coolidge administrations' approach to foreign policy are

  a. internationalism and moralism.
  b. interventionism and militarism.
  c. isolationism and disarmament.
  d. balance of power and alliance-seeking.

5. The proposed ratio of "5-5-3" in the Washington Disarmament Conference of 1921–1922 referred to

  a. the allowable ratio of American, British, and Japanese troops in China.
  b. the respective number of votes Britain, France, and the United States would have in the League of Nations.
  c. the allowable ratio of battleships and carriers among the United States, Britain, and Japan.
  d. the number of nations from Europe, the Americas, and Asia, respectively, that would have to ratify the treaties before they went into effect.

6. The very high tariff rates of the 1920s had the economic effect of

  a. stimulating the formation of common markets among the major industrial nations.
  b. causing severe deflation in the United States and Europe.
  c. turning American trade away from Europe and toward Asia.
  d. causing the Europeans to erect their own tariff barriers and thus severely reduce international trade.

7. The central scandal of Teapot Dome involved members of Harding's cabinet who

  a. sold spoiled foodstuffs to the army and navy.
  b. took bribes for leasing federal oil lands.
  c. violated prohibition by tolerating gangster liquor deals.
  d. stuffed ballot boxes and played dirty tricks on campaign opponents.

8. The "farm bloc's" favorite solution to the severe drop in prices that caused farmers' economic suffering in the 1920s was

  a. direct federal assistance to encourage farmers not to grow grain or cotton.
  b. for the federal government to buy up agricultural surpluses at higher prices and sell them abroad.
  c. for the United States to impose high tariffs on agricultural imports from foreign countries.
  d. for farmers to form "producers' unions" to force consumers to pay higher prices.

9. Besides deep divisions within the Democratic party, the elections of 1924 revealed

  a. Coolidge's inability to attain Harding's level of popularity.
  b. the weakness of profarmer and prolabor Progressive reform.
  c. the turn of the solid South from the Democrats to the Republicans.
  d. The rise of liberalism within the Democratic party.

10. The international economic crisis caused by unpaid war reparations and loans was partially resolved by
    a. private American bank loans to Germany.
    b. forgiving the loans and reparations.
    c. the creation of a new international economic system by the League of Nations.
    d. the rise of Mussolini and Hitler.
11. Al Smith's Roman Catholicism and opposition to prohibition hurt him especially
    a. in the South.
    b. among ethnic voters.
    c. among African Americans.
    d. among women voters.
12. The election of Hoover over Smith in 1928 seemed to represent a victory of
    a. northern industrial values over southern agrarianism.
    b. small business over the ideas of big government and big business.
    c. ethnic and cultural diversity over traditional Anglo-Saxon values.
    d. big business and efficiency over urban and Catholic values.
13. One important cause of the great stock market crash of 1929 was
    a. overexpansion of production and credit beyond the ability to pay for them.
    b. a "tight" money policy that made it difficult to obtain loans.
    c. the lack of tariff protection for American markets from foreign competitors.
    d. excessive government regulation of business.
14. The sky-high Hawley-Smoot Tariff of 1930 had the economic effect of
    a. providing valuable protection for hard-pressed American manufacturers.
    b. lowering the value of American currency in international money markets.
    c. crippling international trade and deepening the depression.
    d. forcing foreign governments to negotiate fairer trade agreements.
15. The federal agency that Hoover established to provide "pump-priming" loans to business was the
    a. Tennessee Valley Authority.
    b. Bonus Expeditionary Force.
    c. Reconstruction Finance Corporation.
    d. American Legion.

C. Identification

Supply the correct identification for each numbered description.

1. _____ Poker-playing cronies from Harding's native state who contributed to the morally loose atmosphere in his administration

2. _____ Supreme Court ruling that removed workplace protection and invalidated a minimum wage for women

3. _____ World War I veterans' group that promoted patriotism and economic benefits for former servicemen

4. _____ Agreement emerging from the Washington Disarmament Conference that reduced naval strength and established a ratio of warships among the major shipbuilding powers

5. _____ Toothless international agreement of 1928 that pledged nations to outlaw war

6. _____ Naval oil reserve in Wyoming that gave its name to one of the major Harding administration scandals

7. _____ Farm proposal of the 1920s, passed by Congress but vetoed by the president, that provided for the federal government to buy farm surpluses and sell them abroad

8. _____ American-sponsored arrangement for rescheduling German reparations payments that only temporarily eased the international debt tangle of the 1920s

9. _____ Southern Democrats who turned against their party's "wet," Catholic nominee and voted for the Republicans in 1938

10. _____ Sky-high tariff bill of 1930 that deepened the depression and caused international financial chaos

11. _____ The climactic day of the October 1929 Wall Street stock-market crash

12. _____ Depression shantytowns, named after the president whom many blamed for their financial distress

13. _____ Hoover-sponsored federal agency that provided loans to hard-pressed banks and businesses after 1932

14. _____ Encampment of unemployed veterans who were driven out of Washington by General Douglas MacArthur's forces in 1932

15. _____ The Chinese province invaded and overrun by the Japanese army in 1932

D. Matching People, Places, and Events

Match the person, place, or event in the left column with the proper description in the right column by inserting the correct letter on the blank line.

1. ___ Warren G. Harding
2. ___ Charles Evans Hughes
3. ___ Andrew Mellon
4. ___ Henry Sinclair
5. ___ John Davis
6. ___ Albert B. Fall
7. ___ Harry Daugherty
8. ___ Calvin Coolidge
9. ___ Robert La Follette
10. ___ Herbert Hoover
11. ___ Al Smith
12. ___ Black Tuesday
13. ___ Charles Dawes
14. ___ Douglas MacArthur
15. ___ Henry Stimson

a. The worst single event of the great stock market crash of 1929

b. Negotiator of a plan to reschedule German reparations payments and Calvin Coolidge's vice president after 1925

c. The "Happy Warrior" who attracted votes in the cities but lost them in the South

d. Harding's interior secretary, convicted of taking bribes for leases on federal oil reserves

e. Weak, compromise Democratic candidate in 1924

f. U.S. attorney general and a member of Harding's corrupt "Ohio Gang" who was forced to resign in administration scandals

g. Strong-minded leader of Harding's cabinet and initiator of major naval agreements

h. Wealthy industrialist and conservative

secretary of the treasury in the 1920s

i.   Weak-willed president whose easygoing ways opened the door to widespread corruption in his administration

j.   Hoover's secretary of state, who sought sanctions against Japan for its aggression in Manchuria

k.   Secretary of commerce through much of the 1920s whose reputation for economic genius became a casualty of the Great Depression

l.   Leader of a liberal third-party insurgency who attracted little support outside the farm belt

m.   Wealthy oilman who bribed cabinet officials in the Teapot Dome scandal

n.   Commander of the troops who forcefully ousted the "army" of unemployed veterans from Washington in 1932

o.   Tight-lipped Vermonter who promoted frugality and pro-business policies during his presidency

E. Putting Things in Order

Put the following events in correct order by numbering them from 1 to 5.

1. _____   Amid economic collapse, Congress raises tariff barriers to new heights and thereby deepens the depression.

2. _____   An American-sponsored plan to ease German reparations payments provides a temporarily successful approach to the international war-debt tangle.

3. _____   An American-sponsored international conference surprisingly reduces naval armaments and stabilizes Far Eastern power relations.

4. _____   The prosperous economic bubble of the 1920s suddenly bursts, setting off a sustained period of hardship.

5. _____   A large number of corrupt dealings and scandals become public knowledge just as the president who presided over them is replaced by his impeccably honest successor.

F. Matching Cause and Effect

Match the historical cause in the left column with the proper effect in the right column by writing the correct letter on the blank line.

	Cause		Effect
1. ___	Republican probusiness policies	a.	Led to a Republican landslide in the election of 1928
2. ___	American concern about the arms race and the danger of war	b.	Weakened labor unions and prevented the enforcement of progressive antitrust legislation
3. ___	The high-tariff Fordney-McCumber Law of 1922	c.	Plunged the United States into the worst economic depression in its history
4. ___	The loose moral atmosphere of Harding's Washington	d.	Drove crop prices down and created a rural economic depression
5. ___	The improved farm efficiency and production of the 1920s	e.	Led to the successful Washington Disarmament Conference and the Five Power Naval Agreement of 1922
6. ___	America's demand for complete repayment of the Allies' war debt	f.	Encouraged numerous federal officials to engage in corrupt dealings
7. ___	Hoover's media campaign and Smith's political liabilities	g.	Helped cause the stock-market crash and deepen the Great Depression
8. ___	The stock-market crash	h.	Failed to end the depression but did prevent more serious economic suffering
9. ___	Domestic overexpansion of production and dried-up international trade	i.	Sustained American prosperity but pushed Europe into economic protectionism and turmoil
10. ___	Hoover's limited efforts at federally sponsored relief and recovery	j.	Aroused British and French anger and toughened their demands for German war reparations

G. Developing Historical Skills

Reading Diagrams

Sometimes a schematic drawing or diagram can help explain a complicated historical process in a simpler way than words. The international financial tangle of the 1920s is an exceptionally complicated affair, but examining the diagram on p. 764 makes it much easier to understand.

Answer the following questions:

1. What two roles did Americans play in the process?

2. What economic relationship did Great Britain and France have with Germany?

3. To whom did Britain owe war debts? To whom did France owe war debts?

4. Why was credit from American bankers so essential to all the European powers? Can you explain what happened when that credit was suddenly cut off after the stock-market crash of 1929?

PART III: APPLYING WHAT YOU HAVE LEARNED

1. What basic economic and political policies were pursued by the conservative Republican administrations of the 1920s?

2. What were the effects of America's international economic and political isolationism in the 1920s?

3. What weakness existed beneath the surface of the general 1920s prosperity, and how did these weaknesses help cause the Great Depression?

4. Why were liberal or "progressive" politics so weak in the 1920s? Discuss the strengths and weaknesses of La Follette and Smith as challengers to the Republicans in 1924 and 1928.

5. The three Republican presidents of the 1920s are usually lumped together as essentially identical in outlook. Is it right to see them that way, or were the personal or political differences between them at all significant?

6. What were the effects of the Great Depression on the American people, and how did President Hoover attempt to balance his belief in "rugged individualism" with the economic necessities of the time? Why do historians today tend to see Hoover as a more tragic figure than people of the time, who bitterly denounced him?

7. How did some of the economic policies of the 1920s and 1930s help cause and deepen the depression?

8. How could the economic and political conservatism of the 1920s coincide with the great cultural and intellectual innovations of the same decade? (See Chapter 31.) Was it fitting or ironic that someone as straight-laced and traditional as Calvin Coolidge should preside over an age of jazz, gangsterism, and Hollywood?

CHAPTER 33

The Great Depression and the New Deal, 1933–1939

PART I: REVIEWING THE CHAPTER

A. CHECKLIST OF LEARNING OBJECTIVES

After mastering this chapter, you should be able to

1. describe the rise of Franklin Roosevelt to the presidency in 1932.

2. explain how the early New Deal pursued the "three Rs" of relief, recovery, and reform.

3. describe the New Deal's effect on labor and labor organizations.

4. discuss the early New Deal's efforts to organize business and agriculture in the NRA and the AAA and indicate what replaced those programs after they were declared unconstitutional.

5. describe the Supreme Court's hostility to many New Deal programs and explain why FDR's "Court-packing" plan failed.

6. explain how Roosevelt mobilized a New Deal political coalition that included the South, Catholics, Jews, African Americans, and women.

7. discuss the changes the New Deal underwent in the late thirties and explain the growing opposition to it.

8. analyze the arguments presented by both critics and defenders of the New Deal.

B. GLOSSARY

To build your social science vocabulary, familiarize yourself with the following terms:

1. **dispossessed** The economically deprived. ". . . she . . . emerged as a champion of the dispossessed. . . ." (p. 778)

2. **rubberstamp** To approve a plan or law quickly or routinely, without examination. ". . . it was ready to rubberstamp bills drafted by White House advisors. . . ." (p. 781)

3. **blank check** Referring to permission to use an unlimited amount of money or authority. ". . . Congress gave the president extraordinary blank-check powers. . . ." (p. 781)

4. **foreign exchange** The transfer of credits or accounts between the citizens or financial institutions of different nations. "The new law clothed the president with power to regulate banking transactions and foreign exchange. . . ." (p. 782)

5. **hoarding** Secretly storing up quantities of goods or money. "Roosevelt moved swiftly . . . to protect the melting gold reserve and to prevent panicky hoarding." (p. 783)

6. **boondoggling** Engaging in trivial or useless work; any enterprise characterized by such work. "Tens of thousands of jobless were employed at . . . make-work tasks, which were dubbed 'boondoggling.' " (p. 785)

7.   **Fascist (Fascism)** A political system or philosophy that advocates a mass-based party dictatorship, extreme nationalism, racism, and the glorification of war. "Fear of Long's becoming a fascist dictator ended. . . ." (p. 786)

8.   **parity** Equivalence in monetary value under different conditions; specifically, in the United States, the price for farm products that would give them the same purchasing power as in the period 1909–1914. ". . . this agency was to establish 'parity prices' for basic commodities." (p. 788)

9.   **holding company** A company that owns, and usually controls, the stocks and securities of another company. "New Dealers . . . directed their fire at public utility holding companies. . . ." (p. 791)

10. **collective bargaining** Bargaining between an employer and his or her organized work force over hours, wages, and other conditions of employment. "The NRA blue eagles, with their call for collective bargaining, had been a godsend. . . ." (p. 795)

11. **jurisdictional** Concerning the proper sphere in which authority may be exercised. ". . . bitter and annoying jurisdictional feuding involving strikes continued. . . ." (p. 797)

12. **checks and balances** In American politics, the interlocking system of divided and counter-weighted authority among the executive, legislative, and judicial branches of government. ". . . Roosevelt was savagely condemned for attempting to break down the delicate checks and balances. . . ." (p. 799)

13. **pinko** Disparaging term for someone who is not a "red," or Communist, but is presumed to be sympathetic to communism. "Critics deplored the employment of 'crackpot' college professors, leftist 'pinkos.'. . ." (p. 802)

14. **deficit spending** The spending of public funds beyond the amount of income. "Despite some $20 billion poured out in six years of deficit spending. . . ." (p. 803)

15. **left (or left-wing)** In politics, groups or parties that traditionally advocate progress, social change, greater economic and social equality, and the welfare of the common worker. (The **right** or **right-wing** is traditionally groups or parties that advocate adherence to tradition, established authorities, and an acceptance of some degree of economic and social hierarchy.) "He may even have headed off a more radical swing to the left. . . ." (p. 804)

PART II: CHECKING YOUR PROGRESS

A. True-False

Where the statement is true, circle **T**; where it is false, circle **F**.

1.   T   F   Roosevelt's call for a "New Deal" in the 1932 campaign included attacks on the Hoover deficits and a promise to balance the federal budget.

2.   T   F   The economy was beginning a turn upward in the months immediately before Roosevelt's inauguration.

3.   T   F   Congress rushed to pass many of the early New Deal programs that granted large emergency powers to the president.

4.   T   F   Roosevelt's monetary reforms were designed to maintain the gold standard and protect the value of the dollar.

5.   T   F   The Civilian Conservation Corps (CCC) and the Public Works Administration (PWA) were designed to reform American business practices.

6.   T   F   Two early New Deal programs, the National Recovery Administration (NRA) and the Agricultural Adjustment Administration (AAA), were both declared unconstitutional by the Supreme Court.

7.   T   F   The primary agricultural problem of the Great Depression was declining farm production caused by the natural disasters of the period.

8.   T   F   The New Deal opened new opportunities for women through appointment to government offices and the new social sciences.

9.   T   F   The Tennessee Valley Authority (TVA) was designed primarily to aid in conserving water and soil resources in eroded hill areas.

10. T   F   The Committee for Industrial Organization (CIO) used sympathetic New Deal laws to unionize many unskilled workers previously ignored by the American Federation of Labor (AF of L).

11. T   F   Roosevelt's political coalition rested heavily on lower-income groups, including African Americans, Jews, Catholics, and southerners.

12. T   F   After Roosevelt's Court-packing plan failed, the conservative Supreme Court continued to strike down New Deal legislation just as it had before.

13. T   F   After 1938 the New Deal lost momentum and ran into increasing opposition from an enlarged Republican bloc in Congress.

14. T   F   The New Deal more than doubled the U.S. national debt through "deficit spending."

15. T   F   By 1939 the New Deal had largely solved the major depression problem of unemployment.

B. Multiple Choice

Select the best answer and circle the corresponding letter.

1.   Franklin Roosevelt's presidential campaign in 1932
   a.   called for large-scale federal spending to reduce unemployment and restore prosperity.
   b.   focused primarily on issues of international trade.
   c.   promised to aid the ordinary person by balancing the federal budget and ending deficits.
   d.   emphasized that there was no way out of the depression in the near future.

2.   Eleanor Roosevelt became an influential figure in the 1930s especially by advocating the cause of
   a.   the impoverished and dispossessed.
   b.   feminists and proponents of sexual liberation.
   c.   farmers and ranchers.
   d.   immigrant ethnic groups and Roman Catholics.

3.   The Roosevelt landslide of 1932 included the shift into the Democratic camp of traditionally Republican
   a.   New Englanders.
   b.   African Americans.
   c.   labor unions.
   d.   southerners.

4.   Roosevelt's first bold action during the Hundred Days was
   a.   taking the nation off the gold standard.
   b.   declaring a national bank holiday.
   c.   legalizing labor strikes and job actions.
   d.   doubling relief for the unemployed.

5. The *primary* purpose of the Civilian Conservation Corps (CCC) was

a. to restore unproductive farmland to productive use.
b. to protect wildlife and the environment.
c. to provide better-trained workers for industry.
d. to provide jobs and experience for unemployed young people.

6. Strong political challenges to Roosevelt came from extremist critics like

a. Father Coughlin and Huey Long.
b. Frances Perkins and Harry Hopkins.
c. Henry Ford and Mary McLeod Bethune.
d. John Steinbeck and John L. Lewis.

7. Roosevelt's National Recovery Administration (NRA) ended when

a. Dr. Francis Townsend attacked it as unfair to the elderly.
b. Congress refused to provide further funding for it.
c. it came to be considered too expensive for the results achieved.
d. the Supreme Court declared it unconstitutional.

8. Roosevelt's Agricultural Adjustment Administration met sharp criticism because

a. it failed to raise farm prices.
b. it actually contributed to soil erosion on the Great Plains.
c. it raised prices by paying farmers to slaughter animals and not grow crops.
d. it relied too much on private bank loans to aid farmers.

9. In addition to the natural forces of drought and wind, the Dust Bowl of the 1930s was also caused by

a. Roosevelt's AAA farm policies.
b. excessive use of dry farming and mechanization techniques on marginal land.
c. the attempted shift from wheat and cotton growing to fruit and vegetable farming.
d. the drying up of underground aquifers used to irrigate the Great Plains.

10. The so-called "Indian New Deal" included an emphasis on

a. local tribal self-government and recovery of Indian identity and culture.
b. the distribution of tribal lands to individual Indian landowners.
c. the migration of Indians from rural reservations to the cities.
d. programs to encourage businesses like gambling casinos to locate on Indian lands.

11. The major New Deal program that attempted to provide flood control, electric power, and economic development occurred in the valley of the

a. Columbia River.
b. Colorado River.
c. Hudson River.
d. Tennessee River.

12. The Social Security Act of 1935 provided for

a. electricity and conservation for rural areas.
b. pensions for older people, the blind, and other categories of citizens.
c. assistance for low-income public housing and social services.
d. unemployment and disability insurance for workers.

13. The new labor organization that flourished under depression conditions and New Deal sponsorship was

a. the Knights of Labor.
b. the American Federation of Labor.
c. the National Labor Relations Board.
d. the Committee for Industrial Organization.

14. Among the groups that formed part of the powerful "Roosevelt coalition" in the election of 1936 were
    a. African Americans, southerners, and Catholics.
    b. Republicans, New Englanders, and "Old Immigrants."
    c. midwesterners, small-town residents, and Presbyterians.
    d. businessmen, prohibitionists, and Coughlinites.
15. Roosevelt's attempt to "pack" the Supreme Court proved extremely costly because
    a. the Court members he appointed still failed to support the New Deal.
    b. Congress began proceedings to impeach him.
    c. its failure ended much of the political momentum of the New Deal.
    d. many of his New Deal supporters turned to back Huey Long.

C. Identification
Supply the correct identification for each numbered description.

1. _____ Term used by FDR in 1932 acceptance speech that came to describe his whole reform program

2. _____ FDR's reform-minded intellectual advisers, who conceived much of the New Deal legislation

3. _____ Popular term for the special session of Congress in early 1933 that passed vast quantities of Roosevelt-initiated legislation

4. _____ The early New Deal agency that worked to solve the problems of unemployment and conservation by employing youth in reforestation and other socially beneficial tasks

5. _____ Large federal employment program, established in 1935 under Harry Hopkins, that provided jobs in areas from road building to art

6. _____ Widely displayed symbol of the National Recovery Administration (NRA), which attempted to reorganize and reform U.S. industry

7. _____ New Deal farm agency that attempted to raise prices by paying farmers to reduce their production of crops and animals

8. _____ The drought-stricken plains areas from which hundreds of thousands of "Okies" were driven during the Great Depression

9. _____ New Deal agency that aroused strong conservative criticism by producing low-cost electrical power in competition with private utilities

10. _____ New Deal program that financed old-age pensions, unemployment insurance, and other forms of income assistance

11. _____ The new union group that organized large numbers of unskilled workers with the help of the Wagner Act and the National Labor Relations Board

12. _____ New Deal agency established to provide a public watchdog against deception and fraud in stock trading

13. _____ Organization of wealthy Republicans and conservative Democrats whose attacks on the New Deal caused Roosevelt to denounce them as "economic royalists" in the campaign of 1936

14. _____ Roosevelt's scheme for gaining Supreme Court approval of New Deal legislation

15. _____   Law of 1939 that prevented federal officials from engaging in campaign activities or using federal relief funds for political purposes

D. Matching People, Places, and Events

Match the person, place, or event in the left column with the proper description in the right column by inserting the correct letter on the blank line.

1. ___ Franklin D. Roosevelt

2. ___ Eleanor Roosevelt

3. ___ Banking holiday

4. ___ Harry Hopkins

5. ___ Father Coughlin

6. ___ Huey ("Kingfish") Long

7. ___ *Schechter* case

8. ___ Harold Ickes

9. ___ John Steinbeck

10. ___ John L. Lewis

11. ___ Frances Perkins

12. ___ Alfred M. Landon

13. ___ Ruth Benedict

14. ___ John Maynard Keynes

15. ___ Justice Roberts

a. Republican who carried only two states in a futile campaign against "The Champ" in 1936

b. The "microphone messiah" of Michigan whose mass radio appeals turned anti-New Deal and anti-Semitic

c. Writer whose best-selling novel portrayed the suffering of dust bowl "Okies" in the Thirties

d. Supreme Court justice whose "switch in time" to support New Deal legislation helped undercut FDR's Court-packing scheme

e. Presidential wife who became an effective lobbyist for the poor during the New Deal

f. Louisiana senator and popular mass agitator who promised to make "every man a king" at the expense of the wealthy

g. Former New York governor who roused the nation to action against the depression with his appeal to the "forgotten man"

h. Roosevelt's secretary of labor, America's first female cabinet member

i. Prominent 1930s social scientist who argued that each culture produced its own type of personality

j. Former New York social worker who became an influential FDR adviser and head of several New Deal agencies

k. Former bull moose progressive who spent billions of dollars on public building projects while carefully guarding against waste

l. Roosevelt-declared closing of all U.S. financial institutions on March 6–10, 1933, in order to stop panic and prepare reforms

m. British economist whose theories helped justify New Deal deficit spending

n. Supreme Court ruling of 1935 that struck down a major New Deal industry-and-labor agency

o. Domineering boss of the mine workers' union who launched the CIO

E. Putting Things in Order

Put the following events in correct order by numbering them from 1 to 5.

1. _____   FDR devalues the dollar to about sixty cents in gold in an attempt to raise domestic prices.

2. _____   Congress passes numerous far-reaching laws under the pressure of a national crisis and strong presidential leadership.

3. _____   Republican attempts to attack the New Deal fall flat, and FDR wins reelection in a landslide.

4. _____   FDR's frustration at the conservative Supreme Court's overturning of New Deal legislation leads him to make a drastic proposal.

5. _____   Passage of new federal pro labor legislation opens the way for a new union group and successful mass labor organizing.

F. Matching Cause and Effect

Match the historical cause in the left column with the proper effect in the right column by writing the correct letter on the blank line.

Cause	Effect
1. ___ The "lame-duck" period from November 1932 to March 1933	a. Succeeded in raising farm prices but met strong opposition from many conservatives
2. ___ Roosevelt's leadership during the Hundred Days	b. Encouraged the CIO to organize large numbers of unskilled workers
3. ___ The Civilian Conservation Corps, the Works Progress Administration, and the Civil Works Administration	c. May have pushed the Court toward more liberal rulings but badly hurt FDR politically
4. ___ New Deal farm programs like the AAA	d. Caused a sharp "Roosevelt Depression" that brought unemployment back up to catastrophic levels
5. ___ The Tennessee Valley Authority	
6. ___ The Wagner (National Labor Relations) Act	e. Caused a political paralysis that nearly halted the U.S. economy
7. ___ FDR's political appeals to workers, African Americans, southerners, and "New Immigrants"	f. Provided federal economic planning, conservation, cheap electricity, and jobs to a poverty-stricken region
8. ___ The Supreme Court's conservative rulings against New Deal legislation	g. Provided federal jobs for unemployed workers in conservation, construction, the arts, and other areas
9. ___ Roosevelt's attempt to "pack" the Supreme Court	h. Caused Roosevelt to propose a plan to "pack" the Supreme Court
10. ___ The rapid cutback in federal "pump-priming" spending in 1937	i. Pushed a remarkable number of laws through Congress and restored the nation's confidence

j.   Forged a powerful political coalition that made the Democrats the majority party

G. Developing Historical Skills

Reading Charts

Charts can classify complex information for ready reference. In this chapter they are an effective way to present the many New Deal laws, agencies, and programs. The chart dealing with the Hundred Days is on p. 781, and that dealing with the later New Deal on p. 784.

Answer the following questions:

1.   Which Hundred Days agency whose primary purpose was recovery also contributed to relief and reform?

2.   List three Hundred Days actions that were aimed *primarily* at recovery.

3.   List three later New Deal measures aimed primarily at reform.

4.   Which later New Deal law aimed primarily at relief also contributed to recovery and reform?

5.   Which was the *last* of the later New Deal laws aimed primarily at providing relief?

6.   Compare the two charts. What can you conclude about the Hundred Days compared to the later New Deal in relation to their relative emphasis on the three goals of relief, recovery, and reform? In which of the areas do you see the most continuity of purpose?

H. Map Mastery

Map Discrimination

Using the maps and charts in Chapter 34, answer the following questions:

1.   *TVA Area*: In which four states was most of the Tennessee Valley Authority located?

2.   *TVA Area*: How many major TVA dams were located in (a) Tennessee and (b) Alabama?

3.   *The Rise and Decline of Organized Labor*: Before the organizing drives of the 1930s, which year saw the highest membership for organized labor?

4.   *The Rise and Decline of Organized Labor*: About how many million members did the CIO *gain* between 1935 and 1945: 2 million, 4 million, 6 million, or 8 million?

Map Challenge

Using the graph of *The Rise and Decline of Organized Labor* on p. 797, write a brief essay explaining the changing fortunes of (a) organized labor in general and (b) the different types of unions—craft, industrial, and independent—from 1900 to 1998.

PART III: APPLYING WHAT YOU HAVE LEARNED

1.   What qualities did FDR bring to the presidency, and how did he display them during the New Deal years? What particular role did Eleanor Roosevelt play in FDR's political success?

2.   How did the early New Deal legislation attempt to achieve the three goals of relief, recovery, and reform?

3.   How did Roosevelt's programs develop such a strong appeal for the "forgotten man," and why did the New Deal arouse such opposition from conservatives, including those on the Supreme Court?

4.   Discuss the political components of the "Roosevelt coalition" formed in the 1930s. What did the New Deal offer to the diverse elements of this coalition?

5.   Was the New Deal essentially a conservative attempt to save American capitalism from collapse, a radical change in traditional American anti-government beliefs, or a moderate liberal response to a unique crisis?

6.   How was the New Deal a culmination of the era of progressive reform, and how did it differ from the pre–World War I progressive era? (See Chapters 28 and 29.)

7.   One of the strongest arguments proponents of the New Deal make was that it saved Depression-plagued America from the radical right-wing or left-wing dictatorships that seized power in much of Europe. Was there ever a serious chance that the United States would have turned to fascism or communism if there had been no New Deal or if Roosevelt had failed as a leader?

8.   Critics of the New Deal have often pointed out that it did not really solve the great Depression problem of unemployment; only World War II did that. Did the New Deal's other positive effects—e.g., in Social Security, labor rights, and regulation of the stock market—counterbalance its inability to overcome the central problem of unemployment?

CHAPTER 34

Franklin D. Roosevelt and the Shadow of War, 1933–1941

PART I: REVIEWING THE CHAPTER

A. CHECKLIST OF LEARNING OBJECTIVES

After mastering this chapter, you should be able to

1.   describe the isolationist motives and effects of FDR's early foreign policies.

2.   explain how American isolationism dominated U.S. policy in the mid-1930s.

3.   explain how America gradually began to respond to the threat from totalitarian aggression while still trying to stay neutral.

4.   describe Roosevelt's increasingly bold moves toward aiding Britain in the fight against Hitler and the sharp disagreements these efforts caused at home.

5.   discuss the events and diplomatic issues in the Japanese American conflict that led up to Pearl Harbor.

B. GLOSSARY

To build your social science vocabulary, familiarize yourself with the following terms:

1.   **exchange rate** The monetary ratio according to which one currency is convertible into another, e.g., American dollars vis-à-vis German deutschmarks, which determines their value relative to one another. "Exchange-rate stabilization was essential to revival of world trade . . ." (p. 806)

2.   **militarist** Someone who glorifies military values or institutions and extends them into the political and social spheres. "Yet in Tokyo, Japanese militarists were calculating that they had little to fear. . . ." (p. 807)

3.   **totalitarianism** A political system of absolute control, in which all social, moral, and religious values and institutions are put in direct service of the state. "Post-1918 chaos in Europe, followed by the Great Depression, fostered the ominous spread of totalitarianism." (p. 809)

4.   **quarantine** In politics, isolating a nation by refusing to have economic or diplomatic dealings with it. ". . . they feared that a moral quarantine would lead to a shooting quarantine." (p. 812)

5.   **division** The major unit of military organization, usually consisting of about 3,000 to 10,000 soldiers, into which most modern armies are organized. " . . . he sent his mechanized divisions crashing into Poland at dawn on September 1, 1939." (p. 813)

6.   **unilateral** In politics, concerning a policy or action undertaken by only one nation. "This ancient dictum [was] hitherto unilateral. . . ." (p. 815)

7.   **multilateral** In politics, referring to a policy or action undertaken by more than one nation. "Now multilateral, [the Monroe Doctrine bludgeon] was to be wielded by twenty-one pairs of American hands. . . ." (p. 815)

8. **steppes** The largely treeless great plains of southeastern Europe and western Asia. "The two fiends could now slit each other's throats on the icy steppes of Russia." (p. 822)

9. **convoy (v.)** To escort militarily, for purposes of protection. (The escorting ships or troops are called a convoy.) "Roosevelt made the fateful decision to convoy in July 1941." (p. 823)

10. **warlord** An armed leader or ruler who maintains power by continually waging war, often against other similar rulers or local military leaders. ". . . Roosevelt had resolutely held off an embargo, lest he goad the Tokyo warlords. . . ." (p. 824)

11. **hara-kiri** Traditional Japanese ritual suicide. "Japan's *hara-kiri* gamble in Hawaii paid off only in the short run." (p. 825)

PART II: CHECKING YOUR PROGRESS

A. True-False

Where the statement is true, circle **T**; where it is false, circle **F**.

1. T F Roosevelt's policy toward the 1933 London Economic Conference showed his concern for establishing a stable international economic order.

2. T F Roosevelt adhered to his Good Neighbor principle of nonintervention in Latin America even when Mexico seized American oil companies in 1938.

3. T F American isolationism was caused partly by deep disillusionment with U.S. participation in World War I.

4. T F The Neutrality Acts of the mid-1930s prevented Americans from lending money or selling weapons to warring nations and from sailing on belligerent ships.

5. T F Despite the neutrality laws, the United States provided some assistance to the democratic Spanish Loyalist government in its Civil War with the Fascistic General Franco.

6. T F America's isolationist mood began to swing toward interventionism immediately after Roosevelt's "Quarantine" speech and Japan's attack on the U.S. gunboat *Panay* in 1937.

7. T F The United States attempted to dissuade the Western European democracies from pursuing their policy of appeasing Hitler's aggressive demands at the Munich Conference and after.

8. T F The "cash-and-carry" Neutrality Act of 1939 allowed America to aid the Allies without making loans or transporting weapons on U.S. ships.

9. T F The fall of France to Hitler in 1940 strengthened U.S. determination to stay neutral.

10. T F Isolationists argued that economic and military aid to Britain would inevitably lead to U.S. involvement in the European war.

11. T F Republican presidential nominee Wendell Willkie joined the isolationist attack on Roosevelt's pro-Britain policy in the 1940 campaign.

12. T F The 1941 Lend-Lease Act marked the effective abandonment of U.S. neutrality and the beginning of naval clashes with Germany.

13. T F The Atlantic Charter was an agreement on future war aims signed by Great Britain, the United States, and the Soviet Union.

14. T F   U.S. warships were already being attacked and sunk in clashes with the German navy before Pearl Harbor.

15. T F   The focal point of conflict between the United States and Japan in the pre–Pearl Harbor negotiations was Japan's refusal to withdraw from the Dutch East Indies.

B. Multiple Choice

Select the best answer and circle the corresponding letter.

1. Roosevelt torpedoed the London Economic Conference of 1933 because
    a. he wanted to concentrate primarily on the recovery of the American domestic economy.
    b. he saw the hand of Hitler and Mussolini behind the conference's proposals.
    c. he was firmly committed to the gold standard.
    d. he wanted economic cooperation only between the United States and Britain, not the rest of Europe.
2. Seeking to withdraw from overseas commitments and colonial expense, the United States in 1934 promised future independence to
    a. Puerto Rico.
    b. the Virgin Islands.
    c. the Philippines.
    d. Cuba.
3. Roosevelt's Good Neighbor policy toward Latin America included
    a. a substantial program of American economic aid for Latin American countries.
    b. a renunciation of American intervention in Mexico or elsewhere in the region.
    c. an American military presence to block German influence in Argentina and Brazil.
    d. an American pledge to transfer the Panama Canal to Panama by the year 2000.
4. The immediate response of most Americans to the rise of the Fascist dictators Mussolini and Hitler was
    a. a call for a new military alliance to contain aggression.
    b. a focus on political cooperation with Britain and the Soviet Union.
    c. support for the Spanish government against Fascist rebels.
    d. a deeper commitment to remain isolated from European problems.
5. The Neutrality Acts of 1935, 1936, and 1937 provided that
    a. the United States would remain neutral in any war between Britain and Germany.
    b. Americans could not sail on belligerent ships, sell munitions, or make loans to nations at war.
    c. no belligerent could conduct propaganda campaigns, sell goods, or make loans within the United States.
    d. the United States would take the lead in neutral efforts to end the wars in China and Ethiopia.
6. The effect of the strict American arms embargo during the civil war between the Loyalist Spanish government and Franco's Fascist rebels was
    a. to encourage a negotiated political settlement between the warring parties.
    b. to strengthen the Spanish government's ability to resist Franco.
    c. to push Britain and the Soviet Union to intervene in the Spanish Civil War.
    d. to cripple the Loyalist government while the Italians and Germans armed Franco.
7. The policy of appeasing the Fascist dictators reached its low point in 1938 when Britain and France sold out Czechoslovakia to Hitler in the conference at
    a. Geneva.
    b. Versailles.

c.   Munich.

d.   Prague.

8.   The "cash-and-carry" Neutrality Act of 1939 was cleverly designed to

a.   guarantee that American policy would not benefit either side in World War II.

b.   enable American merchants to provide loans and ships to the Allies.

c.   prepare America for involvement in the war.

d.   help Britain and France by letting them buy supplies and munitions in the United States.

9.   The "destroyers-for-bases" deal of 1940 provided that

a.   the United States would give Britain fifty American destroyers in exchange for eight British bases in North America.

b.   the United States would give Britain new bases in North America in exchange for fifty British destroyers.

c.   if America entered the war it would receive eight bases in Britain in exchange for American destroyers.

d.   the British would transfer captured French destroyers to the United States in exchange for the use of American bases in East Asia.

10.   The twin events that precipitated the reversal of American policy from neutrality to active, though nonbelligerent, support of the Allied cause were

a.   the Munich Conference and the invasion of Poland.

b.   the fall of France and the Battle of Britain.

c.   the fall of Poland and the invasion of Norway.

d.   the invasion of the Soviet Union and the German submarine attacks on American shipping.

11.   In the campaign of 1940, the Republican nominee Willkie essentially agreed with Roosevelt on the issue of

a.   the New Deal.

b.   the third term.

c.   Roosevelt's use of power in office.

d.   foreign policy.

12.   The Lend-Lease Act clearly marked

a.   the end of isolationist opposition to Roosevelt's foreign policy.

b.   an end to the pretense of American neutrality between Britain and Germany.

c.   a secret Roosevelt plan to involve the United States in war with Japan.

d.   the beginning of opposition in Congress to Roosevelt's foreign policy.

13.   The provisions of the Atlantic Charter signed by Roosevelt and Churchill in 1941 included

a.   self-determination for oppressed peoples and a new international peacekeeping organization.

b.   a permanent alliance between Britain, the United States, and the Soviet Union.

c.   a pledge to rid the world of dictators and to establish democratic governments in Germany and Italy.

d.   an agreement to oppose Soviet communism, but only after Hitler was defeated.

14.   By the fall of 1940, American warships were being attacked by German destroyers near the coast of

a.   Spain.

b.   Ireland.

c.   Iceland.

d.   Canada.

15.   The key issue in the failed negotiations with Japan just before Pearl Harbor was

a.   the refusal of the Japanese to withdraw their navy from Hawaiian waters.

b.   Americans' insistence on their right to expand naval power in Asia.

c.   the Japanese refusal to withdraw from China.

d.   the Japanese refusal to guarantee the security of the Philippines.

C. Identification

Supply the correct identification for each numbered description.

1. _____   International economic conference on stabilizing currency that was sabotaged by FDR

2. _____   Nation to which the U.S. promised independence in the Tydings-McDuffie Act of 1934

3. _____   FDR's repudiation of Theodore Roosevelt's Corollary to the Monroe Doctrine, stating his intention to work cooperatively with Latin American nations

4. _____   A series of laws enacted by Congress in the mid-1930s that attempted to prevent any American involvement in future overseas wars

5. _____   Conflict between the rebel Fascist forces of General Francisco Franco and the Loyalist government that severely tested U.S. neutrality legislation

6. _____   Roosevelt's 1937 speech that proposed strong U.S. measures against overseas aggressors

7. _____   European diplomatic conference in 1938 where Britain and France conceded to Hitler's demands for Czechoslovakia

8. _____   Term for the British-French policy of attempting to prevent war by granting German demands

9. _____   Leading U.S. group advocating American support for Britain in the fight against Hitler

10. _____ Leading isolationist group advocating that America focus on continental defense and non-involvement with the European war

11. _____ Controversial 1941 law that made America the "arsenal of democracy" by providing supposedly temporary military material assistance to Britain

12. _____ Communist nation invaded by Hitler in June 1941 that was also aided by American lend-lease

13. _____ U.S.–British agreement of August 1941 to promote democracy and establish a new international organization for peace

14. _____ U.S. destroyer sunk by German submarines off the coast of Iceland in October 1941, with the loss of over a hundred men

15. _____ Major American Pacific naval base devastated in a surprise attack in December 1941

D. Matching People, Places, and Events

Match the person, place, or event in the left column with the proper description in the right column by inserting the correct letter on the blank line.

1. ___   Cordell Hull

2. ___   Adolf Hitler

3. ___   Benito Mussolini

a.   Courageous prime minister who led Britain's lonely resistance to Hitler

b.   Leader of the "America First" organization and chief spokesman for

4.	___	Gerald Nye	U.S. isolationism
5.	___	Francisco Franco	c. African nation invaded by an Italian dictator in 1935
6.	___	Ethiopia	
7.	___	Czechoslovakia	d. Dynamic dark horse Republican presidential nominee who attacked FDR only on domestic policy
8.	___	Poland	
9.	___	France	e. Fanatical Fascist leader of Germany whose aggressions forced the United States to abandon its neutrality
10.	___	Charles A. Lindbergh	
11.	___	Wendell Willkie	f. Instigator of 1934 Senate hearings that castigated World War I munitions manufacturers as "merchants of death"
12.	___	Winston Churchill	
13.	___	Joseph Stalin	g. Nation whose sudden fall to Hitler in 1940 pushed the United States closer to direct aid to Britain
14.	___	Iceland	
15.	___	Hawaii	

h. Site of a naval base where Japan launched a devastating surprise attack on the United States

i. North Atlantic nation near whose waters U.S. destroyers came under Nazi submarine attack

j. Small East European democracy betrayed into Hitler's hands at Munich

k. The lesser partner of the Rome-Berlin Axis who invaded Ethiopia and joined the war against France and Britain

l. FDR's secretary of state, who promoted reciprocal trade agreements, especially with Latin America

m. Russian dictator who first helped Hitler destroy Poland before becoming a victim of Nazi aggression in 1941

n. East European nation whose September 1939 invasion by Hitler set off World War II in Europe

o. Fascist rebel against the Spanish Loyalist government

E. Putting Things in Order

Put the following events in correct order by numbering them from 1 to 5.

1. _____   FDR puts domestic recovery ahead of international economics, torpedoing a major monetary conference.

2. _____ Western democracies try to appease Hitler by sacrificing Czechoslovakia, but his appetite for conquest remains undiminished.

3. _____ Already engaged against Hitler in the Atlantic, the United States is plunged into World War II by a surprise attack in the Pacific.

4. _____ The fall of France pushes FDR into providing increasingly open aid to Britain.

5. _____ Japan invades China and attacks an American vessel, but the United States sticks to its neutrality principles.

F. Matching Cause and Effect

Match the historical cause in the left column with the proper effect in the right column by writing the correct letter on the blank line.

Cause

1. ___ FDR's refusal to support international economic cooperation in the 1930s

2. ___ Roosevelt's Good Neighbor policy

3. ___ Bad memories of World War I and revelations about arms merchants

4. ___ The U.S. Neutrality Acts of the 1930s

5. ___ Japanese aggression against China in 1937

6. ___ Hitler's invasion of Poland

7. ___ The fall of France in 1940

8. ___ Willkie's support for FDR's pro-British foreign policy

9. ___ The U.S. embargo on oil and other supplies to Japan

10. ___ Roosevelt's decision to convoy lend-lease shipments

Effect

a. Thrust the United States into an undeclared naval war with Nazi Germany in the North Atlantic

b. Prompted FDR to make his "Quarantine Speech," proposing strong action against aggressors

c. Brought new respect for the United States and for democracy in Latin America

d. Shocked the United States into enacting conscription and making the "destroyers-for-bases" deal

e. Forced Japan to either accept U.S. demands regarding China or go to war

f. Caused the United States to institute a "cash-and-carry" policy for providing aid to Britain

g. Deepened the worldwide Depression and aided the rise of Fascist dictators

h. Actually aided Fascist dictators in carrying out their aggressions in Ethiopia, Spain, and China.

i. Promoted U.S. isolationism and the passage of several Neutrality Acts in the mid-1930s

j. Kept the 1940 presidential campaign from becoming a bitter national debate

G. Developing Historical Skills

Reading Text for Sequence and Context

In learning to read for and remember the historical sequence of events, it is often helpful to look for the context in which they occurred.

In the first list below are several major events discussed in the chapter. The second list contains the immediate contexts in which those events occurred. First, link the event to the appropriate context by putting a number from the bottom list to the right of the proper event. Then put the event-with-context in the proper sequence by writing numbers 1 to 7 in the spaces to the left.

Order	Event	Context
_____	Destroyer-for-bases deal	_____
_____	Atlantic Charter	_____
_____	Good Neighbor policy	_____
_____	U.S. Neutrality Acts of 1935–1936	_____
_____	Pearl Harbor	_____
_____	Lend-lease	
_____	Munich Conference	

Context

1. Failure of U.S.–Japanese negotiations

2. Decline of U.S. investment in Latin America

3. Nye Hearings and Italy's invasion of Ethiopia

4. Britain's near-defeat from German bombing

5. The fall of France

6. Hitler's threats to go to war

7. Hitler's invasion of Russia

H. Map Mastery

Map Discrimination

Using the maps and charts in Chapter 35, answer the following questions:

1. *Presidential Election of 1940*: In the 1940 election, how many electoral votes did Willkie win west of the Mississippi River?

2. *Presidential Election of 1940*: How many electoral votes did Willkie win east of the Mississippi River?

3. *Main Flow of Lend-Lease Aid*: Which *continent* received the most U.S. lend-lease aid?

4. *Main Flow of Lend-Lease Aid*: Which nation received lend-lease aid by way of both the Atlantic and Pacific oceans?

PART III: APPLYING WHAT YOU HAVE LEARNED

1. How and why did the United States attempt to isolate itself from foreign troubles in the early and mid-1930s?

2. Discuss the effects of the U.S. neutrality laws of the 1930s on both American foreign policy and the international situation in Europe and East Asia.

3. How did the Fascist dictators' continually expanding aggression gradually erode the U.S. commitment to neutrality and isolationism?

4. How did Roosevelt manage to move the United States toward providing effective aid to Britain while slowly undercutting isolationist opposition?

5. Was American entry into World War II with both Germany and Japan inevitable? Is it possible the U.S. might have been able to fight *either* Germany *or* Japan, while avoiding armed conflict with the other?

6. How did the process of American entry into World War II compare with the way the country got into World War I? (See Chapter 30.) How were the Neutrality Acts aimed at the conditions of 1914–1917, and why did they prove ineffective under the conditions of the 1930s?

7. Argue for or against: America's foreign policy from 1933 to 1939 was fundamentally shaped by domestic issues and concerns, particularly the Great Depression.

8. Isolationists and hostile critics in 1940-41 and even after World War II charged Franklin Roosevelt with deliberately and sometimes deceitfully manipulating events and public opinion so as to lead the United States into war. What factual basis, if any, is there for such a charge? Which of Roosevelt's words and actions tend to refute it?

CHAPTER 35

America in World War II, 1941–1945

PART I: REVIEWING THE CHAPTER

A. CHECKLIST OF LEARNING OBJECTIVES

After mastering this chapter, you should be able to

1. tell how America reacted to Pearl Harbor and prepared to wage war against both Germany and Japan.

2. describe the mobilization of the American economy for war, and the mobilization of manpower and womanpower for both the military and wartime production.

3. describe the war's effects on American society, including regional migration, race relations, and women's roles.

4. explain the early Japanese successes in Asia and the Pacific and the American strategy for countering them.

5. describe the early Western Allies' efforts in North Africa and Italy, the strategic tensions with the Soviet Union over the Second Front, and the invasion of Normandy in 1944.

6. discuss FDR's successful 1944 campaign against Thomas Dewey for a fourth term and controversial choice of a new vice president.

7. explain the final military efforts that brought Allied victory in Europe and Asia and the significance of the atomic bomb.

B. GLOSSARY

To build your social science vocabulary, familiarize yourself with the following terms:

1. **concentration camp** A place of confinement for prisoners or others a government considers dangerous or undesirable. "The Washington top command . . . forcibly herded them together in concentration camps. . . ." (p. 829)

2. **bracero** A Mexican farm laborer temporarily brought into the United States. "The *bracero* program outlived the war by some twenty years. . . ." (p. 833)

3. **U-boat** A German submarine (from the German *Unterseeboot*). "Not until the spring of 1943 did the Allies . . . have the upper hand against the U-boat." (p. 841)

4. **depose(d); deposition** Forcibly remove from office or position. "Mussolini was deposed, and Italy surrendered unconditionally soon thereafter." (p. 843)

5. **beachhead** The first position on a beach secured by an invading force and used to land further troops and supplies. "The Allied beachhead, at first clung to with fingertips, was gradually enlarged, consolidated, and reinforced." (p. 846)

6. **underground** A secret or illegal movement organized in a country to resist or overthrow the government. "With the assistance of the French 'underground,' Paris was liberated. . . ." (p. 846)

7. **acclamation** A general and unanimous action of approval or nomination by a large public body, without a vote. "He was nominated at Chicago on the first ballot by acclamation." (p. 847)

8. **bastion** A fortified stronghold, often including earthworks or stoneworks, that guards against enemy attack. ". . . the 101st Airborne Division had stood firm at the vital bastion of Bastogne." (p. 848)

9. **genocide** The systematic extermination or killing of an entire people. "The Washington government had long been informed about Hitler's campaign of genocide against the Jews. . . ." (p. 849)

10. **bazooka** A metal-tubed weapon from which armor-piercing rockets are electronically fired. "The enemy was almost literally smothered by bayonets, bullets, bazookas, and bombs." (p. 854)

PART II: CHECKING YOUR PROGRESS

A. True-False

Where the statement is true, circle **T**; where it is false, circle **F**.

1. T F   America's major strategic decision in World War II was to fight Japan first and then attack Hitler's Germany.

2. T F   A substantial minority of Americans, particularly those of German and Italian descent, questioned the wisdom of fighting World War II.

3. T F   Government-run rationing and wage-price controls enabled the United States to meet the economic challenges of the war.

4. T F   New sources of labor such as women and Mexican *braceros* helped overcome the human-resources shortage during World War II.

5. T F   World War II stimulated massive black migration to the North and West and encouraged black demands for greater equality.

6. T F   A majority of women who worked in wartime factories stayed in the labor force after the war ended.

7. T F   American citizens at home had to endure serious economic deprivations during World War II.

8. T F   The Japanese navy established its domination of the Pacific sea-lanes in the 1942 battles of Coral Sea and Midway.

9. T F   The American strategy in the Pacific was to encircle Japan by flank movements from Burma and Alaska.

10. T F   In the first years of the war in Europe, Britain and the United States bore the heaviest burden of Allied ground fighting against Hitler.

11. T F   Roosevelt's promise to open a second front in Western Europe by 1942 proved impossible to keep.

12. T F   At the Teheran Conference in 1943, Stalin, Churchill, and Roosevelt planned the D-Day invasion and the final strategy for winning the war.

13. T F   Liberal Democrats rallied to dump Vice President Henry Wallace from FDR's ticket in 1944 and replace him with Senator Harry S Truman.

14. T   F   Roosevelt died just a few weeks before the dropping of the atomic bomb and the surrender of Japan.

15. T   F   The United States modified its demand for "unconditional surrender" by allowing Japan to keep its emperor, Hirohito.

B. Multiple Choice

Select the best answer and circle the corresponding letter.

1. The fundamental American strategic decision of World War II was

    a. to attack Germany and Japan simultaneously with equal force.
    b. to concentrate naval forces in the Pacific and ground forces in Europe.
    c. to attack Germany first while using just enough strength to hold off Japan.
    d. to attack Germany and Japan from the "back door" routes of North Africa and China.

2. The major exception to the relatively good American civil liberties record during World War II was the treatment of

    a. American Fascist groups.
    b. Japanese Americans.
    c. Mexican Americans.
    d. German Americans.

3. Wartime inflation and food shortages were kept partly in check by

    a. price controls and rationing.
    b. government operation of factories and railroads.
    c. special bonuses to farmers and workers to increase production.
    d. importation of additional fuel and food from Latin America.

4. The wartime shortage of labor was partly made up by bringing into the work force such groups as

    a. teenage and elderly laborers.
    b. Japanese and Chinese immigrants.
    c. Mexican *braceros* and women.
    d. sharecroppers and inner-city residents.

5. Compared with British and Soviet women during World War II, more American women

    a. did not work for wages in the wartime economy.
    b. worked in heavy-industry war plants.
    c. served in the armed forces.
    d. worked in agriculture.

6. The Fair Employment Practices Commission was designed to

    a. prevent discrimination against blacks in wartime industries.
    b. guarantee all regions of the country an opportunity to compete for defense contracts.
    c. prevent discrimination in employment against women.
    d. guarantee that those who had been unemployed longest would be the first hired.

7. The wartime migration of rural African Americans to northern urban factories was further accelerated after the war by the invention of

    a. the cotton gin.
    b. the gasoline-powered mechanical combine.
    c. synthetic fibers such as nylon that largely replaced cotton cloth.
    d. the mechanical cotton picker.

8. Besides African Americans, another traditionally rural group who used service in the armed forces as a springboard to postwar urban life were

    a. Scandinavian Americans.

    b.   New England farmers.

    c.   Indians.

    d.   Japanese Americans.

9.   The 1942 battles of Bataan and Corregidor in the Philippines marked the beginning of

    a.   Japanese conquest of key Pacific islands.

    b.   the American comeback from the terrible defeat at Pearl Harbor.

    c.   air warfare conducted from the decks of aircraft carriers.

    d.   a brutal tropical war in which atrocities were committed on both sides.

10.   The essential American strategy in the Pacific called for

    a.   securing bases in China from which to bomb the Japanese home islands.

    b.   carrying the war into Southeast Asia from Australia and New Guinea.

    c.   advancing on as broad a front as possible all across the Pacific.

    d.   "island hopping" by capturing only the most strategic Japanese bases and bypassing the rest.

11.   The U.S.–British demand for "unconditional surrender" was

    a.   a sign of the Western Allies' confidence in its ultimate victory.

    b.   designed to weaken Japan's and Germany's will to resist.

    c.   a weak verbal substitute for the promised "Second Front."

    d.   developed in close cooperation with the Soviet Union.

12.   The American conquest of Guam and other islands in the Marianas in 1944 was especially important because

    a.   it halted the Japanese advance in the Pacific.

    b.   it made possible round-the-clock bombing of Japan from land bases.

    c.   it paved the way for the American reconquest of the Philippines.

    d.   it indicated that the Japanese would surrender without an invasion of the home island.

13.   The most difficult European fighting for American forces through most of 1943 occurred in

    a.   France.

    b.   Italy.

    c.   North Africa.

    d.   Belgium.

14.   Hitler's last-ditch effort to stop the British and American advance in the west occurred at

    a.   the Battle of Normandy.

    b.   the Battle of Château-Thierry.

    c.   the Battle of Rome.

    d.   the Battle of the Bulge.

15.   The *second* American atomic bomb was dropped on the Japanese city of

    a.   Nagasaki.

    b.   Hiroshima.

    c.   Kyoto.

    d.   Okinawa.

C. Identification

Supply the correct identification for each numbered description.

1.   _____   A U.S. minority that was forced into concentration camps during World War II

2.   _____   A federal agency that coordinated U.S. industry and successfully mobilized the economy to produce vast quantities of military supplies

3.   _____   Women's units of the army and navy during World War II

4. _____ Mexican American workers brought into the United States to provide an agricultural labor supply

5. _____ Symbolic personification of female laborers who took factory jobs in order to sustain U.S. production during World War II

6. _____ The federal agency established to guarantee opportunities for African American employment in World War II industries

7. _____ U.S.–owned Pacific archipelago seized by Japan in the early months of World War II

8. _____ Crucial naval battle of June 1942, in which U.S. Admiral Chester Nimitz blocked the Japanese attempt to conquer a strategic island near Hawaii

9. _____ Controversial U.S.–British demand on Germany and Japan that substituted for a "second front"

10. _____ Site of 1943 Roosevelt-Churchill conference in North Africa, at which the Big Two planned the invasion of Italy and further steps in the Pacific war

11. _____ Iranian capital where Roosevelt, Churchill, and Stalin met to plan D-Day in coordination with Russian strategy against Hitler in the East

12. _____ The beginning of the Allied invasion of France in June 1944

13. _____ The December 1944 German offensive that marked Hitler's last chance to stop the Allied advance

14. _____ The last two heavily defended Japanese islands conquered by the United States in 1945

   _____

15. _____ The devastating new weapon used by the United States against Japan in August 1945

D. Matching People, Places, and Events

Match the person, place, or event in the left column with the proper description in the right column by inserting the correct letter on the blank line.

1. ___ Henry J. Kaiser
2. ___ John L. Lewis
3. ___ A. Philip Randolph
4. ___ Detroit
5. ___ Jiang Jieshi (Chiang Kai-shek)
6. ___ Douglas MacArthur
7. ___ Chester W. Nimitz
8. ___ Dwight D. Eisenhower
9. ___ Winston Churchill
10. ___ Joseph Stalin
11. ___ Thomas Dewey

a. Commander of the Allied military assault against Hitler in North Africa and France

b. Japanese emperor who was allowed to stay on his throne, despite unconditional surrender policy

c. FDR's liberal vice president during most of World War II, dumped from the ticket in 1944

d. The Allied leader who constantly pressured the United States and Britain to open a "second front" against Hitler

e. Site of a serious racial disturbance during World War II

12. ___   Henry A. Wallace

13. ___   Harry S Truman

14. ___   Albert Einstein

15. ___   Hirohito

f.   Leading American industrialist and shipbuilder during World War II

g.   Commander of the U.S. Army in the Pacific during World War II, who fulfilled his promise to return to the Philippines

h.   Inconspicuous former senator from Missouri who was suddenly catapulted to national and world leadership on April 12, 1945

i.   Tough head of the United Mine Workers, whose work stoppages precipitated antistrike laws

j.   Commander of the U.S. naval forces in the Pacific and brilliant strategist of the "island-hopping" campaign

k.   Allied leader who met with FDR to plan strategy at Casablanca and Teheran

l.   German-born physicist who helped persuade Roosevelt to develop the atomic bomb

m.   Republican presidential nominee in 1944 who failed in his effort to deny FDR a fourth term

n.   Head of the Brotherhood of Sleeping Car Porters whose threatened march on Washington opened job opportunities for blacks during World War II

o.   U.S. ally who resisted Japanese advances in China during World War II

E. Putting Things in Order

Put the following events in correct order by numbering them from 1 to 4.

1. _____   The United States and Britain invade Italy and topple Mussolini from power.

2. _____   Japan surrenders after two atomic bombs are dropped.

3. _____   The United States enters World War II and begins to "fight Hitler first."

4. _____   The United States stops the Japanese advance in the Pacific and attacks Germany in North Africa.

F. Matching Cause and Effect

Match the historical cause in the left column with the proper effect in the right column by writing the correct letter on the blank line.

Cause	Effect
1. ___ The surprise Japanese attack at Pearl Harbor	a. Kept the Western Allies from establishing a "second front" in France until June 1944
2. ___ Fear that Japanese Americans would aid Japan in invading the United States	b. Slowed the powerful Japanese advance in the Pacific in 1942
3. ___ Efficient organization by the War Production Board	c. Enabled the United States to furnish itself and its allies with abundant military supplies
4. ___ The mechanical cotton picker and wartime labor demand	d. Enabled the United States to set up key bomber bases while bypassing heavily fortified Japanese-held islands
5. ___ Women's role in wartime production	e. Drew millions of African Americans from the rural South to the urban North
6. ___ American resistance in the Philippines and the Battle of the Coral Sea	f. Resulted in Senator Harry S Truman's becoming FDR's fourth-term running mate in 1944
7. ___ The American strategy of "leapfrogging" toward Japan	g. Created a temporary but not a permanent transformation in gender roles for most women
8. ___ The British fear of sustaining heavy casualties in ground fighting	h. Caused innocent American citizens to be rounded up and put in concentration camps
9. ___ Conservative Democrats' hostility to liberal Vice President Henry Wallace	i. Created a strong sense of American national unity during World War II
10. ___ Japan's refusal to surrender after the Potsdam Conference in July 1945	j. Led the United States to drop the atomic bomb on Hiroshima in August 1945

G. Developing Historical Skills

Reading Maps for Routes and Strategy

In order to understand the events and strategies of war, careful reading of military maps is essential. Attention to the routes and dates of the Allied armies, presented in the map of *World War II in Europe and North Africa, 1939–1945* on p. 844, will help you grasp the essentials of Allied strategy and the importance of the postponement of the "second front" in the west, as described in the text. Answer the following questions:

1. Where were (a) the Russians and (b) the Western Allies Britain and America each fighting in January and February of 1943?

2. Approximately where were the central Russian armies when the British and Americans invaded Sicily?

3. Approximately where were the central Russian armies when the British and Americans invaded Normandy in June 1944?

4. It took approximately ten months for the British and Americans to get from the Normandy beaches to the Elbe River in central Germany. How long did it take the Russians to get from Warsaw to Berlin?

5. Besides north-central Germany, where else did the British, American, and Russian invasion routes converge? From what two countries were the British and Americans coming? From what country was the southern Russian army coming?

H. Map Mastery

Map Discrimination

Using the maps and charts in Chapter 36, answer the following questions:

1. *Internal Migration in the United States During World War II*: During World War II, what was the approximate *net* migration of civilian population from the East to the West? (Net migration is the number of westward migrants minus the number of those who moved east.)

2. *Internal Migration in the United States During World War II*: Of the nine fastest-growing cities during the 1940s, how many were located in the West and South? (Consider Washington, D.C., as a southern city.)

3. *Internal Migration in the United States During World War II*: Which were the two fastest-growing cities in the North?

4. *United States Thrusts in the Pacific, 1942–1945*: Which *two* of the following territories were not wholly or partially controlled by Japan at the height of Japanese conquest: India, Philippines, Australia, Netherlands Indies, Thailand, and New Guinea?

5. *World War II in Europe and North Africa, 1939–1945*: From which North African territory did the Allies launch their invasion of Italy?

6. *World War II in Europe and North Africa, 1939–1945*: As the Russian armies crossed into Germany from the east, which three Axis-occupied East European countries did they move through?

7. *World War II in Europe and North Africa, 1939–1945*: As the Western Allied armies crossed into Germany from the west, which three Axis-occupied West European countries did they liberate and move through? (Do not count Luxembourg.)

8. *World War II in Europe and North Africa, 1939–1945*: Along which river in Germany did the Western Allied armies meet the Russians?

Map Challenge

Using the maps of both the Pacific (p. 840) and European (p. 844) theaters in World War II, write an essay explaining the principal movements of Allied armies and navies in relation to the principal Allied strategies of the war determined in the ABC–1 agreement and the various wartime exchanges and meetings among American, British, and Soviet leaders.

PART III: APPLYING WHAT YOU HAVE LEARNED

1. What effects did World War II have on the American economy? What role did American industry and agriculture play in the war?

2. Discuss the effects of World War II on women and on racial and ethnic minorities. Is it accurate to see the war as a key turning point in the movement toward equality for some or all of these groups?

3. Ever since World War II, historians and other scholars have commonly spoken of "postwar American society." How was American society different after the war than before? Were these changes all direct or indirect results of the war, or would many have occurred without it?

4. How did the United States and its allies develop and carry out their strategy for defeating Italy, Germany, and Japan?

5. What were the costs of World War II, and what were its effects on America's role in the world?

6. Compare America's role in World War I—domestically, militarily, and diplomatically—with its role in World War II. (See Chapter 30.) What accounts for the differences in America's participation in the two wars?

7. Examine the controversy over the atomic bomb in the context of the whole conduct of World War II on both sides. Is it correct to say that the bomb did not mark a change in the character of warfare against civilians but only its scope? Despite the larger casualties in other bombings, why did the bombings of Hiroshima and Nagasaki stir a greater concern?

8. World War II has sometimes been called "the good war." Is this an accurate label? Why or why not?

CHAPTER 36

The Cold War Begins, 1945–1952

PART I: REVIEWING THE CHAPTER

A. CHECKLIST OF LEARNING OBJECTIVES

After mastering this chapter, you should be able to

1. explain the causes and consequences of the post–World War II economic boom.

2. describe the postwar migrations to the "Sunbelt" and the suburbs.

3. explain changes in American society and culture brought about by the "baby boom."

4. explain the growth of tension between the United States and the Soviet Union after Germany's defeat and Truman's accession to the presidency.

5. describe the early Cold War conflicts over Germany and Eastern Europe, and the failure of the United Nations to resolve Soviet-American tensions

6. discuss American efforts to "contain" the Soviets through the Truman Doctrine, the Marshall Plan, and NATO.

7. describe the growing concern about Soviet spying and internal Communist subversion, and climate of fear it engendered.

8. describe the expansion of the Cold War to East Asia, including the Chinese Communist revolution and the Korean War.

B. GLOSSARY

To build your social science vocabulary, familiarize yourself with the following terms:

1. **gross national product** The total value of a nation's annual output of goods and services. "Real gross national product (GNP) slumped sickeningly in 1946 and 1947. . . ." (p. 858)

2. **agribusiness** Farming and related activities considered as commercial enterprises, especially large corporate agricultural ventures. ". . . consolidation produced giant agribusinesses able to employ costly machinery." (p. 862)

3. **population curve** The varying size and age structure of a given nation or other group, measured over time. "This boom-or-bust cycle of births begot a bulging wave along the American population curve." (p. 866)

4. **precinct** The smallest subdivision of a city, as it is organized for purposes of police administration, politics, voting, and so on. "He then tried his hand at precinct-level Missouri politics. . . ." (p. 866)

5. **protégé** Someone under the patronage, protection, or tutelage of another person or group. "Though a protégé of a notorious political machine in Kansas City, he had managed to keep his own hands clean." (p. 866)

6. **superpower** One of the two overwhelmingly dominant international powers after World War II—the United States and the Soviet Union. "More specific understandings among the wartime allies—especially the two emerging superpowers—awaited the arrival of peace." (p. 870)

7. **exchange rates** The ratios at which the currencies of two or more countries are traded, which express their values relative to one another. ". . . the International Monetary Fund (IMF) [was established] to encourage world trade by regulating currency exchange rates." (p. 871)

8. **underdeveloped** Economically and industrially deficient. "They also founded the International Bank for Reconstruction and Development . . . to promote economic growth in war-ravaged and underdeveloped areas." (p. 871)

9. **military occupation** The holding and control of a territory and its citizenry by the conquering forces of another nation. ". . . Germany had been divided at war's end into four military occupation zones. . . ." (p. 873)

10. **containment** In international affairs, the blocking of another nation's expansion through the application of military and political pressure short of war. "Truman's piecemeal responses . . . took on intellectual coherence in 1947, with the formulation of the 'containment doctrine.' " (p. 874)

11. **communist-fronter** One who belongs to an ostensibly independent political, economic, or social organization that is secretly controlled by the Communist party. ". . . he was nominated . . . by . . . a bizarre collection of disgruntled former New Dealers . . . and communist-fronters." (p. 881)

12. **Politburo** The small ruling executive body that controlled the Central Committee of the Soviet Communist party, and hence dictated the political policies of the Soviet, Chinese, and other Communist parties (from "Political Bureau"). "This so-called Pied Piper of the Politburo took an apparently pro-Soviet line. . . ." (p. 881)

13. **perimeter** The outer boundary of a defined territory. ". . . Korea was outside the essential United States defense perimeter in the Pacific." (p. 883)

PART II: CHECKING YOUR PROGRESS

A. True-False

Where the statement is true, circle **T**; where it is false, circle **F**.

1. T F   The American consumer economy began to grow dramatically as soon as the war ended, during the years 1945 to 1950.

2. T F   The postwar economic boom was fueled by military spending and cheap energy.

3. T F   Labor unions continued to grow rapidly in the industrial factories throughout the 1940s and 1950s.

4. T F   The economic and population growth of the Sunbelt occurred because the South relied less than the North did on federal government spending for its economic well-being.

5. T F   After World War II, American big cities became heavily populated with minorities, while most whites lived in the suburbs.

6. T F   Government policies sometimes encouraged residential segregation in the cities and new suburbs.

7. T F   Harry S Truman brought extensive experience and confidence to the presidency he assumed in April 1945.

8. T   F   The new United Nations proved more effective than the old League of Nations because it did not give a veto to the great powers represented on its Security Council.

9. T   F   The Western Allies pushed to establish a separate nation of West Germany, while the Russians wanted to restore a unified German state.

10. T   F   The Truman Doctrine was initiated in response to threatened Soviet gains in Iran and Afghanistan.

11. T   F   The Marshall Plan was developed primarily as a response to the possible Soviet military invasion of Western Europe.

12. T   F   The fundamental purpose of NATO was to end the historical feuds among the European nations of Britain, France, Italy, and Germany.

13. T   F   The postwar hunt for communist subversion was supposedly aimed at rooting out American communists from positions in government and teaching.

14. T   F   Truman defeated Dewey in 1948 partly because of the deep splits within the Republican party that year.

15. T   F   Truman fired General MacArthur because MacArthur wanted to expand the Korean War into China.

B. Multiple Choice

Select the best answer and circle the corresponding letter.

1. Besides giving educational benefits to returning veterans, the Servicemen's Readjustment Act of 1944 (the GI Bill of Rights) was partly intended to

    a.   prevent returning soldiers from flooding the job market.
    b.   provide the colleges with a new source of income.
    c.   keep the GIs' military skills in high readiness for the Cold War.
    d.   help to slow down the inflationary economy that developed at the end of World War II.

2. Among the greatest beneficiaries of the post–World War II economic "boom" were

    a.   the industrial inner cities.
    b.   farm laborers.
    c.   labor unions.
    d.   women.

3. Among the primary causes of the long postwar economic expansion were

    a.   foreign investment and international trade.
    b.   military spending and cheap energy
    c.   labor's wage restraint and the growing number of small businesses.
    d.   government economic planning and investment.

4. The two regions that gained most in population and new industry in the postwar economic expansion were

    a.   the Pacific Northwest and New England.
    b.   the Northeast and South.
    c.   the Midwest and West.
    d.   the South and West.

5. The federal government played a large role in the growth of the Sunbelt through

    a.   federal subsidies to southern and western agriculture.
    b.   its policies supporting civil rights and equal opportunity for minorities.
    c.   housing loans to veterans.

    d.   its financial support of the aerospace and defense industries.

6.   Among the federal policies that contributed to the postwar migration from the inner cities to the suburbs were

    a.   housing-mortgage tax deductions and federally built highways.
    b.   public housing and Social Security.
    c.   military and public-works spending.
    d.   direct subsidies to suburban homebuilders.

7.   The postwar "baby-boom" population expansion contributed to

    a.   the sharp rise in elementary school enrollments in the 1970s.
    b.   the strains on the Social Security system in the 1950s.
    c.   the popular "youth culture" of the 1960s.
    d.   the expanding job opportunities of the 1980s.

8.   Among President Harry Truman's most valuable qualities as a leader were

    a.   his considerable experience in international affairs.
    b.   his personal courage, authenticity, and sense of responsibility for big decisions.
    c.   his intolerance of pettiness or corruption among his subordinates.
    d.   his patience and willingness to compromise with honest critics.

9.   The failure of the new United Nations to sustain a spirit of cooperation among the great powers was first demonstrated by

    a.   its inability to defend the Jewish state of Israel that it had created.
    b.   its inability to control atomic energy and prevent the spread of nuclear weapons.
    c.   its failure to address the post-World War II refugee crisis.
    d.   its inability to bring a halt to the civil war between Nationalist and Communist Chinese.

10.   Before World War II, both the United States and the Soviet Union

    a.   had competed with Germany for the role of leading power in Europe.
    b.   had concentrated on practical achievements rather than ideological issues.
    c.   had attempted to build powerful armies and navies in order to gain global power.
    d.   had been largely isolated from international affairs and fervently committed to an ideology.

11.   A crucial early development of the Cold War occurred when

    a.   Germany was divided into an East Germany under Soviet control and a pro-American West Germany.
    b.   American and Soviet forces engaged in armed clashes in Austria.
    c.   the Soviets crushed anticommunist rebellions in Poland and Hungary.
    d.   the French and Italian Communist parties attempted revolutions against their own governments.

12.   The NATO alliance represented an historic transformation in American foreign policy because

    a.   it departed from the principles of the Monroe Doctrine.
    b.   it put the United States into the position of guaranteeing the permanent subordination of Germany.
    c.   it committed the United States to a permanent peacetime alliance with other nations.
    d.   it meant establishing military bases outside the territory of the continental United States.

13.   The Truman Doctrine originally developed because of the communist threat to

    a.   Turkey and Greece.
    b.   France and West Germany.
    c.   Iran and Afghanistan.
    d.   Poland and Hungary.

14.   Senator Joseph McCarthy's anticommunist crusade was first directed primarily against

    a.   the Soviet Union
    b.   potential internal communist party takeovers of France and Italy.

    c.   the Chinese Communists.

    d.   alleged communists employed by the United States government.

15. President Harry Truman fired General Douglas MacArthur from his command of American forces in East Asia because

    a.   MacArthur had bungled the invasion of Inchon.

    b.   MacArthur refused to accept the idea of American forces being under United Nations control.

    c.   MacArthur wanted to widen the Korean War by bombing Communist China.

    d.   MacArthur was effectively becoming the military dictator of South Korea.

C. Identification

Supply the correct identification for each numbered description.

1. _____ Popular name for the Servicemen's Readjustment Act, which provided assistance to former soldiers

2. _____ Shorthand name for the southern and western regions of the U.S. that experienced the highest rates of growth after World War II

3. _____ New York suburb where postwar builders pioneered the techniques of mass home construction

4. _____ Term for the dramatic rise in U.S. births that began immediately after World War II

5. _____ Big Three wartime conference that later became the focus of charges that Roosevelt had "sold out" Eastern Europe to the Soviet communists

6. _____ The extended post–World War II confrontation between the United States and the Soviet Union that stopped just short of a shooting war

7. _____ Meeting of Western Allies during World War II that established the economic structures to promote recovery and enhance FDR's vision of an "open world"

8. _____ New international organization that experienced some early successes in diplomatic and cultural areas but failed in areas like atomic arms control

9. _____ Term for the barrier that Stalin erected to block off Soviet-dominated nations of Eastern Europe from the West

10. _____ American-sponsored effort that provided funds for the economic relief and recovery of Western Europe

11. _____ The new anti-Soviet organization of Western nations that ended the long-time American tradition of not joining permanent military alliances

12. _____ Jiang Jieshi's (Chiang Kai-shek's) pro-American forces, which lost the Chinese civil war to Mao Zedong's (Mao Tse-tung's) communists in 1949

13. _____ Key U.S. government memorandum that militarized American foreign policy and indicated national faith in the economy's capacity to sustain large military expenditures

14. _____ U.S. House of Representatives committee that took the lead in investigating alleged procommunist agents such as Alger Hiss

15. _____ The dividing line between North and South Korea, across which the fighting between communists and United Nations forces ebbed and flowed during the Korean War

D. Matching People, Places, and Events

Match the person, place, or event in the left column with the proper description in the right column by inserting the correct letter on the blank line.

1. ___ Benjamin Spock
2. ___ Hermann Goering
3. ___ Joseph Stalin
4. ___ Berlin
5. ___ Iran
6. ___ George F. Kennan
7. ___ Greece
8. ___ George C. Marshall
9. ___ Japan
10. ___ Nuremberg
11. ___ Richard Nixon
12. ___ Joseph McCarthy
13. ___ Henry A. Wallace
14. ___ Strom Thurmond
15. ___ Douglas MacArthur

a. Top Nazi official who committed suicide after being convicted in war-crimes trials

b. Physician who provided advice on child rearing to baby-boomers' parents after World War II.

c. Young California congressman whose investigation of Alger Hiss spurred fears of communist influence in America

d. Oil-rich Middle Eastern nation that became an early focal point of Soviet-American conflict

e. Originator of a massive program for the economic relief and recovery of devastated Europe

f. American military commander in Korea fired by President Harry Truman

g. Former vice president of the United States whose 1948 campaign as a pro-Soviet liberal split the Democratic party

h. Site of a series of controversial war-crimes trials that led to the execution of twelve Nazi leaders

i. Wisconsin senator whose charges of communist infiltration of the U.S. government deepened the anti-red atmosphere of the early 1950s

j. Nation that was effectively converted from dictatorship to democracy by the strong leadership of General Douglas MacArthur

k. The tough leader whose violation of agreements in Eastern Europe and Germany helped launch the Cold War

l. Southern European nation whose threatened fall to communism in 1947 precipitated the Truman Doctrine

m. Territory deep inside the Soviet zone of Germany that was itself divided into four zones of occupation

n. Southern segregationist who led "Dixiecrat" presidential campaign against Truman in 1948

o. Brilliant U.S. specialist on the Soviet Union and originator of the theory that U.S. policy should be to "contain" the Soviet Union

E. Putting Things in Order

Put the following events in correct order by numbering them from 1 to 5.

1. _____ The threatened communist takeover of Greece prompts a presidential request for aid and a worldwide effort to stop communism.

2. _____ The collapse of Jiang Jieshi's (Chiang Kai-shek's) corrupt government means victory for Mao Zedong's (Mao Tse-tung's) communists and a setback for U.S. policy in Asia.

3. _____ A new president takes charge of American foreign policy amid growing tension between America and its ally, the Soviet Union.

4. _____ A "give-'em-hell" campaign by an underdog candidate overcomes a three-way split in his own party and defeats his overconfident opponent.

5. _____ Communists go on the offensive in a divided Asian nation, drawing the United States into a brutal and indecisive war.

F. Matching Cause and Effect

Match the historical cause in the left column with the proper effect in the right column by writing the correct letter on the blank line.

	Cause		**Effect**
1. ____	Cheap energy, military spending, and rising productivity	a.	Caused an era of unprecedented growth in American prosperity from 1950 to 1970
2. ____	The mechanization and consolidation of agriculture		
3. ____	Job opportunities, warm climates, and improved race relations	b.	Drew millions of white and black Americans to the Sunbelt after World War II
4. ____	"White flight" to the suburbs	c.	Led to the proclamation of the Truman Doctrine and hundreds of millions of dollars in aid for anticommunist governments
5. ____	The post–World War II "baby boom"		
6. ____	The American airlift to West Berlin	d.	Led to the organization of the permanent NATO alliance
7. ____	The British withdrawal from	e.	Caused the rise of big commercial

communist-threatened Greece

8. ___ The threat of Soviet invasion or U.S. isolationist withdrawal from Europe

9. ___ General MacArthur's reform-oriented rule of occupied Japan

10. ___ Mao Zedong's (Mao Tse-tung's) defeat of Jiang Jieshi (Chiang Kai-shek)

agribusiness and spelled the near-disappearance of the traditional family farm

f. Aroused Republican charges that Democrats Truman and Acheson had "lost China"

g. Broke a Soviet ground blockade and established American determination to resist further Soviet advance

h. Left America's cities heavily populated by racial minorities

i. Led to the firm establishment of Japanese democracy and the beginnings of a great Japanese economic advance

j. Caused much school-building in the 1950s, a "youth culture" in the 1960s, and a growing concern about "aging" in the 1980s

G. Developing Historical Skills

Reading a Bar Graph

Read the bar graph of *National Defense Budget* on p. 861 and answer the following questions.

1. In what census year after World War II did the defense budget first decline as a percentage of the federal budget and a percentage of GNP?

2. In what census year after 1960 was the defense budget the same fraction of GNP as it was in 1950?

3. Which decade after World War II saw the largest increase in actual dollar outlays for defense?

4. By approximately what percentage of the federal budget did the defense budget increase from 1950 to 1960? By roughly what percentage did it decrease from 1970 to 1980? By what percentage did it increase from 1980 to 1990? By about what percentage did it decrease from 1990 to 1999?

H. Map Mastery

Map Discrimination

Using the maps and charts in Chapter 36, answer the following questions.

1. *Postwar Partition of Germany*: Which of the Big Four had the smallest occupation zone in postwar Germany?

2. *Postwar Partition of Germany*: Which of the three *Western* occupation zones was closest to Berlin?

3. *Postwar Partition of Germany*: Which two other nations did the American occupation zone border on?

4. *The Shifting Front in Korea*: When General MacArthur attacked at Inchon, did he land above or below the thirty-eighth parallel?

5. *The Shifting Front in Korea*: Besides China, what other nation bordering North Korea presented a potential threat to American forces?

6. *The Shifting Front in Korea*: After the armistice—signed on July 27, 1953—which of the two Koreas had made very slight territorial gains in the Korean War?

Map Challenge

Using the map of *Population Increase, 1950–2000* on p. 863, write an essay explaining the differences in the regional impact of post–World War II migration and population growth from 1950 to 1998. What states and regions exhibited exceptions to the general patterns of growth?

PART III: APPLYING WHAT YOU HAVE LEARNED

1. How and why did the American economy soar from 1950 to 1970?

2. How have economic and population changes shaped American society since World War II?

3. What were the immediate conflicts and deeper causes that led the United States and the Soviet Union to go from being allies to bitter Cold War rivals?

4. Explain the steps that led to the long-term involvement of the United States in major overseas military commitments, including NATO and the Korean War. How did expanding military power and the Cold War affect American society and ideas?

5. Discuss President Harry Truman's role as a leader in both international and domestic affairs from 1945–1952. Does Truman deserve to be considered a "great" president? Why or why not?

6. Why did World War II—unlike World War I—lead to a permanent end to American isolationism? (See Chapter 30.)

7. Was the early Cold War primarily an ideological crusade of democracy against "international communism" and its totalitarian ideas, or was it essentially an American defense of its national security and economic interests against the direct threat of the Soviet Union? Support your answer by considering some of the key events of the early Cold War, including the Korean War.

CHAPTER 37

The Eisenhower Era, 1952–1960

PART I: REVIEWING THE CHAPTER

A. CHECKLIST OF LEARNING OBJECTIVES

After mastering this chapter, you should be able to

1. describe the changes in the American consumer economy in the 1950s, and their relationship to the rise of popular "mass culture."

2. describe the rise and fall of McCarthyism and the beginnings of the civil rights movement.

3. outline the Eisenhower-Dulles approach to the Cold War and the nuclear arms race with the Soviet Union.

4. define the basic principles of Eisenhower's foreign policy in Vietnam, the Middle East, and Cuba.

5. describe the practice of "Eisenhower Republicanism" in the 1950s, including domestic consequences of the Cold War.

6. describe the issues and outcome of the tight Kennedy-Nixon presidential campaign of 1960.

7. summarize some major changes in American culture in the 1950s, including the rise of Jewish and African American writers.

B. GLOSSARY

To build your social science vocabulary, familiarize yourself with the following terms:

1. **Pentecostal** A family of Protestant Christian churches that emphasize a "second baptism" of the holy spirit, speaking in tongues, faith healing, and intense emotionalism in worship. "'Televangelists' like the Baptist Billy Graham, the Pentecostal Holiness preacher Oral Roberts."

2. **McCarthyism** The practice of making sweeping, unfounded charges against innocent people with consequent loss of reputation, job, and so on. "But 'McCarthyism' has passed into the English language as a label for the dangerous forces of unfairness. . . ." (p. 891)

3. **universalism** The belief in the fundamental moral and social unity of humankind, which are held to transcend particular local cultures or beliefs. " . . . published a bestseller in 1943, *One World*, which advocated a new postwar era of racially-blind universalism."

4. **taboo** A social prohibition or rule that results from strict tradition or convention. ". . . Warren shocked the president and other traditionalists with his active judicial intervention in previously taboo social issues." (p. 895)

5. **sheikdom** Small, traditional tribal territory ruled by a **sheik**, an hereditary Arab chieftain. "The poor, sandy sheikdoms increasingly resolved to reap for themselves the lion's share of the enormous oil wealth. . . ."

6. **jury tampering** The felony of bribing, threatening, or otherwise interfering with the autonomous deliberations and decisions of a jury.

"[James R. Hoffa] was later convicted for jury tampering, served part of his sentence, and disappeared. . . ."

7. **secondary boycott** A boycott of goods, aimed not at the employer or company directly involved in a dispute but at those who do business with that company. "The new law also prohibited 'secondary boycotts' and certain kinds of picketing."

8. **thermonuclear** Concerning the heat released in nuclear fission; specifically, the use of that heat in hydrogen bombs. "Thermonuclear suicide seemed nearer in July 1958. . . ." (p. 904)

9. **confiscation** The seizure of property by a public authority, often as a penalty. "Castro retaliated with further wholesale confiscations of Yankee property. . . ." (p. 905)

10. **iconoclastic** Literally, a breaking of sacred images; hence, by extension, any action that assaults ideas or principles held in reverence or high regard. "Gore Vidal penned . . . several impish and always iconoclastic works. . . ."

PART II: CHECKING YOUR PROGRESS

A. True-False

Where the statement is true, circle **T**; where it is false, circle **F**.

1. T F Feminist Betty Friedan's manifesto *The Feminine Mystique* was aimed primarily at reviving labor militancy among working-class women in factories and shops.

2. T F Eisenhower initially hesitated to oppose Senator Joseph McCarthy because of McCarthy's political popularity and power.

3. T F McCarthy lost his power when he attacked alleged communist influence in the U.S. Army.

4. T F The Supreme Court ruled in *Brown* v. *Board of Education* that black schools had to receive additional funding in order to guarantee that racially separate education would be truly equal.

5. T F Martin Luther King, Jr. argued that the civil rights movement needed to cast aside the influence of the traditionally conservative African American churches.

6. T F President Eisenhower and Secretary of State John Foster Dulles promoted a policy of reliance on larger conventional forces rather than nuclear weapons in order to contain the Soviet Union.

7. T F In the Suez crisis of 1956, the United States backed the French and British invasion of Egypt in order to guarantee the flow of oil from the Middle East.

8. T F The Soviet launch of the Sputnik satellite in 1957 fueled criticism of the American educational system and federal funding for teaching the sciences and foreign languages.

9. T F The Paris summit conference of 1960 between President Eisenhower and Soviet Premier Khrushchev signaled the first major thaw in the Cold War.

10. T F The strict American embargo on all trade with Cuba was precipitated by Castro's confiscation of American property for his land reform program.

11. T F Senator Kennedy was able to successfully neutralize the issue of his Roman Catholicism during the 1960 campaign.

12. T F   The admission of Hawaii and Alaska to the Union in 1959 helped turn American attention away from Europe and toward East Asia and the Pacific.

13. T F   In his foreign policies, Dwight Eisenhower attempted to avoid threats to peace without the extensive use of American military power.

14. T F   World War II sparked a great literary outpouring of sober, realistic novels about the realities of warfare.

15. T F   Post-World War II American literature was enriched by African American novelists like Ralph Ellison and Jewish novelists like Saul Bellow.

B. Multiple Choice

Select the best answer and circle the corresponding letter.

1. A key economic transformation of the 1950s was
    a. the displacement of large corporations by smaller entrepreneurial businesses.
    b. the growth of "white collar" office jobs that increasingly replaced "blue collar" factory labor.
    c. the turn from World War II military and defense industries to civilian production.
    d. the replacement of "mass consumer production" by "targeted marketing" aimed at particular segments of the population.

2.   When the 1950s began, a majority of American women were
    a. working in blue-collar factory or service jobs.
    b. raising children and not employed outside the home.
    c. pursuing training and education to prepare them for the new positions in service and high technology.
    d. agitating for federal child care and other assistance to enable them to assume a larger place in the work force.

3. The primary force shaping the new consumerism and mass popular culture of the 1950s was
    a. the computer.
    b. magazines like *Playboy*.
    c. television.
    d. evangelical Protestantism.

4. In the 1952 Republican presidential campaign, the task of attacking the Democratic party and Governor Adlai E. Stevenson as "soft" on Communism fell to
    a. Senator Joseph McCarthy.
    b. vice presidential candidate Senator Richard Nixon.
    c. General Douglas MacArthur.
    d. future Secretary of State John Foster Dulles.

5. As president, Eisenhower enjoyed great popularity by presenting a leadership style of
    a. reassurance, sincerity, and optimism.
    b. aggressiveness, boldness, and energy.
    c. political shrewdness, economic knowledge, and hands-on management.
    d. vision, imagination, and moral leadership.

6. The Korean War ended with
    a. an agreement to unify and neutralize Korea.
    b. a peace treaty that provided for withdrawal of American and Chinese forces from Korea.
    c. an American and South Korean military victory.
    d. a stalemated armistice and continued division of North and South Korea.

7. Senator Joseph McCarthy's anticommunist crusade finally collapsed when

    a.   the FBI demonstrated that it had captured all the Soviet spies inside the United States.
    b.   Eisenhower publicly attacked him as a threat to the Republican party.
    c.   McCarthy failed to prove that there were communists in the federal government.
    d.   McCarthy attacked the U.S. Army for alleged communist influence.

8. The precipitating event that led to the rise of Dr. Martin Luther King, Jr. as the most prominent civil rights leader was

    a.   the lynching of Emmett Till.
    b.   the Little Rock school crisis.
    c.   the Montgomery bus boycott.
    d.   the passage of the 1957 Civil Rights Act.

9. The primary impetus for civil rights within the federal government came from

    a.   the Supreme Court.
    b.   Congress.
    c.   President Eisenhower.
    d.   the armed forces.

10. Martin Luther King, Jr.'s own civil rights organization, the SCLC, rested on the institutional foundation of

    a.   black businesses.
    b.   black churches.
    c.   black colleges.
    d.   northern philanthropic foundations.

11. Eisenhower's basic approach to domestic economic policy was

    a.   to seek to overturn the Democratic New Deal.
    b.   to propose major new federal social programs.
    c.   to turn most New Deal programs over to the states.
    d.   to trim back some New Deal programs but keep most in place.

12. Despite his fiscal conservatism, Eisenhower actually outdid the New Deal with his massive federal spending on

    a.   a transcontinental interstate highway system.
    b.   a system of medical care for the elderly.
    c.   intercontinental military bombers and civilian aircraft.
    d.   agricultural subsidies for American farmers.

13. The United States first became involved in Vietnam by

    a.   providing economic aid to the democratic Vietnamese government of Ngo Dinh Diem.
    b.   providing economic aid to the French colonialists fighting Ho Chi Minh.
    c.   providing aid to Ho Chi Minh in his fight against the French colonialists.
    d.   sending American bombers to defend the French at Dien Bien Phu.

14. Senator John F. Kennedy's main issue in the campaign of 1960 was that

    a.   as a Catholic he would better be able to deal with Catholic Latin America.
    b.   the United States should seek nuclear disarmament agreement with the Soviets.
    c.   the United States had fallen behind the Soviet Union in prestige and power.
    d.   the Eisenhower administration had failed to work hard enough for desegregation.

15. One major breakthrough in American literature in the early post–World War II years was

    a.   the realistic depiction of war and industrial poverty.
    b.   angry social criticism of the "American dream."
    c.   satirical and comic novels by Jewish writers.
    d.   an optimistic vision of nature and love in the work of American poets and playwrights.

C. Identification

Supply the correct identification for each numbered description.

1. _____ Term for making ruthless and unfair charges against opponents, such as those leveled by a red-hunting Wisconsin senator in the 1950s

2. _____ Supreme Court ruling that overturned the old *Plessy* v. *Ferguson* principle that black public facilities could be "separate but equal"

3. _____ The doctrine upon which Eisenhower and Dulles based American nuclear policy in the 1950s

4. _____ An Asian alliance, set up by Secretary Dulles on the model of NATO, to help support the anticommunist regime in South Vietnam

5. _____ The British-and-French-owned waterway whose nationalization by Egyptian President Nasser triggered a major Middle East crisis

6. _____ A soviet scientific achievement that set off a wave of American concern about Soviet superiority in science and education

7. _____ Major international corporation that symbolized the early computer and "information age"

8. _____ High-flying American spy plane, whose downing in 1960 destroyed a summit and heightened Cold War tensions

9. _____ Latin American nation where a 1959 communist revolution ousted a U.S.-backed dictator

10. _____ Betty Friedan's 1963 book that launched a revolution against the suburban "cult of domesticity" that reigned in the 1950s

D. Matching People, Places, and Events

Match the person, place, or event in the left column with the proper description in the right column by inserting the correct letter on the blank line.

1. __ Dwight D. Eisenhower
2. __ Joseph R. McCarthy
3. __ Earl Warren
4. __ Martin Luther King, Jr.
5. __ Ho Chi Minh
6. __ Ngo Dinh Diem
7. __ Betty Friedan
8. __ Adlai E. Stevenson
9. __ Billy Graham
10. __ James R. Hoffa
11. __ John Foster Dulles
12. __ Nikita Khrushchev

a. Eloquent Democratic presidential candidate who was twice swamped by a popular Republican war hero

b. Anticommunist leader who set up a pro-American government to block Ho Chi Minh's expected takeover of all Vietnam

c. Latin American revolutionary who became economically and militarily dependent on the Soviet Union

d. Eisenhower's tough-talking secretary of state who wanted to "roll back" communism

e. Red-hunter turned world-traveling diplomat who narrowly missed becoming president in 1960

13. ___ Fidel Castro

14. ___ Richard Nixon

15. ___ John F. Kennedy

f. Black minister whose 1955 Montgomery bus boycott made him the leader of the civil rights movement

g. The soldier who kept the nation at peace for most of his two terms and ended up warning America about the "military-industrial complex"

h. Popular religious evangelical who effectively used the new medium of television

i. Youthful politician who combined television appeal with traditional big-city Democratic politics to squeak out a victory in 1960

j. Blustery Soviet leader who frequently challenged Eisenhower with both threats and diplomacy

k. Reckless and power-hungry demagogue who intimidated even President Eisenhower before his bubble burst

l. A Vietnamese nationalist and communist whose defeat of the French led to calls for American military intervention in Vietnam

m. Writer whose 1963 book signaled the beginnings of more extensive feminist protest

n. Tough Teamster-union boss whose corrupt actions helped lead to passage of the Landrum-Griffin Act

o. Controversial jurist who led the Supreme Court into previously off-limits social and racial issues

E. Putting Things in Order

Put the following events in correct order by numbering them from 1 to 5.

1. _____ Major crises in Eastern Europe and the Middle East create severe challenges for Eisenhower's foreign policy.

2. _____ An American plane is downed over the Soviet Union, disrupting a summit and rechilling the Cold War.

3. _____ Eisenhower refuses to use American troops to prevent a communist victory over a colonial power in Asia.

4. _____   Eisenhower orders federal troops to enforce a Supreme Court ruling over strong resistance from state officials.

5. _____   Eisenhower's meeting with Soviet leader Khrushchev marks the first real sign of a thaw in the Cold War.

F. Matching Cause and Effect

Match the historical cause in the left column with the proper effect in the right column by writing the correct letter on the blank line.

Cause	Effect
1. ___ Joseph McCarthy's attacks on the U.S. Army	a. Set off "massive resistance" to integration in most parts of the Deep South
2. ___ *Brown* v. *Board of Education*	b. Led to continuing nuclear tests and the extension of the arms race
3. ___ Governor Orval Faubus's use of the National Guard to prevent integration	c. Caused the United States to begin backing an anticommunist regime in South Vietnam
4. ___ The 1956 Hungarian revolt	d. Created widespread resentment of the United States in parts of the Western Hemisphere
5. ___ The Communist Vietnamese victory over the French in 1954	e. Forced Secretary of State Dulles to abandon his plans to "roll back" communism
6. ___ Nasser's nationalization of the Suez Canal	f. Exposed the senator's irresponsibility and brought about his downfall
7. ___ The fears of both the United States and the Soviet Union that the other nation was gaining a lead in rocketry and weapons	g. Forced President Eisenhower to send federal troops to Little Rock
8. ___ The downing of the U-2 spy plane	h. Undermined the Paris summit and weakened Eisenhower's goodwill diplomacy
9. ___ American intervention in Latin America and support for anti-communist dictators in that region	i. Enabled the Democrats to win a narrow electoral victory in 1960
10. ___ Kennedy's television glamour and traditional political skills	j. Led to the 1956 British-French-Israeli invasion of Egypt

G. Developing Historical Skills

Comparing and Interpreting Election Maps

Read carefully the maps for the elections of 1956 (p. 902) and 1960 (p. 907). Answer the following questions:

1. Which was the only nonsouthern state to vote for Democrats Stevenson in 1956 and Kennedy in 1960?

2.   Which three southern states (states of the old Confederacy) voted for Republicans Eisenhower in 1956 and Nixon in 1960?

3.   Which two southern states switched from Republican in 1956 to Democratic in 1960?

4.   How many more electoral votes did Kennedy get in the West (not counting Texas) in 1960 than Stevenson got in the same region in 1956?

5.   How many electoral votes did Kennedy win from states that Stevenson also carried in 1956? (Note the divided electoral vote in one state.)

PART III: APPLYING WHAT YOU HAVE LEARNED

1.   In what ways was the Eisenhower era a time of caution and conservatism, and in what ways was it a time of dynamic economic, social, and cultural change?

2.   How did Eisenhower balance assertiveness and restraint in his foreign policies in Vietnam, Europe, and the Middle East?

3.   What were the dynamics of the Cold War with the Soviet Union in the 1950s, and how did Eisenhower and Khrushchev combine confrontation and conversation in their relationship?

4.   How did America's far-flung international responsibilities shape the U.S. economy and society in the Eisenhower era? Was the American way of life fundamentally altered by the nation's new superpower status, or did it remain largely sheltered from world affairs?

5.   How did television and other innovations of the "consumer age" affect American politics, society, and culture in the 1950s?

6.   Despite widespread power and affluence, the 1950s were often described as an "age of anxiety." What were the major sources of anxiety and conflict that stirred beneath the surface of the time? Could they have been addressed more effectively by Eisenhower and other national leaders? Why or why not?

7.   Argue for or against: American politics, society, and culture in the 1950s were all stagnant and narrow, and did not address the real social problems facing the country.

CHAPTER 38

The Stormy Sixties, 1960–1968

PART I: REVIEWING THE CHAPTER

A. CHECKLIST OF LEARNING OBJECTIVES

After mastering this chapter, you should be able to

1. describe the high expectations Kennedy's New Frontier aroused and the obstacles it encountered in promoting its domestic policies.

2. analyze the theory and practice of Kennedy's doctrine of "flexible response" in Asia and Latin America.

3. describe Johnson's succession to the presidency in 1963, his electoral landslide over Goldwater in 1964, and his Great Society successes of 1965.

4. discuss the course of the black movement of the 1960s, from civil rights to Black Power.

5. outline the steps by which Johnson led the United States deeper into the Vietnam quagmire.

6. explain how the Vietnam war brought turmoil to American society and eventually drove Johnson and the divided Democrats from power in 1968.

7. describe the cultural rebellions of the 1960s, and indicate their short-term and long-term consequences.

B. GLOSSARY

To build your social science vocabulary, familiarize yourself with the following terms:

1. **free world** During the Cold War, the noncommunist democracies of the Western world, as opposed to the communist states. "But to the free world the 'Wall of Shame' looked like a gigantic enclosure around a concentration camp." (p. 919)

2. **nuclear proliferation** The spreading of nuclear weapons to nations that have not previously had them. "Despite the perils of nuclear proliferation or Soviet domination, de Gaulle demanded an independent Europe. . . ." (p. 919)

3. **exile** A person who has been banished or driven from her or his country by the authorities. "He had inherited . . . a CIA-backed scheme to topple Fidel Castro from power by invading Cuba with anticommunist exiles." (p. 921)

4. **peaceful coexistence** The principle or policy that communists and noncommunists—specifically, the United States and the Soviet Union—ought to live together without trying to dominate or destroy each other. "Kennedy thus tried to lay the foundations for a realistic policy of peaceful coexistence with the Soviet Union." (p. 923)

5. **détente** In international affairs, a period of relaxed agreement in areas of mutual interest. "Here were the modest origins of the policy that later came to be known as 'détente.'" (p. 923)

6. **sit-in** A demonstration in which people occupy a facility for a sustained period to achieve political or economic goals. "Following the wave of sit-ins that surged across the South. . . ." (p. 923)

7. **establishment** The ruling inner circle of a nation and its principal institutions. "Goldwater's forces had . . . rid[den] roughshod over the moderate Republican 'eastern establishment.'" (p. 929)

8. **literacy test** A literacy examination that a person must pass before being allowed to vote. "Ballot-denying devices like the poll tax, literacy tests, and barefaced discrimination still barred black people from the political process." (p. 931)

9. **ghetto** The district of a city where members of a religious or racial minority are forced to live, either by legal restriction or by informal social pressure. (Originally, ghettoes were enclosed Jewish districts in Europe.) ". . . a bloody riot exploded in Watts, a black ghetto in Los Angeles." (p. 932)

10. **black separatism** The doctrine that blacks in the United States ought to separate themselves from whites, either in separate institutions or in a separate political territory. ". . . Malcolm X trumpeted black separatism. . . ." (p. 932)

11. **hawk** During the Vietnam War, someone who favored vigorous prosecution or escalation of the conflict. "If the United States were to cut and run from Vietnam, claimed prowar 'hawks,' other nations would doubt America's word. . . ." (p. 935)

12. **dove** During the Vietnam War, someone who opposed the war and favored de-escalation or withdrawal by the United States. "New flocks of antiwar 'doves' were hatching daily." (p. 935)

13. **militant** In politics, someone who pursues political goals in a belligerent way, often using paramilitary means. "Other militants . . . shouted obscenities. . . ." (p. 938)

14. **dissident** Someone who dissents, especially from an established or normative institution or position. ". . . Spiro T. Agnew [was] noted for his tough stands against dissidents and black militants." (p. 939)

15. **coattails** In politics, the ability of a popular candidate at the top of a ticket to transfer some of his or her support to lesser candidates on the same ticket. "Nixon was . . . the first president-elect since 1848 not to bring in on his coattails at least one house of Congress. . . ." (pp. 939–940)

PART II: CHECKING YOUR PROGRESS

A. True-False

Where the statement is true, circle **T**; where it is false, circle **F**.

1. T F   Kennedy's attempt to control rising steel prices met strong opposition from big business.

2. T F   The Kennedy doctrine of "flexible response" was applied primarily to conflicts with Soviet communism in Europe.

3. T F   The U.S.-supported coup against the corrupt Diem regime brought South Vietnam greater democracy and political stability.

4. T F   Kennedy financed and trained the Cuban rebels involved in the Bay of Pigs invasion but refused to intervene directly with American troops or planes.

5. T F   The Cuban missile crisis ended in a humiliating defeat for Khrushchev and the Soviet Union.

6. T F Kennedy encouraged the civil rights movement to become more outspoken in its opposition to segregation and discrimination.

7. T F Johnson's landslide victory came in every part of the country except the traditionally Republican Midwest.

8. T F The Gulf of Tonkin Resolution authorized the president to respond to naval attacks but kept the power to make war in Vietnam firmly in the hands of Congress.

9. T F Johnson's Great Society programs attempted to balance the federal budget and return power to the states.

10. T F The nonviolent civil rights movement, led by Martin Luther King, Jr., achieved great victories in integration and voting rights for blacks in 1964 and 1965.

11. T F The urban riots of the late 1960s demonstrated that the South had not been improved by the civil rights movement.

12. T F The campaigns of Senators McCarthy and Kennedy forced Johnson to withdraw as a presidential candidate and promoted de-escalation of the Vietnam War.

13. T F The deep Democratic divisions over Vietnam helped elect Nixon as president in 1968.

14. T F One major American institution largely unaffected by the cultural upheaval of the 1960s was the Roman Catholic Church.

15. T F The "sexual revolution" of the 1960s included the introduction of the birth control pill and the increasing visibility of gays and lesbians.

B. Multiple Choice

Select the best answer and circle the corresponding letter.

1. President Kennedy's New Frontier proposals for increased federal educational aid and medical assistance to the elderly
   a. succeeded because of his skill in legislative bargaining.
   b. were traded away in exchange for passage of the bill establishing the Peace Corps.
   c. were stalled by strong opposition in Congress.
   d. were strongly opposed by business interests.
2. The industry that engaged in a bitter conflict with President Kennedy over price increases was
   a. the airline industry.
   b. the health care industry.
   c. the steel industry.
   d. the oil industry.
3. The fundamental military policy of the Kennedy administration was to
   a. develop a "flexible response" to fighting "brushfire wars" in the Third World.
   b. threaten massive nuclear retaliation against any communist advances.
   c. build up heavy conventional armed forces in Western Europe against the threat of a Soviet invasion.
   d. provide military assistance to client states in the Third World so that they could fight proxy wars without the need of American forces.
4. The first major foreign-policy disaster of the Kennedy administration came when
   a. Middle East governments sharply raised the price of imported oil.
   b. American-backed Cuban rebels were defeated by Castro's Cuban army at the Bay of Pigs.
   c. Khrushchev forced American missiles out of Turkey during the Cuban missile crisis.

    d.   American Green Beret guerilla forces began suffering heavy casualties in the jungles of Vietnam.

5.   The Cuban missile crisis ended when

    a.   the American-backed Cuban invaders were defeated at the Bay of Pigs.

    b.   the United States agreed to allow Soviet missiles in Cuba as long as they were not armed with nuclear weapons.

    c.   the Soviets agreed to pull all missiles out of Cuba and the United States agreed not to invade Cuba.

    d.   The United States and the Soviet Union agreed that Cuba should become neutral in the Cold War.

6.   The Kennedy administration was pushed into a stronger stand on civil rights by

    a.   the civil rights movement led by the Freedom Riders and Martin Luther King, Jr.

    b.   the political advantages of backing civil rights.

    c.   the pressure from foreign governments and the United Nations.

    d.   the threat of violence in northern cities.

7.   Lyndon Johnson won an overwhelming landslide victory in the 1964 election partly because

    a.   he repudiated many of the policies of the unpopular Kennedy administration.

    b.   he promised to take a tough stand in opposing communist aggression in Vietnam.

    c.   Republican candidate Senator Barry Goldwater was seen by many Americans as a "trigger-happy" extremist.

    d.   Johnson had achieved considerable personal popularity with the electorate.

8.   President Johnson was more successful in pushing economic and civil rights measures through Congress than President Kennedy because

    a.   he was better at explaining the purposes of the laws in his speeches.

    b.   the Democrats gained overwhelming control of Congress in the landslide of 1964.

    c.   Republicans were more willing to cooperate with Johnson than with Kennedy.

    d.   Johnson was better able to swing southern Democrats behind his proposals.

9.   The Civil Rights Act of 1965 was designed to guarantee

    a.   desegregation in interstate transportation.

    b.   job opportunities for African Americans.

    c.   desegregation of high schools and colleges.

    d.   voting rights for African Americans.

10.   Most of the racial riots of the 1960s occurred in

    a.   northern inner cities.

    b.   southern inner cities.

    c.   white neighborhoods where black families attempted to move in.

    d.   college campuses.

11.   The primary political problem that the United States faced in waging the Vietnam War was

    a.   the opposition of America's European allies.

    b.   the danger that the North and South Vietnamese would strike a deal and ask the United States to leave.

    c.   the repeated collapse of weak and corrupt South Vietnamese governments.

    d.   the growing political alliance between North Vietnam and Communist China.

12.   Opposition to the Vietnam War in Congress was centered in

    a.   the House Foreign Affairs Committee.

    b.   the Senate Armed Services Committee.

    c.   the Republican leadership of the House and Senate.

    d.   the Senate Foreign Relations Committee.

13. The *two* antiwar candidates whose strong political showing forced Johnson to withdraw from the 1968 presidential race were

   a. Nelson Rockefeller and Ronald Reagan.
   b. Eugene McCarthy and Robert Kennedy.
   c. J. William Fulbright and George McGovern.
   d. George Wallace and Curtis LeMay.

14. One dominant theme of the 1960s "youth culture" that had deep roots in American history was

   a. conflict between the generations.
   b. distrust and hostility toward authority.
   c. the widespread use of mind-altering drugs.
   d. a positive view of sexual experimentation.

15. The cultural upheavals of the 1960s could largely be attributed to the "three P's" of

   a. pot, promiscuity, and publicity.
   b. presidential failure, political rebellion, and personal authenticity.
   c. poverty, protest, and the "pill."
   d. population bulge, protest against racism, and prosperity.

C. Identification

Supply the correct identification for each numbered description.

1. _____ Kennedy administration program that sent youthful American volunteers to work in underdeveloped countries

2. _____ High barrier between East and West erected during the 1961 Berlin crisis

3. _____ Elite antiguerilla military units expanded by Kennedy as part of his doctrine of "flexible response"

4. _____ An attempt to provide American aid for democratic reform in Latin America that met with much disappointment and frustration

5. _____ Site where anti-Castro guerilla forces failed in their U.S.-sponsored invasion

6. _____ Tense confrontation between Kennedy and Khrushchev that nearly led to nuclear war in October 1962

7. _____ New civil rights technique developed in the 1960s to desegregate lunch counters and other public facilities in the South

8. _____ LBJ's broad program of welfare legislation and social reform that swept through Congress in 1965

9. _____ The 1964 congressional action that became a "blank check" for the Vietnam War

10. _____ Law, spurred by Martin Luther King, Jr.'s march from Selma to Montgomery, that guaranteed rights originally given blacks under the Fifteenth Amendment

11. _____ Racial slogan that signaled a growing challenge to King's non-violent civil rights movement by militant younger blacks

12. _____ The Vietnamese New Year celebration, during which the communists launched a heavy offensive against the United States in 1968

13. _____ Student activist protest at the University of California that criticized corporate interests and impersonal university education

14. _____   Student organization that moved from nonviolent protest to underground terrorism within a few years

15. _____   Site of an off-duty police raid in 1969 that spurred gay and lesbian activism

D. Matching People, Places, and Events

Match the person, place, or event in the left column with the proper description in the right column by inserting the correct letter on the blank line.

1. ___   John F. Kennedy

2. ___   Robert S. McNamara

3. ___   Nikita Khrushchev

4. ___   Martin Luther King, Jr.

5. ___   Lyndon B. Johnson

6. ___   Barry M. Goldwater

7. ___   James Meredith

8. ___   Malcolm X

9. ___   Mario Savio

10. ___   Eugene J. McCarthy

11. ___   Robert F. Kennedy

12. ___   Richard M. Nixon

13. ___   George C. Wallace

14. ___   Hubert Humphrey

15. ___   Alfred Kinsey

a.   First black student admitted to the University of Mississippi, shot during a civil rights march in 1966

b.   Cabinet officer who promoted "flexible response" but came to doubt the wisdom of the Vietnam War he had presided over

c.   New York senator whose antiwar campaign for the presidency was ended by an assassin's bullet in June 1968

d.   Former vice president who staged a remarkable political comeback to win presidential election in 1968

e.   Charismatic Black Muslim leader who promoted separatism in the early 1960s

f.   Minnesota senator whose antiwar "Children's Crusade" helped force Johnson to alter his Vietnam policies

g.   Early student activist and leader of the Free Speech Movement at the University of California

h.   Nonviolent black leader whose advocacy of peaceful change came under attack from militants after 1965

i.   Vice president whose loyalty to LBJ's Vietnam policies sent him down to defeat in the 1968 presidential election

j.   Charismatic president whose brief administration experienced domestic stalemate and foreign confrontations with communism

k.   Third-party candidate whose conservative, hawkish 1968 campaign won 9 million votes and carried five states

l.   Aggressive Soviet leader whose failed gamble of putting missiles in Cuba cost him his job

m. Controversial Indiana University "sexologist" who documented Americans' changing sexual behavior

n. Conservative Republican whose crushing defeat opened the way for the liberal Great Society programs

o. Brilliant legislative operator whose domestic achievements in social welfare and civil rights fell under the shadow of his Vietnam disaster

E. Putting Things in Order

Put the following events in correct order by numbering them from 1 to 5.

1. _____ A southern Texas populist replaces a Harvard-educated Irish American in the White House.

2. _____ An American-sponsored anticommunist invasion of Cuba fails.

3. _____ Kennedy successfully risks nuclear confrontation to thwart Khrushchev's placement of Russian missiles in Cuba.

4. _____ A candidate running on a "peace" platform obtains a congressional "blank check" for subsequent expanded military actions against the Communist Vietnamese.

5. _____ Communist military assaults, political divisions between hawks and doves, and assassinations of national leaders form the backdrop for a turbulent election year.

F. Matching Cause and Effect

Match the historical cause in the left column with the proper effect in the right column by writing the correct letter on the blank line.

Cause

1. ___ Kennedy's unhappiness with the corrupt Diem regime

2. ___ Khrushchev's placement of missiles in Cuba

3. ___ Johnson's landslide victory over Goldwater in 1964

4. ___ The Gulf of Tonkin Resolution

5. ___ Martin Luther King, Jr.'s civil rights marches

6. ___ Angry discontent in northern black ghettos

7. ___ American escalation of the

Effect

a. Pushed Johnson into withdrawing as a presidential candidate in 1968

b. Brought ever-rising American casualties and a strengthened will to resist on the part of the Communist Vietnamese

c. Led to a U.S.-encouraged coup and greater political instability in South Vietnam

d. Helped push through historic civil rights legislation in 1964 and 1965

e. Brought along huge Democratic congressional majorities that passed a

Vietnam War

fistful of Great Society laws

8. ___ The Communist Vietnamese Tet Offensive in 1968

f. Helped Nixon win a minority victory over his divided opposition

9. ___ Senator Eugene McCarthy's strong antiwar campaign

g. Became the questionable legal basis for all of Johnson's further escalation of the Vietnam War

10. ___ The deep Democratic party divisions over Vietnam

h. Led to a humiliating defeat when Kennedy forced the Soviet Union to back down

i. Sparked urban riots and the growth of the militant "Black Power" movement

j. Led to an American military request for 200,000 more troops as well as growing public discontent with the Vietnam War

G. Developing Historical Skills

Interpreting Line Graphs

Read the line graph of *Poverty in the United States* on p. 931 carefully and answer the following questions:

1. In what year did the number of people below the poverty line return to approximately the same level it had been at in 1964?

2. In what two years did the percentage of the American population below the poverty line reach its lowest point since 1960?

3. Between what years did the absolute numbers of people below the poverty line *rise* slightly at the same time those in poverty *declined* slightly as a percentage of the total population? What would explain this difference?

4. The number of people in poverty in 1966 was about the same as the number in poverty in which subsequent year?

H. Map Mastery

Map Discrimination

Using the maps and charts in Chapter 38, answer the following questions.

1. *Vietnam and Southeast Asia*: Besides North Vietnam, which two other Southeast Asian countries bordered on South Vietnam?

2. *Presidential Election of 1964*: How many electoral votes did Barry Goldwater win outside the Deep South in 1964?

3. *Presidential Election of 1968*: What four northeastern states did Nixon carry in 1968?

4. *Presidential Election of 1968*: Which five states outside the Northeast did Humphrey carry in 1968? (One of them is not in the continental United States.)

Map Challenge

Using the electoral maps of the five elections of 1952, 1956, 1960, 1964, and 1968 (pp. 889, 902, 906, 928 and 940 (in Chapters 37 and 38), write a brief essay describing the changing fortunes of the Republican and Democratic parties in different regions of the country from 1952 to 1968. Include a discussion of which states and regions remained relatively loyal to a single party, which shifted loyalties, and which were most contested. What are the most plausible explanations for these patterns?

PART III: APPLYING WHAT YOU HAVE LEARNED

1. What successes and failures did Kennedy's New Frontier experience at home and abroad?

2. How did the civil rights movement progress from difficult beginnings to great successes in 1964–1965 and then encounter increasing opposition from both black militants and "white backlash" after 1965?

3. What were Johnson's major domestic achievements, and why did they come to be overshadowed?

4. Why did the Vietnam War, and the domestic opposition to it, come to dominate American politics in the 1960s?

5. How was the cultural upheaval of the 1960s related to the political and social changes of the decade? Is the "youth rebellion" best seen as a response to immediate events, or as a consequence of such longer-term forces as the population bulge and economic prosperity? What were the long-term results of the "counter-culture" in all its varieties?

6. What led the United States to become so deeply involved in the Vietnam War? (See Chapters 36 and 37 for background on the Cold War, anticolonialism, and earlier events in Vietnam.)

7.   Would the 1960s have unfolded in substantially different ways had President Kennedy not been assassinated? What political strengths did Kennedy possess that Johnson did not, and vice versa?

CHAPTER 39

The Stalemated Seventies, 1968–1980

PART I: REVIEWING THE CHAPTER

A. CHECKLIST OF LEARNING OBJECTIVES

After mastering this chapter, you should be able to

1. describe Nixon's foreign policy in relation to Vietnam, the Soviet Union, and Communist China.

2. analyze Nixon's domestic policies, his opposition to the "Warren Court," his "southern strategy", and his landslide victory against George McGovern in 1972.,

3. examine the conflicts created by the secret bombing of Cambodia, the American withdrawal from Vietnam, and the first Arab oil embargo.

4. discuss the Watergate scandals and Nixon's resignation.

5. explain the related economic, energy, and Middle East crises of the 1970s and why both Republican and Democratic administrations were unable successfully to address them.

6. describe the racial tensions of the 1970s and the rise of the new feminist movement.

7. discuss the Iranian crisis and its disastrous political consequences for President Carter.

B. GLOSSARY

To build your social science vocabulary, familiarize yourself with the following terms:

1. **moratorium** A period in which economic or social activity is suspended, often to achieve certain defined goals. "Antiwar protestors staged a massive national Vietnam moratorium in October 1969. . . ." (p. 948)

2. **Marxism** The doctrines of Karl Marx, advocated or followed by worldwide communist parties and by some democratic socialists. "The two great communist powers . . . were clashing bitterly over their rival interpretations of Marxism." (p. 950)

3. **anti-ballistic missile** A defensive missile designed to intercept and destroy an offensive missile in flight. "The first major achievement was an anti-ballistic missile (ABM) treaty. . . ."

4. **devaluation** In economics, steps taken to reduce the purchasing power of a given unit of currency in relation to foreign currencies. " . . . he next stunned the world by taking the United States off the gold standard and devaluing the dollar." (p. 954)

5. **foray** a single, defined movement or attack by a military unit. "The most disturbing feature of these sky forays. . . ."

6. **Kremlin** The extensive palace complex in Moscow that houses the Soviet (Russian) government; hence, a shorthand term for the Soviet or Russian government. "Believing that the Kremlin was poised to fly combat troops to the Suez area. . . ."

7. **attorney general** The presidentially appointed head of the Department of Justice and chief legal officer of the federal government. ". . . firing his own special prosecutor . . . as well as his attorney general and deputy attorney general. . . ."

8. **executive privilege** In American government, the claim that certain information known to the president or the executive branch of government should be unavailable to Congress or the courts because of the principle of separation of powers. " . . . the Supreme Court unanimously ruled that "executive privilege" gave him no right to withhold evidence. . . ."

9. **recession** A moderate and short-term economic downturn, less severe than a depression. (Economists define a recession as two consecutive quarters, i.e., six months, of declining gross domestic product.) "Lines of automobiles at service stations lengthened as tempers shortened and a business recession deepened." (p. 958)

10. **born-again** The evangelical Christian belief in a spiritual renewal or rebirth, involving a personal experience of conversion and a commitment to moral transformation. ". . . this born-again Baptist touched many people with his down-home sincerity." (p. 967)

11. **balance of payments** The net ratio, expressed as a positive or negative sum, of a nation's exports in relation to its imports. (It may be calculated in relation to one particular foreign nation, or to all foreign states collectively.) "The soaring bill for imported oil plunged America's balance of payments deeply into the red. . . ." (p. 971)

12. **Commando** Member of a small, elite military force trained to carry out difficult missions, often within territory controlled by the enemy. "A highly trained commando team penetrated deep into Iran's sandy interior."

PART II: CHECKING YOUR PROGRESS

A. True-False

Where the statement is true, circle **T**; where it is false, circle **F**.

1. T   F   Nixon's "Vietnamization" policy sought to bring an immediate negotiated end to the Vietnam War.

2. T   F   Nixon's 1970 invasion of Cambodia provoked strong domestic protests and political clashes between "hawks" and "doves."

3. T   F   Nixon's and Kissinger's diplomacy attempted to play the Soviet Union and China off against each other for America's benefit.

4. T   F   Nixon attempted to reverse what he saw as the Warren Supreme Court's excessive turn toward "judicial activism."

5. T   F   Nixon consistently opposed the expansion of social-security and pro-environmental legislation.

6. T   F   The basic issue in the 1972 Nixon-McGovern campaign was inflation and the management of the economy.

7. T   F   The 1973 Paris agreement on Vietnam provided for a cease-fire and American withdrawal but did not really end the civil war among the Vietnamese.

8. T   F   The strongest charge against Nixon during Watergate was that he had used government agencies to burglarize and harass opponents and cover up the Watergate crimes.

9. T F The disclosure of the secret bombing of Cambodia led Congress to acknowledge the president's sole authority to take military action in defense of America's national security.

10. T F The 1973 Arab-Israeli War and OPEC oil embargo added to the inflation that began in the wake of the Vietnam War.

11. T F Republican leaders in Congress strenuously opposed Nixon's resignation and urged him to fight to stay in office even after the Watergate tapes were released.

12. T F President Gerald Ford immediately set out to reverse the Nixon-Kissinger policy of détente toward the Soviet Union.

13. T F The women's movement achieved success in the 1970s by allying itself with the rising antiwar and black power movements of the decade.

14. T F President Carter's declaration that America's problems were due to a "moral and spiritual crisis" led the public to support his proposals to decrease dependency on Middle Eastern oil.

15. T F The Iranian revolution against the shah brought the United States into a confrontation with the new, militant Muslim leaders of the country.

B. Multiple Choice

Select the best answer and circle the corresponding letter.

1. A primary cause of the economic decline that began in the 1970s was
    a. an international trade war.
    b. a rise in the price of agricultural goods.
    c. the breakup of efficient American companies.
    d. a decline in worker productivity

2. The severe inflation of the 1970s was largely caused by
    a. Lyndon Johnson's effort to maintain the Vietnam War and the Great Society programs without raising taxes.
    b. Nixon's decision to devalue the dollar and take the U.S. off the gold standard.
    c. the higher prices for scarce natural resources like iron, coal, and lumber.
    d. the strong demands of unionized workers for substantial wage increases.

3. President Nixon's "Vietnamization" policy provided that
    a. the United States would accept a unified but neutral Vietnam.
    b. the United States would escalate the war in Vietnam but withdraw from Cambodia and Laos.
    c. the United States would gradually withdraw ground troops while supporting the South Vietnamese war effort.
    d. the United States would seek a negotiated settlement of the war.

4. The antiwar movement expanded dramatically in 1970 when
    a. the massacre of civilians at My Lai by some U.S. soldiers was revealed.
    b. Nixon ordered further bombing of North Vietnam.
    c. the communist Vietnamese staged their Tet Offensive against American forces.
    d. Nixon ordered an invasion of Cambodia.

5. Nixon attempted to pressure the Soviet Union into making diplomatic deals with the United States by
    a. playing the "China card" by opening U.S. diplomacy and trade with the Soviets' rival communist power.
    b. using American economic aid as an incentive for the Soviets.

    c.   threatening to attack Soviet allies such as Cuba and Vietnam.

    d.   drastically increasing spending on nuclear weapons and missiles.

6.   The Supreme Court came under sharp political attack in the 1970s especially because of its rulings on

    a.   antitrust laws and labor rights.

    b.   voting rights and election laws.

    c.   criminal defendants' rights and prayer in public schools.

    d.   environmental laws and immigrants' rights.

7.   The most controversial element of Nixon's "Philadelphia Plan" was

    a.   its guarantees of women's equal right to employment in the construction trades.

    b.   the extension of "affirmative action" to promote the employment of groups of minorities and women.

    c.   its insistence that employers and labor provide financial compensation to individuals who had suffered discrimination.

    d.   its attempt to get around Supreme Court decisions prohibiting racial and sexual discrimination by business and labor.

8.   Some of President Nixon's greatest legislative successes came in the area of

    a.   upholding civil rights.

    b.   stopping the growth of inflation.

    c.   protecting the environment.

    d.   maintaining foreign-policy cooperation with Congress.

9.   Among the corrupt Nixon administration practices exposed by the Senate Watergate Committee was

    a.   payments to foreign agents.

    b.   bribes to congressmen and senators.

    c.   the illegal use of the Federal Bureau of Investigation and the Central Intelligence Agency.

    d.   the illegal use of the Environmental Protection Agency and the Treasury Department.

10.   The War Powers Act was passed by Congress in response to

    a.   the Watergate scandal.

    b.   President Nixon's secret bombing of Cambodia.

    c.   the end of the war in Vietnam.

    d.   the Arab oil embargo.

11.   The Arab oil embargo of 1973–1974 affected the American economy primarily by

    a.   causing the successful introduction of alternative energy sources.

    b.   leading the United States to open Alaskan and offshore oilfields to exploration.

    c.   increasing American investment in the Middle East.

    d.   ending the era of cheap energy and fueling severe inflation.

12.   Gerald Ford came to be president because

    a.   he had been elected as Nixon's vice president in 1972.

    b.   he was speaker of the House of Representatives and was next in line after Nixon resigned.

    c.   he was elected in a special national election called after Nixon resigned.

    d.   he had been appointed vice president by Nixon before Nixon resigned.

13.   Despite numerous successes for women in the 1970s, the feminist movement suffered a severe setback when

    a.   the Supreme Court began to oppose the extension of women's rights.

    b.   the Equal Rights Amendment failed to achieve ratification by the states.

    c.   Congress refused to extend women's right to an equal education to the area of athletics.

    d.   the declining economy created a growing gap between men's and women's earning power.

14. President Carter's greatest success in foreign policy was
   a. handling the Arab oil embargo and the energy crisis.
   b. negotiating successful new agreements with the Soviet Union.
   c. negotiating the Camp David peace treaty between Israel and Egypt.
   d. maintaining peace and stability in Central America.
15. President Carter's greatest problem in foreign policy was
   a. the Panama Canal issue.
   b. the Soviet invasion of Afghanistan.
   c. the continuing Arab-Israeli confrontation.
   d. the Iranian seizure of American hostages.

C. Identification

Supply the correct identification for each numbered description.

1. _____ Nixon's policy of withdrawing American troops from Vietnam while providing aid for the South Vietnamese to fight the war

2. _____ The Ohio university where four students were killed during protests against the 1970 invasion of Cambodia

3. _____ Top-secret documents, published by *The New York Times* in 1971, that showed the blunders and deceptions that led the United States into the Vietnam War

4. _____ The first major achievement of the Nixon-Kissinger détente with the Soviet Union, which led to restrictions on defensive missile systems

5. _____ Nixon's plan to win reelection by curbing the Supreme Court's judicial activism and soft-pedaling civil rights

6. _____ Term for the new group affirmative action policy promoted by the Nixon administration

7. _____ A Washington office complex that became a symbol of the widespread corruption of the Nixon administration

8. _____ The law, passed in reaction to the secret Cambodia bombing, that restricted presidential use of troops overseas without congressional authorization

9. _____ Arab-sponsored restriction on energy exports after the 1973 Arab-Israeli war

10. _____ Nixon-Ford-Kissinger policy of seeking relaxed tensions with the Soviet Union through trade and arms limitation

11. _____ International agreement of 1975, signed by President Ford, that settled postwar European boundaries and attempted to guarantee human rights in Eastern Europe

12. _____ Proposed constitutional amendment promoting women's rights that fell short of ratification

13. _____ Supreme Court decision that declared women's right to choose abortion.

14. _____ *Two* historic sites seized by American Indian activists in 1970–1972 to draw public attention to Indian grievances

15. _____   Provision of the 1972 Education Amendments that prohibited gender discrimination and opened sports and other arenas to women

D. Matching People, Places, and Events

Match the person, place, or event in the left column with the proper description in the right column by inserting the correct letter on the blank line.

1. ___ Richard Nixon

2. ___ Spiro Agnew

3. ___ Rachel Carson

4. ___ Daniel Ellsberg

5. ___ Henry Kissinger

6. ___ Earl Warren

7. ___ George McGovern

8. ___ Sam Ervin

9. ___ Gerald Ford

10. ___ John Dean

11. ___ James Earl Carter

12. ___ Anwar Sadat

13. ___ Allen Bakke

14. ___ Shah of Iran

15. ___ Ayatollah Ruhollah Khomeini

a. The Muslim religious leader who dominated the 1979 Iranian revolution

b. The first appointed vice president and first appointed president of the United States

c. Supreme Court justice whose "judicial activism" came under increasing attack by conservatives

d. Nixon's tough-talking conservative vice president, who was forced to resign in 1973 for taking bribes and kickbacks

e. Talented diplomatic negotiator and leading architect of détente with the Soviet Union during the Nixon and Ford administrations

f. Egyptian leader who signed the Camp David accords with Israel

g. California medical school applicant whose case led a divided Supreme Court to uphold limited forms of affirmative action for minorities

h. Environmental writer whose book *Silent Spring* helped encourage laws like the Clean Water Act and the Endangered Species Act

i. South Dakota senator whose antiwar campaign was swamped by Nixon

j. Former Georgia governor whose presidency was plagued by economic difficulties and a crisis in Iran

k. Former Pentagon official who "leaked" the Pentagon Papers

l. Winner of an overwhelming electoral victory who was forced from office by the threat of impeachment

m. White House lawyer whose dramatic charges against Nixon were validated by the Watergate tapes

n.   North Carolina senator who conducted the Watergate hearings

o.   Repressive pro-Western ruler whose 1979 overthrow precipitated a crisis for the United States

E. Putting Things in Order

Put the following events in correct order by numbering them from 1 to 6.

1. _____   The overthrow of a dictatorial shah leads to an economic and political crisis for President Carter and the United States.

2. _____   An impeachment-threatened president resigns, and his appointed vice president takes over the White House.

3. _____   A U.S. president travels to Beijing (Peking) and Moscow, opening a new era of improved diplomatic relations with the communist powers.

4. _____   The American invasion of a communist stronghold near Vietnam creates domestic turmoil in the United States.

5. _____   The signing of an agreement with North Vietnam leads to the final withdrawal of American troops from Vietnam.

6. _____   A plainspoken former governor becomes president by campaigning against Washington corruption and for honesty in government.

F. Matching Cause and Effect

Match the historical cause in the left column with the proper effect in the right column by writing the correct letter on the blank line.

Cause	Effect
1. ___ Nixon's "Vietnamization" policy	a. Spawned a powerful "backlash" that halted federal day care efforts and the Equal Rights Amendment
2. ___ The U.S. invasion and bombing of Cambodia	b. Caused Senate defeat of the SALT II treaty and the end of détente with Moscow
3. ___ Nixon's trips to Beijing (Peking) and Moscow	c. Brought about gradual U.S. troop withdrawal but extended the Vietnam War for four more years
4. ___ The Warren Court's "judicial activism"	d. Prompted conservative protests and Nixon's appointment of less activist justices
5. ___ Pressure on Moscow and renewed bombing of North Vietnam	e. Led to the taking of American hostages and new economic and energy troubles for the United States
6. ___ The growing successes of the women's movement in areas of employment and education	
7. ___ Nixon's tape-recorded	

| | | f. | Brought about a cease-fire and the withdrawal of American troops from Vietnam in 1973 |

words ordering the Watergate cover-up

8. ___   The communist Vietnamese offensive in 1975

g.   Caused protests on U.S. campuses and congressional attempts to restrain presidential war powers

9. ___   The Soviet invasion of Afghanistan

h.   Brought an era of relaxed international tensions and new trade agreements

10. ___   The 1979 revolution in Iran

i.   Caused the collapse of South Vietnam and the flight of many refugees to the United States

j.   Proved the president's guilt and forced him to resign or be impeached

G. Developing Historical Skills

Understanding Political Cartoons

The more controversial a major political figure, the more likely he or she is to be the subject of political cartoons. Richard Nixon was such a controversial figure, and the cartoons in this chapter show several views of him. Answer the following questions:

1.   What is the view of Nixon's diplomacy in the cartoon *Balancing Act* on p. 951? What is the significance of his unusual "balance bar"?

2.   In the cartoon of *Nixon, the Law and Order Man* on p. 960, what aspect of Nixon's earlier career is satirized? What details suggest the cartoonist's view of Nixon's Watergate strategy?

3.   In the cartoon *How Long Will Nixon Haunt the GOP* on p. 960, what is the cartoonist suggesting about Ford's pardon of Nixon? What alleged quality of Nixon's is common to both this cartoon and the previous one on *Nixon, the Law and Order Man*?

4.   In the cartoon *Who Lost Vietnam* on p. 962, Nixon is satirized, but less harshly than in the other cartoons. What changes the perspective on him here?

PART III: APPLYING WHAT YOU HAVE LEARNED

1. Was the Nixon-Kissinger foreign policy of détente with the Soviet Union and engagement with Communist China fundamentally a great success? How does the failed end of the Vietnam War color the assessment of Nixon's overall diplomatic achievements?

2. In what ways did Nixon's domestic policies appeal to Americans' racial and economic fears, and in what ways did he positively address problems like inflation, discrimination, and pollution?

3. How did Nixon fall from the political heights of 1972 to his forced resignation in 1974? What were the political consequences of Watergate?

4. How did the administrations of the 1970s attempt to cope with the interrelated problems of energy, economics, and the Middle East?

5. Why can the 1970s be characterized as a "decade of stalemate?" What caused the apparent inability of the federal government to cope with the new problems of the time?

6. In what ways were the foreign policy and economic issues of the 1970s similar to those of the whole post-World War II era, and in what ways were they different? (See Chapters 36, 37, and 38.)

7. It is sometimes said that the recent American disillusionment and even cynicism about politics dates to the paired tribulations of "Vietnam" and "Watergate." Why were these two events so deeply unsettling to traditional American views of democracy and government? Is the linking of the two events accurate, or were there fundamental differences between them?

CHAPTER 40

The Resurgence of Conservatism, 1981–1992

PART I: REVIEWING THE CHAPTER

A. CHECKLIST OF LEARNING OBJECTIVES

After mastering this chapter, you should be able to

1. describe the rise of Reagan and the "new right" in the 1980s, including the controversies it generated over social issues.

2. explain the "Reagan revolution" in economic policy and indicate its immediate and long-term consequences.

3. describe the revival of the Cold War in Reagan's first term, and Reagan's increased willingness to negotiate with Soviet leader Gorbachev in his second term..

4. discuss the American entanglement in Central American and Middle Eastern troubles, including the Iran-contra affair.

5. analyze the growing power of the religious right in politics, and the impact of issues like abortion and affirmation on the Supreme Court.

6. describe the end of the Cold War, and the results for American society abroad and at home.

7. explain America's growing involvement in the Middle East, including the First Persian Gulf War and its aftermath.

B. GLOSSARY

To build your social science vocabulary, familiarize yourself with the following terms:

1. **neoconservatives (neoconservatism)** Political activists and thinkers, mostly former liberals, who turned to a defense of traditional social and moral values and a strongly anticommunist foreign policy in the 1970s and 1980s. "Though Reagan was no intellectual, he drew on the ideas of a small but influential group of thinkers known as 'neoconservatives.'" (p. 977)

2. **supply side** In economics, the theory that investment incentives such as lowered federal spending and tax cuts will stimulate economic growth and increased employment. "But at first 'supply-side' economics seemed to be a beautiful theory mugged by a gang of brutal facts. . . ." (p. 981)

3. **red ink** Referring to a deficit in a financial account, with expenditures or debts larger than income or assets. "Ironically, this conservative president thereby plunged the government into a red-ink bath of deficit spending. . . ." (p. 981)

4. **oligarchs** A small, elite class of authoritarian rulers. ". . . the aging oligarchs in the Kremlin. . . ." (p. 982)

5. **welfare state** The political system, typical of modern industrial societies, in which government assumes responsibility for the economic well-being of its citizens by providing social benefits. "They achieved, in short, Reagan's highest political objective: the containment of the welfare state." (p. 987)

6. **leveraged buy-out** The purchase of one company by another using money borrowed on the expectation of selling a portion of assets after the acquisition. "A wave of mergers, acquisitions, and leveraged buy-outs washed over Wall Street. . . ." (p. 990)

7. **logistical (logistics)** Relating to the organization and movement of substantial quantities of people and material in connection with some defined objective. "In a logistical operation of astonishing complexity, the United States spearheaded a massive international military deployment on the sandy Arabian peninsula." (p. 995)

PART II: CHECKING YOUR PROGRESS

A. True-False

Where the statement is true, circle **T**; where it is false, circle **F**.

1. T F Ronald Reagan successfully portrayed "big government" as the enemy rather than the friend of the "common man."

2. T F Reagan's landslide victory over Carter in 1980 did not have the coattails to bring his fellow Republicans into office.

3. T F Once in office, Reagan backed away from most of his ideologically conservative election promises and concentrated on practical management of the economy and relations with the Russians.

4. T F The fact that Reagan's "supply-side" economic proposals bogged down in Congress demonstrated the continuing stalemate between Congress and the executive branch.

5. T F "Reaganomics" was successful in lowering interest rates and balancing the budget but had difficulty bringing down inflation and creating economic growth.

6. T F Reagan's revival of the Cold War in the early 1980s caused rising military budgets and growing doubts about American policy in Western Europe.

7. T F Reagan pursued a tough policy of military intervention and aid in opposition to leftist governments in Central America and the Caribbean.

8. T F Soviet leader Mikhail Gorbachev's policies of *glasnost* and *perestroika* helped reduce Soviet-American conflict in Reagan's second term.

9. T F The Iran-contra affair involved the secret exchange of weapons for American hostages and the illegal transfer of funds to Nicaraguan rebels.

10. T F The failure of "Reaganomics" to deliver a balanced federal budget actually served Reagan's political goal of curbing the liberal welfare state.

11. T F The new religious right borrowed many of its tactics and organizing methods from the new left of the 1960s.

12. T F The Supreme Court cases of *Webster* v. *Reproductive Health Services* and *Casey* v. *Planned Parenthood* carved out compromises that softened the conflict between pro-life and pro-choice forces.

13. T F American economic and cultural assistance to dissident groups played a key role in the overthrow of communism in Eastern Europe.

14. T F The overthrow of communism in Eastern Europe and the Soviet Union led to vicious fighting among previously repressed ethnic groups.

15.   T   F   The First Persian Gulf War achieved its goal of liberating Kuwait but left Saddam Hussein in power in Iraq.

B. Multiple Choice

Select the best answer and circle the corresponding letter.

1.   In the 1980 national elections,

   a.   Senator Edward Kennedy's primary challenge to incumbent President Carter revealed the divisions and weakness of the Democratic party.
   b.   Ronald Reagan won the presidency, but both houses of Congress retained Democratic party majorities.
   c.   third-party candidate John Anderson nearly forced the election into the House of Representatives.
   d.   Ronald Reagan won the presidency by the closest margin since the Kennedy-Nixon election of 1960.

2.   Ronald Reagan was similar to Franklin D. Roosevelt in that both presidents

   a.   disliked big business.
   b.   championed the common person against vast impersonal menaces.
   c.   were raised in wealthy families.
   d.   favored social engineering by the government.

3.   Ronald Reagan differed from Franklin D. Roosevelt in that Roosevelt

   a.   saw big government as the foe of the common person, and Reagan said the foe was big business.
   b.   appealed to the working class and Reagan appealed only to the rich.
   c.   advocated a populist political philosophy and Reagan did not.
   d.   branded big business as the enemy of the common person, while Reagan branded big government as the foe.

4.   Conservative Democrats who helped Ronald Reagan pass his budget and tax-cutting legislation were called

   a.   boll weevils.
   b.   Sagebrush rebels.
   c.   scalawags.
   d.   neoconservatives.

5.   The one area of the federal government activity that Ronald Reagan spent lavishly on was

   a.   farm programs.
   b.   social security.
   c.   defense.
   d.   education.

6.   Reagan's fundamental principle in negotiating with the Soviet Union was to

   a.   trade America's minor interests for major concessions from the Soviets.
   b.   to negotiate only from a position of overwhelming military superiority.
   c.   to negotiate only in cooperation with the Western European allies.
   d.   to insist on greater human rights and economic freedoms as conditions of the negotiations.

7.   More than two hundred U.S. marines were killed in a suicide bombing during an American mission in

   a.   Lebanon.
   b.   Grenada.
   c.   Somalia.
   d.   Nicaragua.

8. Reagan's key agreement with Soviet leader Mikhail Gorbachev provided for

    a. the eventual end of communism inside the Soviet Union.

    b. a major reduction in both Soviet and American nuclear weapons and intercontinental missiles.

    d. an end to Soviet and American sponsorship of governments and rebels in the Third World.

    e. the banning of all intermediate-range nuclear missiles from Europe.

9. The Iran-contra scandal reflected a sharp conflict between Congress and President Reagan over

    a. U.S. aid for rebels against the leftist government of Nicaragua.

    b. the American policy of refusing to trade arms for U.S. hostages in the Middle East.

    c. the attitude of American Christian and Jewish leaders toward Iran's Islamic Revolution.

    d. the U.S. economic boycott of Fidel Castro's Cuba.

10. The religious right movement of the 1980s adopted many ideas and tactics from the 1960s new left such as

    a. advertising in newspapers and television.

    b. "identity politics" and civil disobedience.

    c. taking over traditional political party machines.

    d. wearing Native American clothing and hairstyles.

11. Among the issues that many religious right activists were most concerned about were

    a. abortion and gay rights

    b. taxation and economic development.

    c. foreign policy.

    d. Medicare and Medicaid programs.

12. In cases like *Ward's Cove Packing* v. *Antonia*, the more conservative 1980s Supreme Court began to reflect Reagan's political agenda in cutting back

    a. affirmative action.

    b. the teaching of evolution in public schools.

    c. gun control laws.

    d. sex and violence on television.

13. That preference in the admission policies of institutions of higher education could not be based on ethnic or racial identity alone was the Supreme Court's decision in

    a. *Roe* v. *Wade*.

    b. the *Bakke* case.

    c. *Brown* v. *Board of Education*.

    d. the *Miranda* decision.

14. In which of the following Communist nations did protesters' attempts to bring greater liberty and democracy in the years 1989-1991 completely fail?

    a. the Soviet Union.

    b. East Germany.

    c. China.

    d. Poland.

15. The major American and Allied success in the Persian Gulf War was

    a. the overthrow of Saddam Hussein.

    b. the liberation of Kuwait from Iraqi rule.

    c. the freeing of the Kurds from Iraqi oppression.

    d. the achievement of an enduring peace in the Middle East.

C. Identification

Supply the correct identification for each numbered description.

1. _____ Influential group of intellectuals led by Irving Kristol and Norman Podhoretz who provided key ideas for the "Reagan Revolution"

2. _____ California ballot initiative of 1978 that set the stage for the "tax revolt" that Reagan rode to victory in 1980

3. _____ The economic theory of "Reaganomics" that emphasized cutting taxes and government spending in order to stimulate investment, productivity, and economic growth by private enterprise

4. _____ Term for "young urban professionals" of the 1980s who flaunted their wealth through conspicuous consumer spending

5. _____ Conservative southern Democrats who supported Reagan's economic policies in Congress

6. _____ Polish labor union crushed by the communist-imposed martial-law regime in 1983

7. _____ The leftist revolutionary rulers of Nicaragua, strongly opposed by the Reagan administration

8. _____ Popular name for Reagan's proposed space-based nuclear defense system, officially called the Strategic Defense Initiative

9. _____ Physical symbol of the Cold War and divided Europe that came down in 1989

10. _____ Code name for the military operation of the "hundred hour war" that drove Saddam Hussein out of Kuwait

D. Matching People, Places, and Events

Match the person, place, or event in the left column with the proper description in the right column by inserting the correct letter on the blank line.

1. ___ Jimmy Carter

2. ___ Edward Kennedy

3. ___ Ronald Reagan

4. ___ Sandinistas

5. ___ Sandra Day O'Connor

6. ___ Mikhail Gorbachev

7. ___ George Bush, Sr.

8. ___ contras

9. ___ Saddam Hussein

10. ___ Corazon Aquino

11. ___ Walter Mondale

12. ___ Geraldine Ferraro

13. ___ Jerry Falwell

14. ___ Norman Schwartzkopf

a. Prominent evangelical minister, leader of the Moral Majority

b. Filipino leader who ousted dictator Marcos with American backing in 1986 revolt

c. Soviet leader whose summit meetings with Reagan achieved an arms-control breakthrough in 1987

d. Jimmy Carter's vice president who lost badly to Ronald Reagan in the 1984 election

e. Iraqi dictator defeated by the United States and its allies in the Persian Gulf War

f. Brilliant legal scholar appointed by Reagan as the first woman justice on the Supreme Court

g. Well-meaning president who was swamped by the 1980 Reagan landslide

15. ____   Clarence Thomas

but later won the Nobel Peace Prize

h.   Anti-communist Nicaraguan rebels strongly backed by the Reagan administration

i.   First woman to be nominated to a major party ticket as Democratic vice presidential candidate in 1984

j.   Successful commander of American forces in the First Persian Gulf War

k.   Liberal Democratic senator whose opposition to Carter helped divide the Democrats in 1980

l.   Long-time Republican political figure who defeated Dukakis for the presidency in 1988

m.   Controversial Supreme Court justice who narrowly won confirmation despite charges of sexual harassment

n.   Ruling leftist party of Nicaragua fiercely opposed by the Reagan administration

o.   Political darling of Republican conservatives who won landslide election victories in 1980 and 1984

E. Putting Things in Order

Put the following events in correct order by numbering them from 1 to 6.

1. _____   Reagan easily wins reelection by overwhelming divided Democrats.

2. _____   The United States and its allies defeat Iraq in the Persian Gulf War.

3. _____   President Jimmy Carter loses in a landslide to former actor and California governor Ronald Reagan.

4. _____   Reagan's "supply-side" economic programs pass through Congress, cutting taxes and federal spending.

5. _____   George Herbert Walker Bush defeats Michael Dukakis in a "referendum on Reaganism."

6. _____   The Soviet Union dissolves into Russia and other new nations, many plagued by fierce ethnic conflicts

F. Matching Cause and Effect

Match the historical cause in the left column with the proper effect in the right column by writing the correct letter on the blank line.

Cause	**Effect**
1. ___ The intellectual movement called neoconservatism	a. Led to a breakoff of arms-control talks, U.S. economic sanctions against Poland, and growing anxiety in Western Europe
2. ___ Reagan's crusade against big government and social spending	b. Brought about an overwhelming Republican victory in the 1984 presidential election
3. ___ By 1983, Reagan's "supply-side" economic policies	c. Resulted in the failure of the American marines' peacekeeping mission in 1983
4. ___ The revival of the Cold War in the early eighties	d. Helped curb affirmative action and limit the right to abortion
5. ___ Continued political turmoil and war in Lebanon	e. Led to sharp cuts in both taxes and federal social programs in 1981
6. ___ Reagan's hostility to leftist governments in Central America and the Caribbean	f. Strained relations with America's European allies
7. ___ Reagan's personal popularity and Democratic divisions	g. Curbed inflation and spurred economic growth but also caused sky-high deficits and interest rates
8. ___ Reagan's "Star Wars" plan for defensive missile systems in space	h. Prompted Congress to pass the Gramm-Rudman-Hollings Act calling for automatic spending cuts and a balanced budget by 1991
9. ___ The huge federal budget deficits of the 1980s	i. Helped fuel Ronald Reagan's successful presidential campaign in 1980
10. ___ Reagan's and Bush's appointments of conservative justices to the Supreme Court	j. Caused the U.S. invasion of Grenada and the CIA-engineered mining of Nicaraguan harbors
11. ___ The Reagan administration's frustration with hostages and bans on aid to Nicaraguan rebels	k. Led to the overthrow of communist puppet governments in Eastern Europe
12. ___ Dissident movements like that of Solidarity in Poland	l. Brought the killing of many people by tanks and machine guns and a re-assertion of harsh Communist Party rule
13. ___ The widespread student protests in China's Tiananmen Square in 1989	m. Brought a large American army to the Arabian peninsula and naval forces to the Persian Gulf
14. ___ Saddam Hussein's invasion of Kuwait	n. Caused a bitter Senate hearing and a growing "gender gap" between
15. ___ Anita Hill's charges of sexual harassment against Supreme Court nominee Clarence Thomas	

Republicans and Democrats

o.   Led to the Iran-contra affair

G. Developing Historical Skills

Using Chronologies

Properly read, chronologies provide handy tools for understanding not only the sequence of events but also their historical relations.

Examine the Chronology for this chapter (p. 1012), and answer the following questions:

1.   In which year did a number of events indicate deep Soviet-American tension and a revived Cold War?

2.   How many years did it take after the first Reagan-Gorbachev summit to reach agreement on the INF treaty?

3.   List three events *prior* to the Persian Gulf War in 1991 that reflect growing American involvement in the Middle East.

4.   List three events between the imposition of sanctions against Poland (1981) and the dissolution of the Soviet Union (1991) that show the *progress* in easing Cold War tensions.

PART III: APPLYING WHAT YOU HAVE LEARNED

1.   What caused the rise of Reagan and the "new right" in the eighties, and how did their conservative movement re-shape American politics?

2.   What were the goals of Reagan's "supply-side" economic policies, and what were their short-term and long-term effects?

3.   What led to the revival of the Cold War in the early 1980s, and how did Ronald Reagan turn the conflict with the Soviet Union to American advantage?

4.   Describe the major changes affecting American foreign policy from 1980 to 1992 in Central America, the Middle East, and Eastern Europe. Which of these changes occurred as a result of American policy and which occurred primarily as a result of developments within those regions?

5. Some historians have compared the "Reagan revolution" with the New Deal because of the way it seemed to transform radically American economics and politics. Is this a valid comparison? Is it correct to see the "Reagan legacy" as a reversal or overturning of the New Deal and the Great Society of Lyndon Johnson?

6. To what extent were American policies responsible for the overthrow of communism in Eastern Europe and the Soviet Union in 1989-1991?

7. Was the first Persian Gulf War fundamentally based on America's "Wilsonian" foreign policy of promoting democracy, liberty, and self-determination for small nations (in this case, Kuwait), or was it primarily a defense of national self-interest, e.g., in protecting oil supplies and strengthening America's allies in the Middle East? Use evidence from the chapter to support your answer.

CHAPTER 41

America Confronts the Post-Cold War Era, 1992-2004

PART I: REVIEWING THE CHAPTER

A. CHECKLIST OF LEARNING OBJECTIVES

After mastering this chapter, you should be able to

1. explain the Clinton victory in 1992, and describe Clinton's attempt to navigate between traditional liberal Democratic values and his centrist "new Democrat" policies.

2. discuss the causes and consequences of the violence that plagued American society in the 1990s.

3. describe Clinton's economic policies, and the impact of the economic boom of the 1990s on issues of global trade.

4. discuss the Clinton administration's intervention in the Balkans, and its failed efforts to broker a Middle East peace agreement.

5. analyze the fierce partisan warfare between Clinton and the "Gingrich Republicans," and discuss the causes and consequences of Clinton's impeachment and acquittal.

6. describe the disputed 2000 election and its partisan impact on American politics.

7. discuss the impact of the September 11 terrorist attacks on American society and global involvements, including the wars in Afghanistan and Iraq.

8. describe President George W. Bush's domestic and foreign policies, and explain why there were such deep divisions in American politics in the early 2000s.

B. GLOSSARY

To build your social science vocabulary, familiarize yourself with the following terms:

1. **sect** A separatist religious group that claims for itself exclusive knowledge of truth and a superior method of salvation over all other religious organizations. "That showdown ended in the destruction of the sect's compound and the deaths of many Branch Davidians. . . ."

2. **paramilitary** Unauthorized or voluntary groups that employ military organization, methods, and equipment outside the official military system of command and organization. "These episodes brought to light a lurid and secretive underground of paramilitary private 'militias'. . . ."

3. **protectionism (protectionists)** The policy of promoting high tariff taxes on imported goods or services in order that domestic producers can sell at lower prices than foreign manufacturers or service providers. " . . . he reversed his own stand in the 1992 election campaign and bucked the opposition of protectionists in his own party. . . . "

4. **vouchers** Officially granted certificates for benefits of a particular kind, redeemable by a designated agency or service provider. "Bush championed private-sector initiatives, such as school vouchers. . . ."

5.   **junta** From Latin America politics: a small armed group, usually military officers, who seize power and rule as a collective dictatorship. " . . . surely it was better to have the buck stop with the judges, not with a junta."

6.   **autocratic (autocracy)** Relating to authoritarian or repressive government or institutional practices. "There was little evidence that Saddam's downfall might topple other autocratic regimes in the region."

PART II: CHECKING YOUR PROGRESS

A. True-False

Where the statement is true, circle **T**; where it is false, circle **F**.

1.   T   F   Bill Clinton's presentation of himself as a "new" Democrat was designed to emphasize his commitment to reversing past Democratic party positions on civil rights.

2.   T   F   Clinton's ambitious reform goals suffered a severe setback when his health-care proposal failed to pass Congress.

3.   T   F   After victory in the 1994 congressional elections, the militant conservatism of Speaker Newt Gingrich stumbled when it shut down the federal government for a time.

4.   T   F   Clinton's liberal reforms put conservative Republicans on the defensive and led to substantial Democratic gains in the 1994 mid-term Congressional elections.

5.   T   F   The Oklahoma City bombing of 1995 and the Columbine High School shootings of 1999 led to new public demands to toughen gun laws.

6.   T   F   The struggling economy of the 1990s led President Clinton to support increased protectionism and restrictions on the export of American jobs overseas.

7.   T   F   The Clinton administration's major foreign policy success came in laying the groundwork for a peace settlement between Israelis and Palestinians in the Middle East.

8.   T   F   The two charges on which President Clinton was impeached and then acquitted were perjury before a grand jury and obstruction of justice.

9.   T   F   In the 2000 election, George W. Bush defeated Albert Gore in the Electoral College but not in the popular vote.

10. T   F   The Supreme Court's majority ruling that settled the 2000 election controversy was based on the idea that Florida's hand counting of ballots violated the equal protection clause of the Fourteenth Amendment.

11. T   F   Once in office, President George W. Bush pursued strongly conservative policies on abortion, the environment, and taxes.

12. T   F   Osama bin Laden, the mastermind of the September 11 terrorist attacks, was an Afghan Taliban leader who had originally fought the Soviet invasion of his country.

13. T   F   The United Nations in 1993 declined to authorize the use of force against Iraq to compel compliance with its resolutions.

14. T   F   The USA-Patriot Act passed in response to the September 11 authorized the detention and deportation of immigrants suspected of terrorism.

15.   T   F   In the cases of *Gratz* v. *Bollinger* and *Grutter* v. *Bollinger*, the Supreme Court banned numerical affirmative action university admissions policies but permitted more flexible approaches.

B. Multiple Choice

Select the best answer and circle the corresponding letter.

1.   Bill Clinton defeated incumbent President George Bush in 1992 by focusing especially on the issue of
   a.   women's rights and gay rights.
   b.   the environment.
   c.   the economy.
   d.   health care.

2.   In 1992, businessman H. Ross Perot made the strongest showing of any third-party presidential candidate since Theodore Roosevelt by winning approximately _____ of the popular vote.
   a.   five percent
   b.   ten percent
   c.   twenty percent
   d.   forty percent

3.   Two areas where President Clinton's initial attempts at liberal reform failed badly were
   a.   health care and gay rights.
   b.   the environment and consumer protection.
   c.   gun control and deficit reduction.
   d.   affirmative action and education funding.

4.   Two areas where the first Clinton administration achieved the most success in domestic affairs was
   a.   health care and gay rights.
   b.   political campaign reform and term limits.
   c.   gun control and deficit reduction.
   d.   immigration reform and improved race relations.

5.   The assault on the Branch Davidian compound in Waco, Texas, and the bombing of the Oklahoma City federal building were extreme, violent expressions of a growing 1990s atmosphere of
   a.   religious belief in the imminent end of the world.
   b.   disillusionment with government and hostility to politicians.
   c.   hostility to free market capitalism.
   d.   anger toward ethnic minorities and immigrants.

6.   The new Republican congressional majority led by House Speaker Newt Gingrich caused a severe backlash in favor of President Clinton in 1995 when it
   a.   restricted "unfunded mandates" imposed on state and local governments.
   b.   supported the Welfare Reform Act cutting welfare benefits and requiring recipients to seek employment.
   c.   tried to restrict illegal immigration.
   d.   shut down the federal government for a time and proposed sending children on welfare to orphanages.

7.   Despite the great prosperity of the 1990s economy, President Clinton experienced controversy and strong opposition to his policy of
   a.   expanding global free trade and supporting the World Trade Organization.
   b.   reducing the power and benefits of American unions.

    c.   imposing regulations on the highly speculative "dot.com" internet businesses and their stock offerings.

    d.   demanding that China allow full human rights in exchange for greater American trade.

8.   During the Clinton administration, American troops were deployed on military missions in all of the following countries *except*

    a.   Somalia.

    b.   Haiti.

    c.   Rwanda.

    d.   Serbia.

9.   The Democratic minority's fundamental defense of the impeachment charges against President Clinton was that

    a.   Clinton had not committed the acts with which he was charged.

    b.   Clinton's actions were personal failings that did not rise to the constitutional level of "high crimes and misdemeanors."

    c.   Newt Gingrich and other leading Republicans had also engaged in sexual misconduct.

    d.   the nation could not afford to remove an incumbent president during a time of international crisis.

10.   The fundamental issue in the presidential election of 2000 was

    a.   foreign policy toward China, Russia, and Latin America.

    b.   trade policy toward Europe and nations of the Third World.

    c.   whether to use projected budget surpluses for tax cuts or for debt reduction and Medicare.

    d.   whether to build a unilateral American missile defense system.

11.   Victory in the 2000 presidential election was eventually awarded to George W. Bush

    a.   when the Florida legislature awarded that state's electoral votes to Bush.

    b.   when the Supreme Court ruled in Bush's favor that Florida's hand counting of ballots was illegal.

    c.   when Al Gore conceded that it was impossible for him to win.

    d.   when a joint session of Congress declared Bush the winner.

12.   One of George W. Bush's first vigorously conservative and nationalistic actions in office was to repudiate American participation in

    a.   the International Atomic Energy Agency.

    b.   the United Nations World Health Organization.

    c.   the International Criminal Court and the Geneva Conventions on the treatment of prisoners.

    d.   the Kyoto Global Warming Treaty.

13.   The fundamentalist Islamic party that ruled Afghanistan and shielded Osama bin Laden prior to the September 11 attacks was

    a.   the Party of God.

    b.   the Taliban.

    c.   Hamas.

    d.   the Baath Party.

14.   Which of the following was *not* among the reasons offered by President George W. Bush for America's 1993 invasion of Iraq?

    a.   Possible Iraqi involvement in the September 11 attacks

    b.   The need for the U.S. to control Iraqi oil supplies

    c.   Saddam Hussein's possession of weapons of mass destruction

    d.   The idea that the creation of a peaceful, democratic Iraq would inspire hope and reform throughout the Middle East

15. Which of the following was *not* among the controversial Bush administration policies that led to increased polarization between supporters and opponents of the administration?
    a. Attorney General Ashcroft's zealous enforcement of the USA-Patriot Act
    b. Bush's strong anti-abortion policies
    c. The reduction of benefits for Gulf War veterans
    d. Approaches to gay and lesbian rights

C. Identification

Supply the correct identification for each numbered description.

1. _____ "Centrist" Democratic organization that promoted Bill Clinton's candidacy as a "new" Democrat

2. _____ Shorthand phrase for compromise policy that emerged after Clinton's failed attempt to end ban on gays and lesbians in the military

3. _____ Fundamentalist group whose compound in Waco, Texas, was assaulted by federal agents in 1993

4. _____ Colorado high school where a deadly shooting in 1999 stirred a national movement against guns and gun violence

5. _____ Conservative campaign platform that led to a sweeping Republican victory in the 1994 mid-term elections

6. _____ H. Ross Perot's third party that in 1996 received less than half the votes Perot had garnered in 1992

7. _____ International trade organization that prompted strong protests from anti-global trade forces in Seattle, Washington in 1999

8. _____ Caribbean nation where Clinton sent twenty thousand American troops to restore ousted President Jean-Bertrand Aristide to power

9. _____ Clinton Arkansas investment deal that spurred a federal special prosecutor and led to widespread investigations of his administration

10. _____ Third party led by environmentalist Ralph Nader that took votes from Democratic presidential nominee Albert Gore in 2000 election

11. _____ Constitutional institution for choosing presidents that came under severe criticism after the 2000 popular vote winner failed to win the office

12. _____ The other site of direct attack by terrorists on September 11, 2001, besides the twin towers of the World Trade Center

13. _____ The international terrorist network headed by Osama bin Laden

14. _____ Controversial law restricting civil liberties passed in the immediate aftermath of the September 11 attacks

15. _____ Iraqi prison where alleged American abuse of Iraqi prisoners inflamed anti-American sentiment in Iraq and beyond

D. Matching People, Places, and Events

Match the person, place, or event in the left column with the proper description in the right column by inserting the correct letter on the blank line.

1. _____ William J. Clinton

2. _____ H. Ross Perot

3. _____ Hillary Rodham Clinton

4. _____ Robert Dole

5. _____ Newt Gingrich

6. _____ John McCain

7. _____ Slobodan Milosevic

8. _____ Monica Lewinsky

9. _____ William Rehnquist

10. _____ Al Gore

11. _____ George W. Bush

12. _____ Richard Cheney

13. _____ Osama bin Laden

14. _____ Saddam Hussein

15. _____ John Ashcroft

a. Young White House intern whose sexual affair with President Clinton led to his impeachment

b. President Clinton's loyal vice president who won the most popular votes but lost the election of 2000

c. George W. Bush's vice president who vigorously promoted conservative domestic policies and the invasion of Iraq

d. Texas billionaire who won nearly twenty percent of the popular vote as third-party candidate in 1992

e. George W. Bush's controversial attorney general who sharply restricted civil liberties and detained or deported immigrants suspected of terrorism

f. Serbian president who conducted vicious "ethnic cleansing" campaigns and was eventually forced from office

g. Son of a former president whose narrow election as president in 2000 did not prevent him from pursuing a strong conservative agenda in office

h. The first "baby boomer" president who was the first Democrat elected to two full terms since Franklin Roosevelt

i. Long time Iraqi dictator who was overthrown by invading American armies in 2003

j. First presidential spouse to be given major policy responsibilities and to win election to the United States Senate

k. Fiery Republican Speaker of the House who led his party to great victory in 1994 but resigned after Republican losses in 1998

l. Wealthy Saudi Arabian exile who formed a global terrorist network that assaulted the United States

m. Moderate Republican senator who

led the crusade for campaign finance reform but lost 2000 presidential nomination to George W. Bush

n.   1996 Republican presidential nominee who was soundly defeated by Bill Clinton

o.   Chief Justice of the United States who presided at the impeachment trial of President Clinton

E. Putting Things in Order

Put the following events in correct order by numbering them from 1 to 5

1. _____   George W. Bush loses the popular vote but wins the presidency with a majority of the Electoral College

2. _____   Republicans win a majority in the House of Representatives after Newt Gingrich promotes the strongly conservative "Contract with America."

3. _____   Arkansas Governor Bill Clinton defeats incumbent President George H. W. Bush.

4. _____   With authorization from the U.S. Congress but not the United Nations, President George Bush launches a preemptive American invasion of Iraq.

5. _____   Terrorists conduct the first major attack on American soil in two hundred years.

PART III: APPLYING WHAT YOU HAVE LEARNED

1. Was Bill Clinton's election in 1992 a positive mandate for change, or was it primarily a repudiation of the first Bush administration's record on the economy?

2. How did the antigovernment mood of the 1990s affect both Bill Clinton and his Republican opponents? In what ways did Clinton attempt to uphold traditional Democratic themes, and in what ways did he serve to consolidate the conservative Bush-Reagan era?

3. What new foreign policy challenges did the United States face after the end of the Cold War? What were the principal themes of U.S. relations with the world in the Clinton administration?

4. Why was their so much anti-government rhetoric, political action, and even violence in the 1990s? To what extent did the Clinton administration attempt to counter this mood, and to what extent did it bend to it?

5. Argue for or against: the presidential election of 2000, despite its controversies, demonstrated the strength and resiliency of America's democracy.

6. What was the impact of the September 11, 2001, terrorist attacks on America's national priorities and foreign policies? Is it true that "everything changed" after September 11, or were there significant areas in which America's global aims remained essentially the same?

7.   What caused the increased polarization in American politics in the early 2000s? Is it appropriate to align this polarization with the two political parties and their respective strengths in "red states" and "blue states"? Are there significant issues that have not been affected by this political polarization?

CHAPTER 42

The American People Face a New Century

PART I: REVIEWING THE CHAPTER

A. CHECKLIST OF LEARNING OBJECTIVES

After mastering this chapter, you should be able to

1. describe the changing shape of the American economy and work force, and the new social and ethical challenges facing the United States in a global economy dominated by high technology and scientific innovation.

2. explain the impact of the feminist revolution on women's roles and on American society as a whole.

3. analyze the changing structure and character of American families, and explain the social consequences of the "aging of America."

4. describe the impact of the great wave of immigration from Asia and Latin America since the 1970s, and the challenge it posed to the traditional ideals of the "melting pot."

5. describe the difficulties and challenges facing American cities, including the increasing split between central cities and outer suburbs.

6. describe the changing condition of African Americans in American politics and society, including the impact of economic differences within the African American community.

7. discuss the major developments in American thought, culture and the arts since the 1970s.

B. GLOSSARY

To build your social science vocabulary, familiarize yourself with the following terms:

1. **biosphere** The earth's entire network of living plants and organisms, conceived as an inter-connected whole. ". . . the fragile ecological balance of the wondrous biosphere in which human-kind was delicately suspended."

2. **nuclear family** A parent or parents and their immediate offspring. "The nuclear family, once prized as the foundation of society. . . ." (p. 1020)

3. **undocumented** Lacking official certification of status as a legal immigrant or resident alien. ". . . attempted to choke off illegal entry by penalizing employers of undocumented aliens. . . ." (p. 1023)

4. **amnesty** An official governmental act in which some general category of offenders is declared immune from punishment. ". . . by granting amnesty to many of those already here." (p. 1023)

5. **civil trial** A trial before a judge or jury instigated by a private lawsuit in which one party seeks relief, compensation, or damages from another. A **criminal trial** is instigated by an indictment for criminal law violations brought by a state prosecutor on behalf of the government ("the people"); it may result in fines, imprisonment, or execution. "In a later civil trial, another jury found Simpson liable for the 'wrongful deaths' of his former wife and another victim." (p. 1025)

PART II: CHECKING YOUR PROGRESS

A. True-False
Where the statement is true, circle **T**; where it is false, circle **F**.

1. T F   The communications and genetics revolutions in postwar America created new social and moral dilemmas as well as widespread economic growth.

2. T F   After World War II, America's leading research universities concentrated on basic research and scholarship, while scientists in private industry focused on applied research and product development.

3. T F   The gap between America's wealthiest citizens and its poorest continued to grow in the 1990s and early 2000s.

4. T F   By the year 2000, almost all women without children at home were employed, but a majority of mothers with small children remained outside the workplace.

5. T F   One of the greatest issues affecting the character of American families in the 1990s and after was the growing poverty of the nation's elderly.

6. T F   One factor that made Hispanic immigration to the U.S. unique was the close proximity of Mexican Americans to their former homeland across the border.

7. T F   The percentage of foreign-born people in the United States at the end of the 1990s was the highest ever in American history.

8. T F   By the mid-1990s, a majority of Americans lived in suburbs rather than central cities or rural areas.

9. T F   Reactions to the O.J. Simpson case and the controversial 2000 election in Florida demonstrated that both whites and blacks were increasingly able to make political judgments without considering race.

10. T F   African Americans attained considerable success in being elected to both local and national political leadership positions in the late twentieth and early twenty-first centuries.

11. T F   Immigration from Latin America and Asia along with black disillusionment with racial integration created a focus on "multiculturalism" rather than the traditional melting pot.

12. T F   The rise of television and rock music caused a sharp decline in the number of Americans who patronized the "high culture" of museums and symphony orchestras.

13. T F   The tradition of fictional and nonfiction writing about the American West declined sharply in the late twentieth century.

14. T F   The center of the American and international art world after World War II was San Francisco.

15. T F   The greatest challenge to American values posed by the terrorist attacks of September 11, 2001, was how to maintain national security without eroding traditional freedoms and isolating the United States in the world.

B. Multiple Choice
Select the best answer and circle the corresponding letter.

1. The "flagship business" of the heavy industrial economy of the *early* twentieth century was

    a.   the International Business Machines Company.
    b.   the Microsoft Corporation.
    c.   the U.S. Steel Corporation.
    d.   the General Mills Corporation.

2. The primary engine driving the U.S. economy of the early twenty-first century is

    a.   scientific research.
    b.   corporate mergers and acquisitions.
    c.   labor union activism.
    d.   international investment in American companies.

3. The greatest controversy regarding fundamental scientific research in the early 2000s concerned

    a.   stem cell research using human embryos.
    b.   biological research on increasing plant yields.
    c.   artificial computer aids to human intelligence.
    d.   artificial insemination and organ transplants.

4. One of the greatest concerns regarding the continuing success of American science in the early twentieth century was

    a.   that America's research universities were affected by anti-scientific ideologies.
    b.   that American industry no longer sought to take advantage of scientific breakthroughs.
    c.   that women and minorities were still largely unable to pursue scientific careers.
    d.   that the United States was no longer producing scientists or even attracting top scientists from abroad.

5. The most striking development in the American economic structure in the 1990s and 2000s was

    a.   the growing inequality between rich and poor.
    b.   the slow general decline in the American standard of living.
    c.   the growing reliance on investments and real estate rather than jobs for income.
    d.   the increasing concentration of wealth in certain regions and affluent suburbs.

6. Which of the following was *not* among the causes of the income gap in the United States?

    a.   Intensifying global economic competition
    b.   The shrinkage in manufacturing jobs for unskilled and semi-skilled labor
    c.   The decline of labor unions
    d.   The weakening family structure

7. The most dramatic change in the patterns of women's employment from the 1950s to the 2000s was

    a.   the end of "occupational segregation" in certain female job categories.
    b.   that the majority of mothers with young children went to work outside the home.
    c.   that women were unable to break through into traditional single-sex colleges and universities.
    d.   that married women worked at a higher rate than single women.

8. Perhaps the most significant sign of the pressures on the traditional American family in the late twentieth century was

    a.   that television no longer portrayed family situations.
    b.   that a majority of children no longer lived with their birth parents.
    c.   that families were increasingly slow to form at all.
    d.   that the elderly were no longer likely to live with their adult children.

9. The increasingly longer lives of America's senior citizens were often eased by

    a.   the ability of the potent elderly lobby to obtain government benefits for seniors.
    b.   the willingness of younger generations to provide income support for aged parents.
    c.   the large-scale migration of senior citizens to the West Coast.

    d.   the more positive portrayals of the elderly in movies and television.

10.   The deepest problem caused by federal programs like Social Security and Medicare in the twenty-first century was likely to be

    a.   that benefits could not keep up with rising inflation.

    b.   that the Social Security and Medicare trust funds would exercise too great a control over the economy.

    c.   that the higher taxes necessary to support benefits would create a generational war with younger workers.

    d.   that the health care system could no longer meet the rising demand for services to the elderly.

11.   The "new immigrants" of the late twentieth and early twenty-first centuries came to the United States primarily because

    a.   they wanted jobs and economic opportunities unavailable in their homelands.

    b.   they were fleeing religious and political repression.

    c.   they admired American cultural and intellectual achievements.

    d.   they wanted to strengthen the minority voting bloc in the United States.

12.   The largest group of the "new immigrants" came from

    a.   East Asia.

    b.   Mexico and other Latin American countries.

    c.   Africa and the Middle East.

    d.   South Asia.

13.   The period between 1920 and the mid-1990s will likely be seen as a unique but passing age in American demographic history because

    a.   a majority of people lived in the Northeast rather than the South and West.

    b.   a majority of people were of European rather than African American or Hispanic ancestry.

    c.   a majority of people were the children or grandchildren of immigrants.

    d.   a majority of people lived in central cities rather than in rural areas or suburbs.

14.   The primary goals of modern "multiculturalists" was

    a.   to end traditional American national literature and culture.

    b.   to make Spanish an official American language equal to English.

    c.   to preserve and promote rather than crush distinct ethnic and racial cultures in the United States.

    d.   to emphasize the human rights and human values common to all people regardless of nationality.

15.   The most striking development in American literature in the past two decades has been

    a.   the importance of the fantastic literature of absurdism and "black comedy."

    b.   the rise of writers from once-marginal regions and ethnic groups.

    c.   the focus on themes of nostalgia and lost innocence.

    d.   the rise of social realism and attention to working-class stories.

C. Identification

Supply the correct identification for each numbered description.

1. _____   The computer corporation that symbolized the U.S. economy in the 1990s much as U.S. Steel did in 1900

2. _____   Health care program for the elderly, enacted in 1965, that created large economic demands on the American economy by the 1990s

3. _____ Law of 1986 that granted amnesty to past illegal immigrants and penalized employers of future illegal workers

4. _____ The largest of the "new immigrant" groups

5. _____ Organization headed by Cesar Chavez that worked to improve conditions for migrant workers

6. _____ City where major racial disturbance erupted in 1992

7. _____ American region that saw a particularly rich literary revival beginning in the 1980s

8. _____ Tax-funded federal agency created in 1965 that provided support for American art and artists

9. _____ Avant-garde painting movement pioneered by Jackson Pollock and others in the 1940s and 1950s

10. _____ Oil tanker whose 1989 spill off the coast of Alaska sparked deep concern over oil drilling and transportation on the world's oceans

D. Matching People, Places, and Events

Match the person, place, or event in the left column with the proper description in the right column by inserting the correct letter on the blank line.

1. ___ O. J. Simpson
2. ___ L. Douglas Wilder
3. ___ Carol Mosely-Braun
4. ___ Larry McMurtry
5. ___ Norman MacLean
6. ___ August Wilson
7. ___ Toni Morrison
8. ___ N. Scott Momaday
9. ___ David Mamet
10. ___ Eve Ensler
11. ___ Jackson Pollock
12. ___ Frank Gehry

a. Leading Indian writer, author of *House Made of Dawn*

b. Pioneer artistic creator of "abstract expressionism" in the 1940s and 1950s

c. The first African American state governor

d. Leading twenty-first century American architect whose works like the Disney Concert Hall used fanciful metallic forms

e. Feminist playwright whose *Vagina Monologues* blended comedy and sharp social commentary

f. Playwright who deployed gritty American slang in socially critical dramas like *Glengarry Glen Ross*

g. Former football star whose murder trial became a focus of racial tension

h. Author of *Beloved* and winner of the Nobel Prize for Literature

i. Western writer who portrayed small towns in *Last Picture Show* and the cattle-drive era in *Lonesome Dove*

j. First African American woman elected

to the U.S. Senate

k. African American playwright who portrayed the psychological costs of the northern migration

l. Former English professor who wrote memorable tales of his Montana boyhood

E. Putting Things in Order

Put the following events in correct order by numbering them from 1 to 5.

1. _____   F. Douglas Wilder is elected the first African American governor.

2. _____   Congress passes the Immigration Reform and Control Act to try to thwart illegal immigration.

3. _____   Jackson Pollock and others pioneer "abstract expressionism" and the leading form of modern American painting.

4. _____   Los Angeles experiences a major riot as the result of a racial incident involving police brutality.

5. _____   California voters approve Proposition 209 in an attempt to overturn affirmative-action policies.

F. Matching Cause and Effect

Match the historical cause in the left column with the proper effect in the right column by writing the correct letter on the blank line.

Cause	Effect
1. ___ Decline of manufacturing jobs and higher pay for educated workers	a. Made the American southwest increasingly a "bicultural" zone
2. ___ The computer revolution and the new trend toward "genetic engineering"	b. Changed both child-rearing patterns and men's social roles
3. ___ Expanding economic opportunities for women	c. Led to sharp attacks on "Eurocentrism" in American education
4. ___ Rise of the median age of the population since the 1970s	d. Contributed to sharply increased income inequality in the U.S.
5. ___ Growing numbers and political power for Hispanic Americans	e. Made the elderly a powerful political force
6. ___ The growth of the African American middle class and their migration to the suburbs	f. Further isolated the poverty-stricken lower class in the inner cities
7. ___ Poverty and economic upheavals in Latin America and Asia	g. Made New York City the art capital of the world
	h. Created the highest rates of immigration to the United States since

8. ___   The resentment against many affirmative action measures

the early 1900s

i.   Led California voters to pass measures restricting the use of racial categories

9. ___   The reaction against integration and the rise of "multiculturalism"

10. ___   The success of modernist American art movements since the 1940s

j.   Expanded the economy but threatened many traditional jobs while creating new ethical dilemmas for society

PART III: APPLYING WHAT YOU HAVE LEARNED

1.   What were the consequences of the dramatically changed American economy in the 1990s? What caused the rapidly increasing gap between rich and poor in this period?

2.   How did women's new economic opportunities affect American society? What barriers to women's complete economic equality proved most difficult to overcome?

3.   How did the "new immigration" and the rise of ethnic minorities transform American society by the beginning of the twenty-first century? Were the effects of the new immigration similar to that of earlier waves of immigration, or fundamentally different?

4.   How were the changes in American society reflected in literature and the arts in the late twentieth and early twenty-first centuries?

5.   What is the central social and moral challenge America faces in the first half of the twenty-first century? How is the way the nation approaches that challenge shaped by American history, and how does understanding that history contribute to address that challenge in productive ways?

6.   How does the relative "uniqueness" of America's history and culture affect its relationship to such increasingly international issues as economic development, the environment, immigration, and terrorism?

Answer Key to Volume 2 of the Guidebook

CHAPTER 22

II. A.

1. True
2. False. White Southerners strongly rejected Northern political domination.
3. True
4. True
5. True
6. False. Johnson had been a poor white who opposed the planter elite.
7. True
8. False. It weakened the moderates and strengthened the radicals.
9. True
10. False. Redistribution of land was opposed by moderates and never became part of reconstruction policy.
11. False. Blacks controlled only one house of one state legislature—South Carolina.
12. True
13. False. The Klan was organized primarily because of resentment over blacks' growing political power.
14. True
15. False. The moderate plan failed to deal with the deeper economic and social aftermath of slavery.

II. B.

1. c
2. c
3. b
4. b
5. c
6. a
7. a
8. c
9. c
10. b
11. c

12. c
13. a
14. b
15. d

II. C.

1. freedmen
2. Freedmen's Bureau
3. Baptist
4. 10 percent plan
5. Thirteenth Amendment
6. Black Codes
7. Fourteenth Amendment
8. moderates
9. radicals
10. Union League
11. *Ex parte Milligan*
12. scalawags
13. carpetbaggers
14. Fifteenth Amendment
15. Alaska

II. D.

1. H
2. K
3. C
4. M
5. B
6. J
7. O
8. I
9. F
10. G
11. E
12. A
13. L

14. N

15. D

II. E.

4

1

5

3

2

II. F.

1. D

2. E

3. J

4. C

5. I

6. F

7. H

8. B

9. A

10. G

II. G.

1. Eight whites, three blacks; the white woman seated in the center; they are in the rear and partly hidden, suggesting that they might hold subordinate positions on the staff.

2. The shabby clothes of the boy and young woman; the crude log cabin dwelling. The people seem weary but hopeful: at least three of them have partial smiles.

3. The men in the line appear to be working people—perhaps farmers in their best clothes. The voting officials, black and white, appear more affluent and well-dressed. The drawing shows the new voters as somewhat hesitant and uncertain, perhaps being manipulated by the more politically knowledgeable officials.

CHAPTER 23

II. A.

1. False. Grant's lack of political experience hurt, and he did engage in Republican party politics.

2. True

3. False. The political mistakes of the Liberal Republicans caused them to fail.

4. True

5. False. The parties agreed on national issues; their disagreements were at the local level.

6. True

7. False. The Republicans got the presidency and the Democrats other political and economic concessions.

8. True

9. True

10. True

11. True

12. False. The campaign was based on personal mudslinging rather than issues.

13. True

14. True

15. False. The gold deal made Cleveland extremely unpopular among Democrats and Populists.

II. B.

1. c
2. c
3. b
4. b
5. a
6. d
7. c
8. a
9. a
10. b
11. d
12. b
13. b
14. a
15. d

II. C.

1. (waving the) bloody shirt
2. Credit Mobilier
3. Liberal Republican party
4. silver
5. Greenback Labor party

6. Gilded Age

7. Grand Army of the Republic

8. Stalwarts

9. Half-Breeds

10. Compromise of 1877

11. Chinese

12. civil service

13. McKinley Tariff

14. Populists (People's Party)

15. grandfather clause

II. D.

1. D

2. B

3. A

4. N

5. J

6. H

7. I

8. K

9. O

10. C

11. G

12. E

13. L

14. F

15. M

II. E.

4

1

5

3

2

II. F.

1. G

2. E

3. C

4. I

5. A

6. J

7. B

8. F

9. D

10. H

II. G.

1. The fundamental difference was in their ethnic and religious composition. The Republicans were based on morally-oriented groups with Puritan backgrounds; the Democrats on immigrant ethnic groups of Catholic or Lutheran background.

2. Most of the controversial issues existed at the state or local level.

3. The two parties each had well-mobilized machines that got out the vote no matter who the candidates were.

4. Winning elections was crucial for patronage—passing out jobs to party supporters.

II. H.

1. none

2. Connecticut, New Jersey, New York, and Indiana

3. four

4. Texas

5. none

CHAPTER 24

II. A.

1. False. The railroads received subsidies and land grants to build the rail lines.

2. True

3. True

4. False. Railroads were often unfair and corrupt in their dealings with shippers, the government, and the public.

5. True

6. False. The description applies to Carnegie's technique of "vertical integration." Rockefeller's "horizontal integration" meant consolidating with competitors in the same market.

7. True

8. True

9. False. The South remained poor and dependent, despite the "new South."

10. True

11. False. Industrialization gave the wage earner less control and status.

12. True

13. True

14. True

15. False. The AFL did not even attempt to organize these categories of workers.

II. B.

1. b

2. d

3. b

4. d

5. c

6. c

7. c

8. d

9. d

10. b

11. b

12. d

13. a

14. c

15. b

II. C.

1. land grants

2. Union Pacific Railroad

3. Central Pacific Railroad

4. Great Northern Railroad

5. stock watering

6. *Wabash* case

7. Interstate Commerce Commission

8. telephone

9. Standard Oil Company

10. United States Steel Corporation

11. New South
12. Colored National Labor Union
13. Knights of Labor
14. craft unions
15. American Federation of Labor (or AF of L)

II. D.

1. J
2. H
3. M
4. G
5. F
6. O
7. A
8. I
9. E
10. B
11. D
12. L
13. N
14. C
15. K

II. E.

5
4
3
2
1

II. F.

1. I
2. D
3. E
4. H
5. A
6. B

7. J

8. F

9. G

10. C

II. G.

1. The family of "pieceworkers" are in their own home; each concentrates on their own single tasks, but they are able to relate to one another and perhaps offer advice and assistance around the table. The black textile workers are at separate posts, but the women and children can also probably converse and assist one another. In both these two cases the children and adult workers are mingled and performing the same tasks. By contrast, the adult male Westinghouse workers are dwarfed by their industrial machinery and serve its demands. In the final photo, the child textile workers are by themselves and almost encased by the machines. They are evidently without adult assistance or supervision, and plainly in danger of industrial accident.

2. The scene takes place in front of the owner's house. The men have evidently come directly from the factory. There appears to have been some conflict over wages or working conditions.

3. The owner and the woman—evidently his wife—are very well dressed. The workers, and worker's family on the left, are shabbily dressed. The painting illustrates the considerable class difference between the owner and his immigrant work force.

4. The workers are conversing with the owner and his wife, and also with one another. The first conversation is probably about the grievance. The second may be about what the workers should do next—whether to strike or resort to violence (as the one worker seems about to do).

5. The presence of women and children points out that factory conditions affected families as well as employees. The woman at the center is probably the owner's wife. Her fine dress and vigorous manner is contrasted with the poverty and passive condition of the worker's wife.

CHAPTER 25

II. A.

1. True

2. False. They came from southern and eastern Europe.

3. False. Most were originally peasants driven from the countryside.

4. True

5. True

6. True

7. False. Many Protestant and Catholic religious thinkers attempted to reconcile Darwinian evolution and Christianity.

8. False. Secondary education was increasingly carried out in public schools.

9. False. Washington advocated economic equality but not social equality.

10. True

11. True

12. False. They favored social realism in their fiction.

13. True

14. True

15. True

II. B.

1. c

2. c

3. c

4. c

5. a

6. b

7. d

8. d

9. c

10. b

11. d

12. b

13. a

14. a

15. d

II. C.

1. dumbbell tenement

2. New Immigration

3. birds of passage

4. social gospel

5. Hull House

6. social work

7. American Protective Association

8. Roman Catholicism

9. Tuskegee Institute

10. National Association for the Advancement of Colored People (or NAACP) (Niagara Movement less preferable but OK)

11. *Progress and Poverty*

12. Comstock Law

13. *Women and Economics*
14. National American Women's Suffrage Association (or NAWSA)
15. Women's Christian Temperance Union (or WCTU)

II. D.
1. M
2. E
3. J
4. N
5. D
6. F
7. L
8. G
9. A
10. O
11. B
12. H
13. K
14. I
15. C

II. E.
4
2
3
5
1

II. F.
1. G
2. B
3. E
4. I
5. H
6. C
7. F
8. A

9. J

10. D

II. G.

1. five peaks: end of Civil War, anti-Jewish pogroms, early twentieth-century prosperity, the end of World War I, and the end of World War II and the quota system

    four valleys: Panic of 1873, Panic of 1893, World War I, and the introduction of quotas

2. Each major period lasted 15–20 years. The most recent growth period has lasted for 40 years.

3. sharpest rise: 1900–1905; sharpest decline: 1915–1920

4. 800,000: approximately 1882, 1910, 1923

    200,000: about 1867, 1875, 1880, 1898–99, 1917, 1932, 1948–49

5. about a million fewer (1.2 million to 200,000)

    about 350,000 to 400,000 more (about 225,000 to 600,000)

CHAPTER 26

II. A.

1. True

2. False. The Indians were defeated only slowly and with difficulty.

3. True

4. False. Humanitarian reformers did not respect the Indians' culture and tried to destroy their tribal way of life.

5. True

6. True

7. False. More families acquired land from the states and private owners than from the federal government under the Homestead Act.

8. True

9. True

10. False. Their greatest problem was that they produced too much grain, causing prices to fall.

11. True

12. True

13. False. Hanna had no difficulty raising large sums of money for McKinley's campaign.

14. True

15. True

II. B.

1. d

2. c

3. a

4. c

5. b

6. b

7. d

8. c

9. c

10. b

11. d

12. b

13. a

14. a

15. b

II. C.

1. Sioux

2. Apaches

3. reservations

4. Ghost Dance

5. Dawes Severalty Act

6. Comstock Lode

7. long drive

8. Homestead Act

9. barbed wire

10. Oklahoma

11. Populists (People's Party)

12. Coin's Financial School

13. Pullman strike

14. Cross of Gold speech

15. "goldbugs"

II. D.

1. H

2. J

3. E

4. B

5.   G

6.   I

7.   F

8.   C

9.   K

10.   D

11.   L

12.   A

II. E.

3

5

2

1

4

II. F.

1.   J

2.   E

3.   I

4.   D

5.   H

6.   C

7.   G

8.   B

9.   A

10.   F

II. G.

1.   All six (Kansas, Nebraska, Colorado, Wyoming, Nevada, Idaho) were carried by Bryan.

2.   Any six of the following: New Jersey, Delaware, Maryland, Pennsylvania, West Virginia, Kentucky, Ohio, Indiana, Illinois, Wisconsin, California. Most were in the Midwest or Middle Atlantic region.

3.   Republican: any five of the following: Maine, Vermont, New Hampshire, Connecticut, New York, Michigan, Iowa, Minnesota, South Dakota, North Dakota, Washington.

Democratic: any five of the southern states, plus Missouri.

4.   Three went Republican (North Dakota, South Dakota, and Oregon); six went Democratic (Nebraska, Kansas, Colorado, Idaho, Wyoming, Nevada).

II. H.

1. Montana, Washington, and California

2. Texas, North Carolina, Oklahoma, and Georgia

3. Thirty-seven

4. none

CHAPTER 27

II. A.

1. False. America was unconcerned and isolated from international affairs in those decades..

2. False. It nearly resulted in a war with Britain.

3. True.

4. True.

5. True

6. False. The invasion was inefficient, but America suffered few battlefield casualties.

7. True.

8. False. The peace treaty was very controversial.

9. False. It ruled that the constitution and bill of rights did not apply to American colonies.

10. True

11. False. Foreign nations continued to intervene in China.

12. False. Roosevelt believed that the United States should pursue an assertive foreign policy.

13. True.

14. True.

15. True

II. B.

1. b

2. c

3. a

4. a

5. c

6. b

7. b

8. a

9. b

10. a

11. c
12. c
13. c
14. b
15. c

II. C.

1. Samoa (Samoan Islands)
2. Chile
3. Monroe Doctrine
4. yellow journalism or yellow press
5. *Maine*
6. Manila Bay
7. Rough Riders
8. Puerto Rico
9. insular cases
10. Open Door notes
11. Boxer Rebellion
12. Hay-Pauncefote-Treaty
13. Colombia
14. Roosevelt Corollary (to the Monroe Doctrine)
15. Gentlemen's Agreement

II. D.

1. J
2. F
3. K
4. D
5. N
6. C
7. H
8. L
9. G
10. A
11. O
12. E

13.   B

14.   M

15.   I

II. E.

1

3

2

4

5

II. F.

1.   F

2.   C

3.   E

4.   G

5.   B

6.   D

7.   A

8.   I

9.   J

10.   H

II. G.

1.   Great Britain

2.   (a) Pago Pago Harbor; (b) Pearl Harbor

3.   Luzon

4.   San Juan Hill

5.   Puerto Rico

CHAPTER 28

II. A.

1.   False. Progressives favored the growth of government power over the economy and society.

2.   True

3.   False. The progressives arose mostly from the middle class.

4.   True

5.   False. He threatened the owners with federal intervention, saying he would seize their mines.

6. True

7. False. He believed that there were "good trusts" and "bad trusts," and that only the bad trusts should be broken up.

8. False. It was intended to focus attention on the plight of the meat-packing workers.

9. True

10. True

11. True

12. FalseTaft was an unskilled politician and campaigner.

13. False. Progressives grew angry over his tariff and conservation policies

14. True

15. True

II. B.

1. c

2. a

3. c

4. c

5. d

6. b

7. a

8. c

9. b

10. a

11. d

12. a

13. a

14. c

15. c

II. C.

1. progressivism

2. muckrakers

3. initiative

4. recall

5. Square Deal

6. Hepburn Act

7.   Triangle Shirtwaist Fire

8.   *The Jungle*

9.   Women's Christian Temperance Union

10. Roosevelt panic (Panic of 1907)

11. dollar diplomacy

12. Standard Oil Company

II. D.

1.   E

2.   I

3.   F

4.   K

5.   D

6.   C

7.   H

8.   J

9.   B

10. A

11. L

12. G

II. E.

5

1

4

2

3

II. F.

1.   I

2.   B

3.   G

4.   C

5.   J

6.   D

7.   A

8.   F

9.   H
10. E

II. G.

1.   D
2.   B
3.   A
4.   B
5.   A
6.   C
7.   C
8.   A
9.   B
10. B
11. D
12. B

CHAPTER 29

II. A.

1.   True
2.   False. Wilson's "New Freedom" favored small enterprise and antitrust activities; Roosevelt's "New Nationalism" favored federal regulation and social activism.
3.   True
4.   True
5.   False. Wilson's policies were unfavorable to blacks.
6.   True
7.   False. Wilson sent troops to Haiti and Santo Domingo.
8.   True
9.   True
10. False. It was sent in response to Villa's raids into New Mexico and the killing of United States citizens.
11. False. Most Americans sympathized with Britain from the beginning.
12. True
13. False. The East was ready to go to war; the Midwest and West favored attempts at negotiation.
14. True
15. True

II. B.

1. c
2. b
3. c
4. b
5. d
6. a
7. b
8. c
9. b
10. a
11. c
12. d
13. c
14. d
15. d

II. C.

1. bull moose
2. Socialist Party
3. New Freedom
4. Federal Reserve Board
5. Federal Trade Commission
6. Clayton Anti-Trust Act
7. Railway Labor Act
8. Haiti
9. ABC Powers
10. Central Powers
11. Allies
12. submarine
13. *Lusitania*
14. *Sussex* pledge
15. California

II. D.

1. H

2. K
3. L
4. I
5. D
6. O
7. M
8. C
9. B
10. G
11. F
12. A
13. N
14. J
15. E

II. E.

5
2
1
4
3

II. F.

1. D
2. B
3. I
4. E
5. J
6. G
7. H
8. A
9. F
10. C

II. G.

1. German policy was that they would not *try* to sink neutral shipping, but they warned that mistakes might occur.

2.   America was an important neutral, and Germany had no reason to want American civilians to be killed. The warning could be used to take the burden of responsibility off Germany and put it on those passengers who chose to travel anyway.

3.   Germany knew that the *Lusitania* was in fact carrying 4200 cases of ammunition.

4.   America claimed a complete right of neutral and unarmed civilian travel on the high seas. Issuing a warning did nothing to affect that.

CHAPTER 30

II. A.

1.   False. Germany responded by resuming unrestricted submarine warfare.

2.   True

3.   True

4.   True

5.   False. The primary targets were antiwar Socialists and members of the Industrial Workers of the World (IWWs).

6.   True

7.   True

8.   True

9.   False. It signaled political suffrage but not economic advance.

10.   True

11.   True

12.   False. His poor handling of the Republican opposition weakened his hand in Paris.

13.   True

14.   True

15.   False. Cox supported the League, while Harding tried to evade the issue.

II. B.

1.   b

2.   c

3.   c

4.   b

5.   d

6.   a

7.   a

8.   b

9.   a

10.   b

11. c

12. a

13. b

14. d

15. b

II. C.

1. "peace without victory"

2. Zimmerman note

3. Fourteen Points

4. Committee on Public Information (CPI)

5. Industrial Workers of the World (IWWs)

6. War Industries Board

7. Nineteenth Amendment (Women's Suffrage Amendment OK)

8. Liberty Loans

9. Big Four

10. League of Nations

11. Treaty of Versailles

12. Foreign Relations Committee

13. irreconcilables

14. Lodge reservations

15. "solemn referendum"

II. D.

1. E

2. O

3. N

4. H

5. K

6. I

7. C

8. G

9. A

10. M

11. D

12. B

II. C.

1. red scare
2. Ku Klux Klan
3. Immigration Act of 1924
4. Eighteenth Amendment (Prohibition or Prohibition Amendment OK)
5. Bible Belt
6. Scopes trial ("monkey trial")
7. advertising (credit or installment buying OK)
8. Model T
9. airplane
10. radio
11. birth control
12. jazz
13. Universal Negro Improvement Association (UNIA)
14. *American Mercury*
15. stock market

II. D.

1. E
2. C
3. G
4. L
5. H
6. D
7. J
8. A
9. M
10. O
11. K
12. F
13. N
14. B
15. I

II. E.

4

1

5

2

3

II. F.

1. C

2. A

3. J

4. E

5. F

6. I

7. B

8. H

9. D

10. G

II. G.

1. Hollywood's movies, like Henry Ford's cars, were mass-produced consumer products created by industry.

2. New products helped free women from the home and from their traditional roles.

3. Fitzgerald's novel idealized the moral and sexual liberation of youth from the past, and suggested that personal freedom and pleasure were goals of the new affluent American society.

4. These writers all endorsed new moral and social values at odds with those of the American past. Before the 1920s most Americans lived on farms or in small towns, and such values were widely shared. Now there was an audience ready to hear what such writers were saying.

CHAPTER 32

II. A.

1. False. The corrupt cabinet officers were the secretary of the interior and the attorney general (Fall and Doherty).

2. False. The antitrust laws were generally not enforced.

3. False. They pursued disarmament policies and reduced military spending.

4. True

5. True

6. True

7. False. The main source of La Follette's support was farmers.

8. True

9. True

10. True

11. False. The Hawley-Smoot Tariff represented a policy of economic isolationism and helped undercut international trade.

12. True

13. True

14. False. He modified his policies somewhat and provided some federal funds for relief and recovery.

15. True

II. B.

1. d
2. a
3. b
4. c
5. c
6. d
7. b
8. b
9. b
10. a
11. a
12. d
13. a
14. c
15. c

II. C.

1. Ohio Gang
2. *Adkins* v. *Children's Hospital*
3. American Legion
4. Five-Power Naval Treaty
5. Kellogg-Briand Pact
6. Teapot Dome
7. McNary-Haugen Bill
8. Dawes plan
9. Hoovercrats

10.   Hawley-Smoot Tariff
11.   Black Tuesday
12.   Hoovervilles
13.   Reconstruction Finance Corporation
14.   Bonus Army (Bonus Expeditionary Force)
15.   Manchuria

II. D.

1.   I
2.   G
3.   H
4.   M
5.   E
6.   D
7.   F
8.   O
9.   L
10.   K
11.   C
12.   A
13.   B
14.   N
15.   J

II. E.

5
2
1
4
3

II. F.

1.   B
2.   E
3.   I
4.   F
5.   D

6. J

7. A

8. C

9. G

10. H

II. G.

1. Americans were private investors in Germany. America also collected allied war debts from France and Britain.

2. France and Britain collected war reparations from Germany.

3. Britain and France both owed war debts to the U.S.

4. Credit from U.S. bankers was the only thing that enabled the whole international financial system to function. When Wall Street collapsed in 1929, Europe and the whole financial system collapsed with it.

CHAPTER 33

II. A.

1. True

2. False. The economy was turning downward.

3. True

4. False. FDR took the United States off the gold standard and devalued the dollar.

5. False. They were designed for relief.

6. True

7. False. It was excessive farm production, causing falling prices.

8. True

9. False. It was also designed to provide jobs, electricity, and low-income housing to residents of the area.

10. True

11. True

12. False. The Supreme Court "switched" and began approving New Deal measures.

13. True

14. True

15. False. Unemployment remained high despite the New Deal.

II. B.

1. c

2. a

3. b

4. b

5. d

6. a

7. d

8. c

9. b

10. a

11. d

12. b

13. d

14. a

15. c

II. C.

1. New Deal

2. brain(s) trust

3. Hundred Days

4. Civilian Conservation Corps

5. Works Progress Administration (WPA)

6. blue eagle

7. Agricultural Adjustment Administration (AAA)

8. Dust Bowl

9. Tennessee Valley Authority (TVA)

10. Social Security

11. Committee for Industrial Organization (CIO) (Congress of Industrial Organizations OK)

12. Securities and Exchange Commission (SEC)

13. American Liberty League

14. court packing plan

15. Hatch Act

II. D.

1. G

2. E

3. L

4. J

5.   B

6.   F

7.   N

8.   K

9.   C

10. O

11. H

12. A

13. I

14. M

15. D

II. E.

2

1

4

5

3

II. F.

1.   E

2.   I

3.   G

4.   A

5.   F

6.   B

7.   J

8.   H

9.   C

10. D

II. G.

1.   National Recovery Administration (NRA)

2.   FDR closes banks, Emergency Banking Relief Act.

   FDR orders gold surrender and abandons gold standard.

   Gold-payment clause repealed. (any three)

3.   Securities Exchange Commission, Social Security Act, Public Utilities Holding Company Act

4.   National Housing Act creating the FHA.

5.   Second Agricultural Adjustment Act

6.   The Hundred Days was aimed primarily at recovery, the later New Deal at relief and reform. The most continuity was seen in measures aimed at relief.

II. H.

1.   Tennessee, Alabama, North Carolina, Virginia

2.
   a.   five
   b.   three

3.   1920

4.   8 million

CHAPTER 34

II. A.

1.   False. It showed that he put domestic recovery ahead of establishing a stable international economic order.

2.   True

3.   True

4.   True

5.   False. The United States adhered to its neutrality laws and refused to help the Loyalist government.

6.   False. There was a strong isolationist reaction

    to both Roosevelt's speech and the *Panay* incident.

7.   False. The United States did not object to the appeasement policy, and in effect endorsed it.

8.   True

9.   False. It strengthened the movement to give aid to Britain.

10.   True

11.   False. Willkie agreed with Roosevelt's pro-British stance and did not attack him on foreign policy.

12.   True

13.   False. It was an agreement between Britain and the United States only.

14.   True

15.   False. The point of conflict was Japan's refusal to withdraw from China.

II. B.

1.   a

2. c
3. b
4. d
5. b
6. d
7. c
8. d
9. a
10. b
11. d
12. b
13. a
14. c
15. c

II. C.

1. London Conference
2. Philippines
3. Good Neighbor policy
4. Neutrality Acts
5. Spanish Civil War
6. Quarantine Speech
7. Munich
8. appeasement
9. Committee to Defend America by Aiding the Allies
10. America First
11. lend-lease
12. Soviet Union
13. Atlantic Charter
14. *Reuben James*
15. Pearl Harbor

II. D.

1. L
2. E
3. K

4.   F
5.   O
6.   C
7.   J
8.   N
9.   G
10.   B
11.   D
12.   A
13.   M
14.   I
15.   H

II. E.

1
2
5
4
3

II. F.

1.   G
2.   C
3.   I
4.   H
5.   B
6.   F
7.   D
8.   J
9.   E
10.   A

II. G.

Order	Context
4	4
6	7
1	2

2	3
7	1
5	5
3	6

II. H

1. 41

2. 41

3. Europe

4. Soviet Union

CHAPTER 35

II. A.

1. False. The decision was to fight Hitler first and then Japan.

2. False. Americans nearly all supported World War II.

3. True

4. True

5. True

6. False. Most women left the labor force after the war.

7. False. Americans enjoyed economic prosperity during World War II.

8. False. The battles of the Coral Sea and Midway enabled the United States to block Japanese domination of the Pacific sea-lanes.

9. False. The plan was to "island-hop" directly toward Japan.

10. False. The Soviet Union bore the heaviest burden of the ground fighting.

11. True

12. True

13. False. It was conservative Democrats who dumped Wallace for Truman.

14. False. He died a few weeks before Germany surrendered, but four months before Japan's surrender.

15. True

II. B.

1. c

2. b

3. a

4. c

5. a

6. a

7. d
8. c
9. d
10. d
11. c
12. b
13. b
14. d
15. a

II. C.

1. Japanese Americans
2. War Production Board
3. WAACS and WAVES
4. *braceros*
5. "Rosie the Riveter"
6. Fair Employment Practices Commission (FEPC)
7. Philippines
8. Battle of Midway
9. Unconditional Surrender
10. Casablanca
11. Teheran
12. D-Day
13. Battle of the Bulge
14. Iwo Jima and Okinawa
15. atomic bomb

II. D.

1. F
2. I
3. N
4. E
5. O
6. G
7. J
8. A

9. K
10. D
11. M
12. C
13. H
14. L
15. B

II. E.

3

4

1

2

II. F.

1. I
2. H
3. C
4. E
5. G
6. B
7. D
8. A
9. F
10. J

II. G.

1.

  a.   Russians: Leningrad and Stalingrad

  b.   Americans and British: Tunisia, North Africa

2. driving the Germans out of Russia

3. in Poland

4. about ten months (July 1944 to May 1945)

5. southern Germany (Austria). The British and Americans were coming from Italy and France, the Russians from Hungary.

II. H.

1. 116,000

2. 7

3. Detroit and New York

4. India and Australia

5. Tunisia

6. Poland, Hungary, and Romania

7. France, Netherlands, and Belgium

8. Elbe

CHAPTER 36

II. A.

1. False. The economy struggled from 1945 to 1950, and only began to grow dramatically after 1950.

2. True

3. False. Unions declined by the 1950s.

4. False. The Sunbelt relied more than the North on federal spending.

5. True

6. True

7. False. Truman had little experience or confidence.

8. False. The United Nations was not dramatically more effective than the League of Nations, and it did give a veto to the Great Powers.

9. False. The reverse is true; the Western Allies wanted a united Germany, while the Soviets endorsed a separate East Germany.

10. False. The threat was to Greece and Turkey.

11. False. It was developed in response to the economic weakness and threat of domestic communism in Western Europe.

12. False. The fundamental purpose of NATO was to defend Europe against the Soviets.

13. True

14. False. Truman defeated Dewey despite splits in his own Democratic party.

15. True

II. B.

1. a

2. d

3. b

4. d

5. d

6. a

7. c
8. b
9. b
10. d
11. a
12. c
13. a
14. d
15. c

II. C.

1. GI Bill of Rights
2. Sunbelt
3. Levittown
4. baby boom
5. Yalta
6. Cold War
7. Bretton Woods
8. United Nations
9. iron curtain
10. Marshall Plan
11. North Atlantic Treaty Organization (NATO)
12. Nationalists
13. NSC-68
14. House Un-American Activities Committee
15. 38th parallel

II. D.

1. B
2. A
3. K
4. M
5. D
6. O
7. L
8. E

9.   J

10.   H

11.   C

12.   I

13.   G

14.   N

15.   F

II. E.

2

4

1

3

5

II. F.

1.   A

2.   E

3.   B

4.   H

5.   J

6.   G

7.   C

8.   D

9.   I

10.   F

II. G.

1.   1970

2.   1980

   1980–1990

3.

1950–1960:	+20%
1970–1980:	–20%
1980–1990:	+5%
1990–1999:	–10%

II. H.

1. France
2. British
3. Austria and Czechoslovakia
4. below
5. U.S.S.R.
6. South Korea

CHAPTER 37

II. A.

1. False. The book was aimed primarily at explaining suburban women's discontent with their lives.
2. True
3. True
4. False. It held that segregation was inherently unequal and that the schools had to be integrated.5. False. King made the African American churches the basis of his movement.
6. False. The reverse is true: they relied more on nuclear weapons than on conventional forces.
7. False. The United States opposed the British-French invasion of Suez.
8. True
9. FalseThe summit was never held, and its collapse deepened Cold War tensions.
10. True
11. True
12. True
13. True
14. False. Most of the World War II novels were not realistic but "absurdist" in tone.
15. True

II. B.

1. b
2. b
3. c
4. b
5. a
6. d
7. d
8. c
9. a

10. b
11. d
12. a
13. b
14. c
15. c

II. C.

1. McCarthyism
2. *Brown* v. *Board of Education*
3. massive retaliation
4. SEATO or Southeast Asia Treaty Organization
5. Suez Canal
6. *Sputnik*
7. International Business Machines (IBM)
8. U-2
9. Cuba
10. *The Feminine Mystique*

II. D.

1. G
2. K
3. O
4. F
5. L
6. B
7. M
8. A
9. H
10. N
11. D
12. J
13. C
14. E
15. I

II. E.

3

5

1

4

2

II. F.

1. F

2. A

3. G

4. E

5. C

6. J

7. B

8. H

9. D

10. I

II. G.

1. Missouri

2. Virginia, Florida, Tennessee

3. Texas and Louisiana

4. ten: Nevada: 3, Hawaii: 3, New Mexico: 4

5. 60

CHAPTER 38

II. A.

1. True

2. False. It was applied mostly to struggles with communism in the underdeveloped world—Asia and Latin America.

3. False. The coup brought military dictatorships and political instability.

4. True

5. True

6. False. It was the civil rights movement that encouraged Kennedy to become more outspoken.

7. False. Johnson won in every part of the country except the traditionally Democratic Deep South.

8. False. The Gulf of Tonkin Resolution gave the president a blank check for the whole war in Vietnam.

9. False. The Great Society authorized deficit spending and gave more power to the federal government.

10. True

11. False. Most of the riots were in the North, which showed that race was a national and not just a southern problem.

12. True

13. True

14. False. The Catholic Church also underwent major change and upheaval.

15. True

II. B.

1. c
2. c
3. a
4. b
5. c
6. a
7. c
8. b
9. d
10. a
11. c
12. d
13. b
14. b
15. d

II. C.

1. Peace Corps
2. Berlin Wall
3. Special Forces or Green Berets
4. Alliance for Progress
5. Bay of Pigs
6. Cuban missile crisis
7. sit-in

8. Great Society
9. Gulf of Tonkin Resolution
10. Voting Rights Act of 1965
11. Black Power
12. Tet
13. Free Speech Movement
14. Students for a Democratic Society (SDS)
15. Stonewall Inn raid

II. D.
1. J
2. B
3. L
4. H
5. O
6. N
7. A
8. E
9. G
10. F
11. C
12. D
13. K
14. I
15. M

II. E.
3
1
2
4
5

II. F.
1. C
2. H
3. E

4. G

5. D

6. I

7. B

8. J

9. A

10. F

II. G.

1. 1974 (1973 or 1975 are acceptable answers)

2. 1973, 1978

3. From about 1974 to 1976. The difference would be explained by a rise in the total U.S. population.

4. 1980

II. H.

1. Laos and Cambodia

2. five

3. Vermont, New Hampshire, New Jersey, and Delaware

4. Michigan, Minnesota, Washington, Texas, and Hawaii

CHAPTER 39

II. A.

1. False. It sought to transfer the burden of the war to the South Vietnamese while Americans withdrew.

2. True

3. True

4. True

5. False. He supported new social security and environmental laws.

6. False. The basic issue was Vietnam.

7. True

8. True

9. False. It led to the War Powers Act, which put congressional restraints on presidential authority to take military action.

10. True

11. False. Conservative Republicans joined in calling for Nixon's resignation.

12. False. Ford continued to pursue Nixon's policies of détente.

13. True

14. False. The public largely ignored Carter's call for energy sacrifices and for decreased dependence on foreign oil.

15. True

II. B.

1. d

2. a

3. c

4. d

5. a

6. c

7. b

8. c

9. c

10. b

11. b

12. d

13. d

14. c

15. d

II. C.

1. Vietnamization

2. Kent State

3. Pentagon Papers

4. ABM (Anti–Ballistic Missile) Treaty

5. southern strategy

6. Philadelphia Plan

7. Watergate

8. War Powers Act

9. oil embargo

10. detente

11. Helsinki accords

12. Equal Rights Amendment (ERA)

13. *Roe* v. *Wade*

14. Alcatraz (Island) and Wounded Knee (South Dakota)
15. Title IX

II. D.
1. L
2. D
3. H
4. K
5. E
6. C
7. I
8. N
9. B
10. M
11. J
12. F
13. G
14. O
15. A

II. E.
6
4
2
1
3
5

II. F.
1. C
2. G
3. H
4. D
5. F
6. A
7. J
8. I

9. B

10. E

II. G.

1. Nixon's diplomacy involved a delicate and dangerous effort to deal with both the communist powers. His balance bar is a head of wheat—showing his use of American grain sales as a key to his diplomatic effort.

2. Nixon's career as a tough "law and order" anti-crime politician is satirized. The attempt to "cover up" the Watergate crimes is not very successful, since the burglar's tools and tapes are plainly visible.

3. The cartoon suggests that Nixon was really behind the "Ford mask." Both cartoons portray Nixon as deceptive.

4. Nixon is portrayed as only one of the long line of presidents involved in Vietnam.

CHAPTER 40

II. A.

1. True

2. False. Reagan's victory brought many other Republicans into office.

3. False. Reagan kept his conservative promises.

4. False. Reagan's supply-side economic policies did not bog down, and actually broke the stalemate in Congress.

5. False. The reverse is true: Reaganomics lowered inflation and created economic growth but raised interest rates and caused budget deficits.

6. True

7. True

8. True

9. True

10. True

11. True.

12. False. The minor restraints on *Roe* v. *Wade* only heightened the political conflict over abortion.

13. False. The rebellions in Eastern Europe were almost entirely home grown.

14. True.

15. True

II. B.

1. a

2. b

3. a

4.   c
5.   c
6.   b
7.   a
8.   d
9.   a
10. b
11. a
12. a
13. b
14. c
15. b

II. C.

1.   Proposition 13
2.   supply-side economics
3.   yuppies
4.   boll weevils
5.   Solidarity
6.   Sandinistas
7.   Star Wars
8.   Berlin Wall
9.   Operation Desert Storm

II. D.

1.   G
2.   K
3.   O
4.   N
5.   F
6.   C
7.   L
8.   H
9.   E
10. B
11. D

12. I
13. A
14. J
15. M

II. E.

3

6

1

2

4

5

II. F.

1. I
2. E
3. G
4. A
5. C
6. J
7. B
8. F
9. H
10. D
11. O
12. K
13. L
14. M
15. N

II. G.

1. 1983
2. two years (1985 to 1987)
3. any three of the following:

     1981   Iran releases American hostages

     1983   U.S. marines killed in Lebanon

     1986   U.S. bombing raid on Libya

Iran-contra scandal revealed

1987   U.S. naval escorts begin in Persian

Gulf

4.   any three of the following:

1985   U.S.-Soviet arms-control talks

resume

Mikhail Gorbachev comes to

power in the Soviet Union

First Reagan-Gorbachev summit

meeting, in Geneva

1986   Second Reagan-Gorbachev summit

meeting, in Reykjavik, Iceland

1987   Third Reagan-Gorbachev summit

meeting in Washington, D.C.;

INF Treaty signed

1988   Fourth Reagan-Gorbachev summit

meeting, in Moscow

1989   Eastern Europe throws off

communist regimes

5.   seven

CHAPTER 41

II. A.

1.   False. Clinton endorsed past Democratic traditions on civil rights. He sought to alter Democrats' previous positions on the economy and defense.

2.   True

3.   True

4.   False. The failure of Clinton's reform measures strengthened the Republicans, who made large gains in the mid-term Congressional elections.

5.   True

6.   False. The strong economy of the 1990s encouraged Clinton to lower international trade barriers and promote free trade.

7.   False. The Clinton administration attempted but failed to achieve an Israeli-Palestinian peace agreement.

8.   True

9.   True

10. True

11. True

12. False. Bin Laden was a Saudi Arabian citizen who took refuge in Afghanistan.

13. True

14. True

15. True

II. B.

1. c

2. c

3. a

4. c

5. b

6. d

7. a

8. c

9. b

10. c

11. b

12. d

13. b

14. b

15. c

II. C.

1. Democratic Leadership Council

2. Don't ask, don't tell

3. Branch Davidians

4. Columbine High School

5. Contract with America

6. Reform Party

7. World Trade Organization (WTO)

8. Haiti

9. Whitewater

10. Green Party

11. Electoral College

12. Pentagon

13. Al Qaeda

14. USA-Patriot Act

15. Abu Ghraib

II. D.

1. H
2. D
3. J
4. N
5. K
6. M
7. F
8. A
9. O
10. B
11. G
12. C
13. L
14. I
15. E

II. E.

1. 5
2. 2
3. 1
4. 3
5. 4

CHAPTER 42

II. A.

1. True

2. False. The U.S. fell behind several other nations in per capita income.

3. True

4. False. A majority of mothers with small children worked outside the home.

5. False. The elderly became more affluent through programs like Social Security and Medicare.

6. True

7. False.   The percentage of foreign-born Americans was higher in the early twentieth century. True

8. False. Race still heavily influence the reaction to such events.

9. True

10. True

11. False. Both popular culture and "high culture" enjoyed expanded audiences

12. False. Writing about the West increased in quantity and quality.

13. False. The art capital was New York City.

14. True

II. B.

1. a

2. a

3. a

4. d

5. a

6. d

7. b

8. c

9. a

10. c

11. a

12. b

13. d

14. c

15. b

II. C.

1. Microsoft Corporation

2. Medicare

3. Immigration Reform and Control Act

4. Hispanics (Latin Americans or Mexican Americans OK)

5. United Farm Workers

6. Los Angeles

7. the West (Northwest or Pacific Northwest OK)

8. National Endowment for the Arts (NEA)

9. Abstract expressionism
10. *Exxon Valdez*

II. D.
1. G
2. C
3. J
4. I
5. L
6. K
7. H
8. A
9. F
10. E
11. B
12. D

II. E.
2
3
1
4
5

II. F.
1. D
2. J
3. B
4. E
5. A
6. F
7. H
8. I
9. C
10. G